PARISIAN LIVES

ALSO BY DEIRDRE BAIR

Al Capone: His Life, Legacy, and Legend

Saul Steinberg: A Biography

Calling It Quits: Late-Life Divorce and
    Starting Over

Jung: A Biography

Anaïs Nin: A Biography

Simone de Beauvoir: A Biography

Samuel Beckett: A Biography

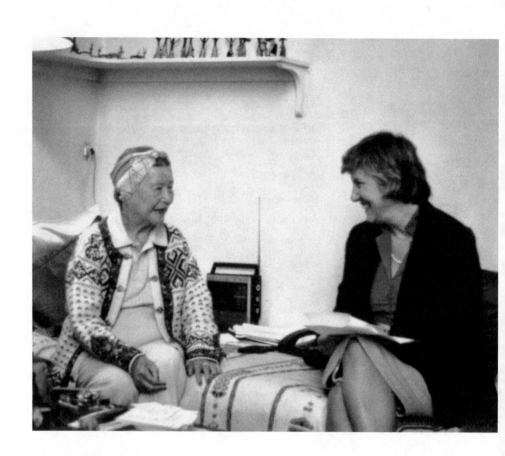

PARISIAN
LIVES

samuel beckett,

simone de beauvoir,

and me:

a memoir

DEIRDRE BAIR

 NAN A. TALESE · DOUBLEDAY · NEW YORK

www.nanatalese.com

DOUBLEDAY is a registered trademark of Penguin Random House LLC.
Nan A. Talese and the colophon are trademarks of Penguin Random House LLC.

Book design by Maria Carella
Jacket image: Samuel Beckett by Thierry Orban/Sygma and Simone de Beauvoir
    by François Lochon/Gamma-Rapho, both Getty Images; (skyline) Stockleb/
    Shutterstock
Jacket design by Michael J. Windsor

Library of Congress Cataloging-in-Publication Data
Names: Bair, Deirdre, author.
Title: Parisian lives : Samuel Beckett, Simone de Beauvoir, and me : a memoir /
    Deirdre Bair.
Other titles: Samuel Beckett, Simone de Beauvoir, and me : a memoir
Description: First edition. | New York : Nan A. Talese / Doubleday, 2019.
Identifiers: LCCN 2019006879 (print) | LCCN 2019021111 (ebook) |
    ISBN 9780385542463 (ebook) | ISBN 9780385542456 (hardcover)
Subjects: LCSH: Bair, Deirdre. | Women authors, American—Biography. | Authors,
    American—20th century—Biography. | Autobiography—Women authors. |
    Biography as a literary form. | Beckett, Samuel, 1906–1989—Psychology. |
    Beauvoir, Simone de, 1908–1986—Psychology. | BISAC: BIOGRAPHY &
    AUTOBIOGRAPHY / Personal Memoirs. | BIOGRAPHY & AUTOBIOGRAPHY /
    Literary. | BIOGRAPHY & AUTOBIOGRAPHY / Women.
Classification: LCC PS3602.A5635 (ebook) | LCC PS3602.A5635 Z46 2019
    (print) | DDC 818/.5403 [B]—dc23
LC record available at https://lccn.loc.gov/2019006879

MANUFACTURED IN THE UNITED STATES OF AMERICA

10 9 8 7 6 5 4 3 2 1

First Edition

PREFACE

Whenever I meet someone new and tell them that I have written biographies of Samuel Beckett and Simone de Beauvoir, their first question is usually "What made you choose those subjects?" I've honed a ready answer over the years, one designed to be brief and polite and to let me change the subject. "They were remarkable people," I say. "Truly extraordinary. Great privilege to have known them." Most of the time I don't get away with it, and the question that routinely follows is "What were they *really* like?" That one is never easy to answer.

Over the years I wrote several other biographies about equally fascinating people, but the interest in Beckett and Beauvoir remained out of proportion to all the rest. With every lecture or seminar, I found myself fielding questions about what was it like to be with them, and what did we talk about, and why did I write the books as I did. I was bombarded with remarks along the lines of "Weren't you awestruck, terrified, humble, wowed"—you pick the adjective here—"to be in the presence of Samuel Beckett and Simone de Beauvoir?" Yes, I admit; yes, I felt all those emotions and many more besides. I can't count how many times I was asked to sing for my supper at dinners and parties, or relate how hard I searched for anecdotes to amuse other guests without inappropriately revealing anything personal I had come to know about these literary giants.

But the questions persisted, and I began to think that perhaps— someday in the far distant future—perhaps I might write a little book, a "book about the writing of the books." The original idea was to write something primarily for scholars and writers that would cover all my biographies, to concentrate on the decisions I made when dealing with structure and content, or how I worked in foreign archives and languages, or how I dealt with reluctant heirs and troublesome estates. Each time I suggested this possible project, even to fellow biographers or academics, the response was always "That's all very nice, but please just tell us what Beckett and Beauvoir were really like." And for many years that was something I simply could not bring myself to do.

I wrote those two biographies during the most eventful years of my own life, and to write about Beckett and Beauvoir meant that I would have to write about myself as well. If I described the professional decisions that I made, I would also have to describe the brash young woman I was then: a journalist not yet thirty who became an accidental biographer, one who had never read a biography before she decided that Samuel Beckett needed one and she was the person to write it. And I would have to tell of a somewhat wiser woman a decade later, who formed a feminist consciousness during tumultuous years when she worked hard to stay married, raise children, keep a household running, forge an academic career, and scrounge enough money to go to Paris to confer with Simone de Beauvoir—because Simone de Beauvoir appeared to be the only contemporary role model who had made a success of both her personal and her professional lives, and I was searching desperately for someone to tell me how to do the same.

My writing life began as a reporter for newspapers and magazines. Even though it was the era of the New Journalism, I never adopted those techniques and kept myself scrupulously out of everything I wrote. That decision was largely made for me by the fact that I wrote hard news much of the time—from actions of the zoning board of appeals to city council shenanigans, the sort of thing that allowed me to concentrate on the story at hand and not on the role I played in getting it. When I began to write biography, a biographer friend who also started in journalism told me how she melded her old career with the new one: "Biographers are essentially storytellers. So, then, tell the story, but stay the hell out of it."

Since that was my natural impulse, this approach suited me just fine until I became both source and subject.

In the last several years, I was contacted by several biographers whose subjects figured in my books, and thus in my life. I gave them interviews in which I described my interactions with their subjects, and I gave them letters, photos, and other documents to support what I told them. Imagine then my horror when their books were published and I was quoted and thanked effusively but with everything they attributed to me either twisted or subverted. I checked their notes to see if they were using multiple sources, for if so, the weight of information from others might explain how they had changed my testimony. But no, I was their only source, so it was obvious that they had contorted my words to support their theory or thesis. It put me in a terrible position, because much of what they wrote was simply not true. That was the moment when I began to give serious consideration to committing my own version of my working history to print, to set the record straight as I remember it and to let future generations of readers assess it and decide for themselves whether I was an objective witness and a reliable narrator. Or not.

And yet I was still not ready to confront my own story. I am sure I bored my sister-writers in the Women Writing Women's Lives seminar at CUNY, when I sought their counsel for the better part of a year as I asked repeatedly how I could bring myself to reveal so much that was personal, not only about Beckett and Beauvoir but about myself. For every embarrassing or unpleasant or unsavory aspect of their behavior, mine was at least doubly so. I had begun to write biography as a curious combination of seasoned, hardened journalist and total novice in the genre. Did I really want to put all the mistakes I made out there for the world to see? My dilemma was expressed perfectly when Margo Jefferson spoke to the seminar about her memoir, *Negroland,* and said the self she wanted to put on the page was the hardest to write about: "How do you reveal yourself without asking for love or pity?" How, indeed.

I found an interesting example of my problem at a lunchtime

talk at New York University's Institute for the Humanities, when Phillip Lopate said it took him thirty-one years to write a memoir about his mother, because every time he approached the truth he found himself backing away from it. I suppose I was more fortunate, because for me approaching, backing away from, and revealing my own truth took only nineteen years.

How then to construct my story? Of my three subjects—Samuel Beckett, Simone de Beauvoir, and myself—the first two became much easier to remember and recount after I waded through the ceiling-high stacks of boxes of papers in my storage room, what the neighbors call our local fire hazard. Everything I needed to jog my memory was there, from interview transcripts to news clips, photos, and correspondence; looking through this material helped me to remember how the decisions I made when writing the biographies were rooted in the facts. A central tenet of my writing credo is that if memory is to serve as one of the two basic pillars of support for any biography, it must be coupled with fact. But what about me and my story? Where would I find the facts of my life to balance my memories?

I solved that problem when I found boxes I had entirely forgotten, those containing what I called the *Daily Diaries,* or as I abbreviate them here, the *DD.* It was a shock to find the big red "page-a-day" books where I wrote down everything and anything connected with the work I did for the biographies. I did not remember how much detail I had confided to those notebooks, everything from capsule profiles of the people I met, to long philosophical meditations on my life, to the wide, colorful range of emotions (negative as well as positive) I felt for my subjects. Here was the record of the several selves I would have to portray in this book, from the neophyte to the mature woman who reads these journals now with a deep appreciation for how those experiences helped her to become who she is today. That would be the most important self, the one who explains every step of the process.

With the *DD* in hand I could buttress and fortify so many aspects of the shifting and varied self who displayed her emotions and passions those many years ago. Applying the filter of time to these in-the-moment accounts lets me be present but also lets me distance myself, and to create another self, one better suited to a dispassionate telling of the most objective tale possible. Once I mined these layers, I knew I could write this curious hybrid of a book, a "bio-memoir" that does indeed tell my story, but only as it first tells the story of my subjects and how I wrote their books. I was able to combine literary imagination—all the things I thought then, later proven right or wrong—with the authority of facts as time has revealed them. The reader will see me, I hope, standing above or outside my story, looking down on all the players in it, as I thought of them then, as I think of them now.

I think my years of hesitation led me to wait for the perfect moment to tell this story. Enough time has passed that I can set the record straight (as I see it) with little risk of hurting anyone; most of the people I wrote about have died, and the survivors I know of are unlikely to be surprised by what I write here. Even so, writing bio-memoir has not been easy, particularly because so much writing today is self-referential and it was a struggle to find my place within shifting genres. Memoir is no longer bound by the need for absolute truth, nor is it constrained by the concerns of decorum and decency that prevailed in our recent past. We live now in an age of indecency, when nothing is off-limits. Fiction is often prefaced with terms like "auto," "self," and "reality," a practice that allows novelists to creep under the fences and invade the turf of autobiography. Autobiographers, meanwhile, no longer hesitate to fictionalize the history of others. And contemporary biographers who find little or no information about their subjects feel scant compunction about inserting themselves into lives in which they played no part, either as authoritative characters or as commentators.

I was well aware of all these genre-boundary breakdowns and did my best to avoid them, but on the few occasions when I crossed borders, I tried to explain my reasons. For me, biography will always require the writer to be "the artist under oath," as the critic Desmond MacCarthy decreed, and that was how I tried to write this hybrid of memoir and biography. There was no hiding, and sometimes it was painful. Writing was a slow process of discovery; I have always lived in the present day, and to recall my professional coming-of-age was to explore an almost unknown country that was long gone, one that I had not paid much attention to but one that was now demanding thorough examination. I paraphrase here the French writer Sainte-Beuve, who believed that you never understand a writer's work until you understand her life. The only way I could understand mine was to get outside myself and make myself both subject and object, to discover those selves as I went along, in real life and on the page. Call it serendipity, synchronicity, happenstance, or accident—whatever it was, I became the biographer of two of the most remarkable people the world has ever known, and those adventures became this book.

PARISIAN LIVES

"*So you are the one* who is going to reveal me for the charlatan that I am." It was the first thing Samuel Beckett ever said to me on that bitter cold day, November 17, 1971, as we sat in the minuscule lobby of the Hôtel du Danube on the rue Jacob. I had gone to Paris at his express invitation, to meet him and talk about writing his biography. We were originally scheduled to meet on November 7, and for ten days I had no idea where he was, because he never showed up and never canceled. When we made the initial appointment, he told me I should phone when I arrived in Paris on the sixth and we would confirm the time and place. I was to call precisely at one o'clock, because he disliked the telephone and answered only during the hour between one and two. When he did not pick up, I spent that hour phoning every five minutes, becoming more anxious and upset each time as I let it ring and ring.

In those days Paris had a system of *pneumatiques*, little blue messages that looked like telegrams and went through tubes all over Paris, to be delivered within the hour. I wrote several little "blue pneus" during the days that followed, and still I did not hear from Beckett. I had no idea what to do, and fluctuated between disappointment and fear that he was avoiding me because he had changed his mind about cooperating. And yet I did not think anyone could be so deliberately callous and cruel, so I set about keeping other appointments related to the book I wanted to write until I could find out what was going on with him.

On November 16 he phoned my hotel to arrange a meeting for the next day. He apologized for going off without contacting me and said he would explain in full in person. On the phone he said only that he had been felled by a terrible cold and was so weak and debilitated that he had allowed his wife to take him to Tunisia for sun and warmth. They left in such a hurry that he had not been able to cancel all his appointments. I was relieved beyond measure.

The Hôtel du Danube was not the chic and expensive place it is now. In 1971 it was a $19-a-night shabby dump favored by poor graduate students and budget tourists. The hotel was in such poor repair that there had been neither heat nor hot water for the twenty-four hours before our meeting, so there was no coffee at breakfast and no hot bath. The only staff around to deal with disgruntled lodgers were the two Portuguese maids, whose French accents were so incomprehensible that I did not know whether the inconvenience was the result of yet another of the many utility strikes that roiled Paris that winter or if the decrepit plumbing and heating had simply given out.

I was hungry, cold, and desperately in need of caffeine, but I was too nervous to go out to get it. Because of the missed connections during the previous week, I was superstitious enough to think that if I left the hotel, some terrible accident would happen to make me miss my first meeting with Samuel Beckett. So I decided to bundle up and wait for his arrival in my cold room, where, with the noisy radiator gone silent, the only sound was my growling stomach.

At precisely two o'clock, the time he said he would arrive, my phone rang. "Beckett here," he said in the high-pitched, reed-thin nasal voice I would come to know well. I mumbled something into the receiver as I slammed it down and bolted for the stairs to the lobby, where I found Samuel Beckett peering intently into the gloom through which I made my clattering descent.

I recognized his hawklike visage at once, his slightly crooked nose and the tuft of white hair that reared straight up from his forehead. I don't think I have ever met anyone whose physical reality was so accurately captured in photographs. He was a tall man, but I was also struck by the discrepancy between his elongated torso and his legs, which appeared short in comparison. We shook hands

and murmured greetings. He was bundled against the weather
in a sheepskin jacket and heavy white Irish-knit sweater with a
high turtleneck collar. It reminded me of the ruff worn by British Cavaliers in earlier times, particularly after I gestured toward
the lobby's tiny table and two chairs and he swayed toward them,
sweeping into one with a courtly half-bow. I took the one opposite
and smiled, waiting for him to begin the conversation. There was
no other furniture in the lobby, and the arrangement worked fine
for Beckett's diminished vision, but it was so tight that our knees
touched underneath, even though we struggled to situate ourselves
so they would not. I knew that he had recently had eye surgery, but
I did not know that his general vision was still impaired and that
his peripheral vision had not returned at all. The only way he could
see someone was to sit or stand directly in front of them, as close as
decorum would allow.

So he stared at me intently, because it was the only way he
could see me. I thought perhaps he was puzzled by my heavy coat,
woolen hat, and gloves, all of which I had been wearing since I got
out of bed that morning. I thought he might be afraid that I was
dressed for the outdoors because I intended to spend the rest of the
day trailing after him all over Paris, so I quickly explained about
the hotel's lack of amenities. It did not have the effect I intended,
which was to put him at ease, because I had to shout over the two
Portuguese maids, who were busily trading obscenities in two languages right next to us as they pulled at opposite ends of an old
treadle sewing machine that each was determined would be hers.

When they were gone and quiet fell, Beckett and I managed
to arrange our legs on the diagonal so they did not brush. He took
out a lighter and a pack of something brown, whether tiny cigars
or cigarettes I was too nervous to determine. He fidgeted with the
lighter, all the while staring in silence straight at me through the
pale blue "gull's eyes" he gave to Murphy, the hero of his first published novel. I was disconcerted by what I mistook for the apprais-
ing boldness of his gaze. As he fidgeted with the lighter, I picked
up his packet of smokes and twisted and turned it in my hands. In

one swift motion, Beckett reached across the table, snatched the packet, and spat out those first alarming words, that I would be the one to reveal him as a charlatan.

I was struck by what I thought was scorn in his voice and a cold lack of expression on his face, and I was unable to speak. The silence deepened as he stared and stared—and stared. I don't remember my exact reply to such a stunning declaration, but it was probably something stammering, perhaps even silly, for I was a young woman proposing an ambitious project for which I wanted his cooperation, even though I had no idea how to go about it. Several months earlier I had sent Beckett a letter volunteering to write his biography, and to my amazement he had replied immediately, saying that any biographical information he had was at my disposal and if I came to Paris he would see me. Imagine then, my shock at his initial greeting.

Beckett saw the look on my face and, courtly Old World gentleman that he was, began to stammer an apology for having upset me. No, no, I insisted, I was not upset. He had just taken me by surprise, for after all, I was in Paris at his invitation. What I remember most clearly of that awkward beginning is how so many thoughts raced through my mind. I wondered what sort of game he was playing and whether his invitation was little more than a bait-and-switch meant to sound me out before deciding whether—or how—to put insurmountable obstacles in my way so that I would never write the book. After all, wasn't he one of the most secretive and private of all writers, one about whose personal life almost nothing was known?

Then there was the business of him calling himself a charlatan. I struggled to comprehend how he could possibly believe that his writing was a joke that had somehow gotten beyond his control and managed to hoodwink the reading and theatergoing public. He was a Nobel Prize winner whose novels and plays had changed literature and drama irrevocably in our time, so how could he think of himself as a sham and a hoax? Perhaps this was just his way of testing me, to see if I would respond with flattering and insincere disavowals intended to curry his favor, to determine how serious I was about writing an "objective" biography, as I had stated in my letter.

All this went through my mind in a matter of seconds as I dropped my head into my hands and said, "Oh dear. I don't know if I'm cut out for this biography business."

His demeanor changed immediately, as did his tone of voice. "Well, then," he replied, "why don't we talk about it?"

Beckett seemed nervous as he launched into an apology for having to meet me in midafternoon instead of inviting me for drinks or a meal. He apologized several times, each with increasing agitation, for needing to rush off as he had to do, saying how he hoped that this long-delayed rendezvous had not inconvenienced me and explaining again about how the last-minute trip to Tunisia had caused his appointments to pile up.

He spoke kindly when he asked me to tell him why I wanted to take on "this impossible task" and was smiling when he said, "I would have thought a young woman like you would have more interesting things with which to amuse herself."

And so I began to talk, most of the time coherently, because I had practiced what I wanted to say, memorizing the key arguments. Even so, there were times when I lapsed into unorganized or unrelated remarks, because there was so much I wanted to tell him. I did not touch on any of the many questions that I wanted to ask about his life or his work. Instead I told him a little bit about myself and a lot about the current state of academic theory in the United States, particularly at Columbia University, where I had written a dissertation about his life and work, for which I would receive a doctorate in comparative literature in spring 1972. He sat there quietly, giving me no visible sign that he was receiving my remarks in any way other than just listening—keenly, deeply, and intently listening. In years to come, he often responded to things I told him in this same neutral manner, and each time I found it as disconcerting as I did on this first occasion.

However, he must have found what I said interesting enough.

Time passed, and the hour he said he could spare lengthened into almost two before he realized that he was now behind schedule for the rest of his appointments. Before leaving, he made the remark that has since come to haunt me: "I will neither help nor hinder you. My friends and family will assist you and my enemies will find you soon enough." He began to gather his things and said we could meet again in a day or two, but he could not confirm the time or date just then and would have to phone later. And with that he was gone, leaving me to wonder when (or even if) another meeting was going to happen.

I went back to my room, and as I opened the door, I heard the radiator cranking on. With the promise of heat, I decided that coffee could wait a little longer. Beckett had made so many remarks—cryptic, sarcastic, friendly and open, evasive and unfriendly—that I wanted to record them while I still remembered what he said. It was the first of the many times after our meetings that I hurried back to a place of splendid isolation where I could transcribe everything I retained. And after this first meeting I also needed to recall everything that I had told him about myself.

"You need to know about me," I had insisted. "Before we get started on a biography, I can answer your question about why I want to write yours only by telling you who I am." And so I had. Looking over my notes, his remark about his friends, family, and enemies resonated. Indeed, in the seven years to come, those people did exactly what Beckett had said they would.

2

A *circuitous route had brought* me to that tiny round table in the shabby hotel. I went to Paris because I had the grandiose idea that I would be doing the literary world a service by demonstrating in a biography (as I had done in the dissertation) that Samuel Beckett was not (as the reigning view in the academic community then held) a writer steeped in alienation, isolation, and despair, but rather one who was deeply rooted in his Irish heritage and who portrayed that world through his upper-class Anglo-Irish background and sensibility. Such a high-minded mission had taken root in 1969, the year I left a newspaper career to enroll in graduate school. At the start I was not really committed to a life of scholarship but was there only because I needed a break from the pressures of being a beat reporter on constant call in the world of print journalism.

I spent the decade between my undergraduate and graduate education writing for magazines (*Newsweek* very briefly) and newspapers (at that time the *New Haven Register*), specializing when I could in short features and in-depth profiles of local luminaries. News doesn't happen just during business hours, which made life especially difficult for a woman who had married directly after university, was the mother of two small children, and was the main family support with a husband in graduate school. I was in my late twenties and was exhausted from trying to combine a career with family life, and I felt myself quite alone doing so. Very few married women in my social circle held jobs in the greater New Haven area, where I lived, simply because they were not expected to. Their husbands were either academic or professional men, and if any of these women did work outside the home, it was at something temporary, just until their husbands established careers. Most of those who had jobs did not have children, while I already had two. I was an anomaly who did not know that I was "trying to have it all," for the phrase had not yet found its way into women's consciousness. I knew only that I was burned out. I could not go on volunteering at the PTA and the Junior League while also carving out time to bake cookies for my children's classes or provide refreshments when it was my turn for my husband's graduate study group. Nor could I participate in the local newcomers' group dinner parties, because I couldn't find the time to prepare the elaborate gourmet dishes; also, they ended late and I had to get up early to be at the police station by 6 a.m. to check the police blotter before I went into the newsroom to write that day's feature story. Trying to be and do it all had become too much.

When the opportunity of a writing fellowship in a newly formed program at Columbia University's School of the Arts came along in 1968, I embraced it. I thought it would be a peaceful respite for several years during which I could read novels and write about them without the pressure of daily deadlines. I thought it would enable me to recharge while also sharpening my skills for a writing career as a cultural critic in journalism. At that time it never occurred to me that I might become a professor, let alone a biographer.

My first year at Columbia coincided with the student protests in spring 1968. "Come on," shouted one of my new classmates as I sat in the sun on the steps before the statue of Alma Mater on a sunny April day, "we're going to seize Schermerhorn Hall." I couldn't, I said with regret, because I had to go home to New Haven and cook dinner for my children. It was clear from the start that I was a most unusual graduate student, a reputation I cemented when I told my classmates that I did have to rush home but first I had to stop at Saks for a sale on purses. From that day forward they joked that I was the "Bloomingdale Marxist," never mind how many times I corrected them about the store's name. This is a rather embarrassing story that I still blush to tell, but I do so because it shows how uncommitted I was to a life of serious scholarship, and how, even after one year of course work, I still thought of myself as a journalist in search of a story.

I loved being in the School of the Arts, where indeed I did get to sit around and read novels to my heart's content. But I was not learning anything new in the nonfiction program, where my instructors, many of whom had not seen the inside of a newsroom for years, were teaching my classmates somewhat outmoded explanations of what I had actually been doing every day for almost a decade. The only part of the program that energized me was the literature courses I took in the Graduate School, where I read Joyce's *Ulysses* line by line with William York Tindall and modern poetry with John Unterecker. The 1968 uprising threw the university into crisis, but for me it brought resolution. I discovered that I wanted to read literature, not listen to someone tell me how to prepare copy. I already knew how to do that. I don't exaggerate when I say that I had fallen in love with reading and talking about literature, and somehow I wanted to find a future career that would let me continue.

And so in the fall of 1968 I went to John Unterecker, who was then chairperson of the graduate Department of English and Comparative Literature, and I said, in effect, "Let me in." Instead of spending a second year in the School of the Arts, I wanted to transfer to the Graduate School to get a master's degree, with the possibility of continuing on to the PhD. I thought that no matter what my next job would be, if I became a woman who held an advanced degree, whatever I wrote would command authority. I saw myself becoming a writer more than a teacher, but if a professorship would further my writing, it seemed an excellent way to proceed.

John Unterecker was perfectly willing to sponsor the transfer, because the tuition covering the master's degree was already paid, but he cautioned that I would have to bring my own money if I wanted to study beyond that. The Graduate School's admissions committee would probably be reluctant to admit a woman approaching thirty, married and with two small children, and the scholarship committee surely would not fund her. He said the committee members making these decisions were all men and they would probably think of me as a gamble that would not pay off. And besides, I would be taking a place that could better be given to a man. I nodded in agreement, for at that time I agreed with cultural norms and thought this was a perfectly reasonable attitude. I thanked him kindly and set out to find a way to pay my tuition so I could enroll in the doctoral program.

My quest began at a fortunate moment in women's history, when the lack of women professors and administrators in higher education became a subject of national concern. The St. Louis–based Danforth Foundation decided that something had to be done to rectify the situation, and in 1965 a fellowship program was set up for "mature women" who could get themselves admitted to a graduate school (no easy task in a male-dominated world). These women were expected to work hard and study fast enough to earn advanced degrees in a few short years, after which they were expected to glide easily into full-time positions in colleges and universities. The Danforth Graduate Fellowships for Women was a remarkable program, and everyone I know who became a GFW alumna will tell you how it changed her life. It certainly changed mine.

Even though staying at Columbia meant continuing the commute on the old New York, New Haven, and Hartford trains, then taking the shuttle from Grand Central to Times Square and the subway to 116th Street—two hours door to door in each direction—I never thought of taking my GFW to Yale. You could say I was put off by a conversation with the chair of the Medieval Studies Department, who once told me casually at a party that I would never be admitted to any graduate school because I was "too old [I was twenty-seven at the time], too poorly prepared [I was a Penn honors graduate], and . . . a faculty wife [of a teaching graduate student]." But such banal chauvinism didn't touch on my real reason, one that I later learned was common among women throughout the 1970s. I was afraid I might fail, and if I did, everyone in my circle would know about it. I reasoned that if I failed at Columbia, I could save face by saying that I had decided to drop out because commuting proved too difficult. That was how women thought in those days, even women like me, who had been on the front lines of their professions and subject to all sorts of rejections, insults, and abuse. Looking back, my reasoning may have been faulty, but it turned out to be the right decision.

Columbia was a graduate school for grown-ups. There were many students just like me, who had been in the world of work, and there were professors who understood that when students returned to school after years in "real life," the curriculum had to accommodate them. At Columbia, professors seldom required routine papers and tests. Students were expected to do their course work and, when ready, to present themselves for exams, written and oral. This atmosphere led to an urban legend about the English and Comparative Literature Department, of the student who had just finished his fifteenth year and still believed he didn't know enough to answer questions on the two-hour oral exam that was the prelude to writing a dissertation. I had an entirely different attitude: The Danforth GFW gave its women three years from start to finish and supported a fourth year only under extraordinary circumstances. Relating this fact to my classmates, I said that if I could not manage to bullshit my way through two hours of chattering about literature, I did not deserve the degree.

And so I set myself to it. I began by concentrating on medieval studies for two reasons: because I wanted the deep background and because I thought I needed to prove that I could do "hard work." Reading novels had been "fun," but now it was time for "real" scholarship. Still, I found myself constantly drawn to the novelists of the twentieth century and Irish writers in particular. I grew up with parents who were both serious readers and who established an impressive home library and encouraged regular visits to the local public one. They belonged to several book clubs and were devoted to contemporary literature. Joyce had been my

lodestone since I first read *Ulysses* in high school and was barely
able to comprehend such an astonishing novel. I read it again as
an undergraduate, and at Columbia I devoted my year-long master's thesis to a single chapter (17, *"Ithaca"*). Studying Joyce led to
immersion in Irish culture, in everything from history and politics
to landscape and real people. Thus Joyce led naturally to Beckett,
whose fiction I read with more of the same astonishment. But no
matter how compelling modern literature was, I still thought of it
as something I read for pleasure, and I had the misguided notion
that if I were to become a professor, I would have to "work." And
work meant medieval studies, which for me meant plodding slowly
through Anglo-Saxon and Latin. I started on a dissertation about
garden symbols that required a thorough understanding of medieval Latin because a central text was Saint Bernard's *Sermons on
the Song of Songs*. As I recall, there were eighty-six and at that time
none had been translated from Latin into English.

I began to read them in February 1970, huddled in a cubicle
in Butler Library, bundled in coat, hat, and gloves, sure that my
breath was freezing on my upper lip and icicles were forming on my
eyelashes. I was still reading them in that same cubicle in the swel-
tering heat of July when I realized how many months had passed
and I was only on Sermon 11. At that rate, I envisioned myself as a
stooped, white-haired old lady in a pilled sweater and coke-bottle
glasses and still a graduate student. The Danforth Foundation had
given me three years, maybe four, and I knew I had to find a different subject—and fast—or I would never meet my funding cutoff
date. Thus I made a life-changing decision that was based not on
aesthetic concerns but rather on one that was financially practical.

I used three-by-five note cards in those precomputer days, and
I took a pile of blank ones and fanned them across the desk as if
they were playing cards, which in a sense they were. On each one
I wrote the name of a contemporary writer whose work I admired
enough to want to write about it. As a journalist, I knew how to write
fast when on deadline, and if I could define a topic that required no

waiting for libraries to find crumbling old books and manuscripts and no ancient languages, I could pull together one hundred or so pages in a year's time. Joyce, Yeats, Woolf, Conrad, Beckett—I forget who else, but there were just under a dozen names on the little cards. Without thinking about which name might present the best opportunity for original research, or even which I liked the most, I shuffled them into alphabetical order. There were no A's, and Beckett came first, before Joseph Conrad and E. M. Forster. Beckett it shall be, I said to myself, and that was how my life in biography began.

Like a dutiful beginning academic (powerless and lacking authority), I decided at first to follow the rules and write a dissertation about Beckett that was based primarily on literary theory. I entered the academic world in the waning days of the New Criticism and the heyday of what has since been jumbled together under the broad title of "French critical theory." The only valid interpretation of literature came from the work itself, not from the author's life or the world in which he lived ("he" being the pronoun of choice, because the accepted canon then was composed almost entirely of male writers). Never mind that a work might have been produced in haste by a writer who could not pay his rent or take his sick child to a doctor, or by a political ideologue who was writing in fury about his country's regressive government, or by a frustrated person who had to live a deeply closeted life and could only hint at sexual preference in carefully guarded references. None of this mattered then; only the text itself was relevant.

I remember a little ditty coined during those days that I read in *The New York Review of Books,* one that perfectly captured the zeitgeist: "This is the story of Jacques Derrida; there ain't no writer, there ain't no reader either." The "holy trinity" of Barthes, Lacan, and Derrida ruled, and there was no place in such an environment for anyone who considered them, as I did, convincing in the main but still unholy. Reading Beckett's work made me want answers to a lot of questions, all of which were based on the life from which the work sprang rather than from any theorizing of my own or others. And as I wrote, my thoughts called me back to my days as a journalist who knew the tingle that came from identifying a good story.

I was initially attracted to Beckett's fiction rather than his plays, and in his novels I found many fond and loving references to actual places in the Wicklow Hills and the countryside surrounding his family's suburban home in Foxrock. Besides recognizing real places, I wondered why others did not see the wit and humor in his descriptions of the thinly disguised Dublin characters who peopled his novels. There were times when I literally laughed out loud as I read his prose descriptions of their real-life antics. I wondered why other scholars and critics didn't see these aspects of his writing. Were they so intimidated by the political correctness of literary theory that they had no room for real life? Or was I reading his novels with a warped sensibility, particularly as it might have reflected my own skewed sense of humor? I decided to keep an open mind while I read, one that would allow me to decipher his intentions and not impose my interpretations on them. As I listed the questions I wanted the dissertation to answer, I realized that, in short, they were all one and the same: who was the man whose imagination had managed to puzzle and perplex an international coterie of readers, leaving them to wonder about the novels they read and the plays they saw?

I came to realize that I still revered the writer and the creative process; I embraced my status as the renegade student who had the temerity to ask *how* a literary work came into being, *what* had inspired it, and *who* had been the shaping intelligence behind it. "All you need is the *when* and *where*," said the skeptical Professor Unterecker, who knew of my background in journalism and was the only one to whom I confided my "aberrant" interests. He warned me that even to think of investigating such issues in the work of Samuel Beckett would be akin to committing academic suicide. If I wrote what amounted to a biography, he said, I would never get the PhD, never mind a teaching job. At that point I was not sure I wanted one, so I forged ahead.

Unterecker reluctantly agreed to advise the dissertation after I assured him that I was planning to demonstrate sound critical analysis of new and never-before-known information I had collected about Beckett's writing. But I may have been a touch disingenuous when I told him I would tailor my essay to emphasize theory and stressed that it was merely the foundation for a future in-depth study that could become the all-important first book a scholar needs for tenure. In reality I had no intention of writing such a book. The answers to my questions about Beckett's work could be found only by looking at the writer who created them, and the only way to do that was through an extended profile or—heaven forfend in the academic world of the 1970s—a biography. (I did admit that the dissertation would have some biographical underpinnings, but they would be so slight that the evaluating committee would have to agree they were there just to provide a basis for my theoretical conclusions.)

Professional considerations aside, this was a challenging proposition. Not only had I never considered writing biography before, but with the exception of some of the classics, I had never read them. On my own as an undergraduate, I discovered and admired Suetonius, Plutarch, and Vasari, and I chuckled over Charlemagne's two biographers, Notker and Einhard. In graduate school I read the icons, Boswell and Johnson, whom I found delightful but not particularly important as models for my own critical writing. I made the obligatory glance at Froude's *Carlyle* and Lockhart's *Walter Scott*, but only long enough to agree with various professors who espoused the theory that they were not important for any significant understanding of their subjects' writings. Even as I enjoyed Lytton Strachey's scathing *Eminent Victorians,* I struggled to shake off the theorists who advised students not to mistake any of these "lives" for serious scholarship. They were to be enjoyed in passing, as little more than gossip, for as one professor told me in a statement I would hear all too frequently in years to come, "It's not scholarship; it's *only* biography."

Meanwhile I wrote the dissertation and was about to get the

degree in record time, in spring 1972. I didn't find a teaching job right away because there were very few in the 1970s, and despite the Danforth Foundation's entreaties that they should be given to women, those that were available usually went to men. I made desultory applications to some of the colleges in Connecticut and nearby New York, but nothing full-time materialized, and I wasn't interested in tying myself down to teach an overload of composition courses on a part-time basis for a pittance of a salary. As my dissertation bubbled away in my mind, I realized that I had had so many fascinating experiences and encounters while writing it that I was more determined than ever to write a biography about Samuel Beckett's life and work.

During this period I often thought of John Unterecker shaking his head, warning about "academic suicide" and how I would "never get a teaching job." For five years he would be proven right, but neither of us knew it at the time, and one of us really didn't care.

3

Like Scarlett O'Hara, who always put off worrying about things until the time came to do so, I planned not to worry about getting a job, because first I had Beckett's biography to consider. When Jack Unterecker (once I had the degree we became friends on a first-name basis) asked how I planned to begin, I replied blithely that I would probably model it after a newspaper profile. Jack had an extremely droll way of speaking and an equally dry sense of humor. He raised one skeptical eyebrow and said, "Don't you think that before you do anything, you should tell Beckett about it?" As I knew nothing about how biographies got themselves written, and as I was basing my decision on how journalism profiles came into being, it had never occurred to me that I might need "permission," or an "agreement," or even a "legal contract"— all expressions I heard for the first time when Jack spoke of them. Undeterred and blithely confident that I already had the necessary skill set, I said yes, of course, and wrote a letter to Beckett.

Once I started to write it, I realized how persuasive it had to be, and I agonized over it as I discarded enough drafts to overflow a wastebasket. In the end, the one I mailed in that hot July of 1971 was fairly brief, written in haste, and taken directly to the post office before I lost my nerve. I didn't keep a carbon, and after I sent it off, I feared that I had probably portrayed myself foolishly, like a literary Joan of Arc, clad in shining armor and clutching my reporter's notebook as I rode in to save the day. I do remember writing to Beckett that a biography was a necessary addition to all the critical writing about him, because I read his novels very differently from most other scholars, and I found so much vitality and humor in his prose and such deadly accuracy in his depictions of people and descriptions of places. I must have come off as extremely pompous in that impassioned paragraph, which I hoped would persuade him of the importance of my argument. I concluded the letter with a brief, to-the-point description of myself: a woman who had married young, had two school-age children, and was a journalist and reporter at heart. I asked for the favor of a reply because I did not want to write such a book without his cooperation.

The mail between New Haven and Paris was probably never again as swift as it was during that exchange. A week to the day after I mailed my letter, I received his reply. He began by telling me that his life was "dull and without interest" and "the professors know more about it than I do." He wrote all that in a tiny, careful, and meticulous hand, on tissue-thin unlined paper, with his writing proceeding in a straight line from left to right. Then came a curious second paragraph, in a larger hand and a scrawl that began at bottom left and rose to top right in several unpunctuated lines: "Any biographical information I possess is at your disposal if you come to Paris I will see you."

I couldn't believe my eyes. I kept rubbing the paper, thinking it would say something quite different if I just blinked for a moment. I looked out the window and saw my neighbor across the street, the writer-professor Ernest Lockridge, and I rushed out, waving the letter at him. He was teaching at Yale then, and while I had been studying for my dissertation oral exam, he used to sing a little ditty to the tune of the Miss America song whenever he saw me: "There she goes—think of all the crap she knows." He had been a cheerful and encouraging voice of reason during my student years, giving me a necessary nudge not to give up whenever I was down. I showed him Beckett's letter to make sure its content was real, and he assured me that it was. When my husband came home that night, he did the same. A practical man, he said I should call the Danforth Foundation, tell them of this extraordinary invitation, and ask for a special grant to go to Paris. The exceptional woman who ran the GFW program, Mary Brucker, listened as I blurted out my request and said so quietly that I almost didn't hear, "Of course you must go. We'll send you the check."

It was early August when I replied to Beckett to say that I could come in October or November, and he agreed that either month would be fine. My Columbia classmate Nancy MacKnight was planning to spend several days in Paris before going to London for her own research, so we arranged to travel together. At the same time, another Columbia classmate played a major role in helping me get started on the undertaking that would become the biography. Nancy Milford had just bucked the antibiography attitude at Columbia by publishing to great success her groundbreaking feminist study of Zelda Fitzgerald. We were having lunch one day when Nancy asked if I had found a teaching job. I didn't want one, I replied, because I was going to Paris to meet Samuel Beckett and write his biography.

Several days later, when I was sitting at my desk trying to figure out how biographies are written, never mind how to undertake the many household things I had to do to prepare my family for my absence, my phone rang. A man identified himself as Carl Brandt, Nancy Milford's literary agent. Nancy had relayed my news, and Carl Brandt told me that if it was true, it would be an astonishing coup in the literary world; he was sure he could arrange a book contract and would like to represent me. I knew that his father had founded the highly respected literary agency Brandt & Brandt, so I was thrilled to join their list of distinguished writers and accepted at once. I could hardly believe all my good luck.

Thus, happily situated with the Danforth Foundation guaranteeing travel money for my initial meeting with Beckett and Carl Brandt holding out the possibility of a book contract and an advance against royalties, I was truly on my way. When I tell this story today, other writers shake their heads in wonder at how easily a new career fell into my lap. They are not alone, for as I reflect back upon my amazing good fortune, I marvel at the ease of it myself.

I was wildly excited when I told Jack Unterecker about all the amazing things that were happening, and he remained his usual calm and tranquil self as he listened. He was also practical: if I intended to pursue such madness, he said, I should go to Dublin and London as well as Paris, and he would provide me with a list of the names of his friends who were also friends of Beckett. Jack had already demonstrated how invaluable such connections could be by introducing me to two New Yorkers who were his close friends and even closer friends of Beckett, the actor Jack MacGowran and the poet George Reavey. Both had enriched my academic work as I finished the dissertation, and now that a proper biography was in the works they were eager to contribute even further. Conversations with them would grant my first insights into Beckett the man rather than Beckett the author. And the letters and other documents they could share would be invaluable.

During Beckett's unhappy London years in the 1930s, George Reavey was the friend who was determined to help him get his novel *Murphy* published and who took it upon himself to be Beckett's agent. Their correspondence covered the years of rejections from forty-two publishers before George finally succeeded in persuading Routledge to bring out the book in 1938. During those frustrating years, as rejections mounted, Beckett wrote letters both amusing and scathing. One I particularly liked was the limerick he composed after a rejection by the American publisher Doubleday, Doran: "Oh Doubleday Doran/More oxy than moron/ you've a mind like a whore on/the way to Bundoran." When I used this letter in my dissertation, it was one of the earliest indications I had of how Beckett used his withering sense of humor to respond to adversity.

I first met George at his apartment in a tenement walk-up on East Eighty-Fifth Street where he lived with his playwright wife, Jean. It was truly the home of a hoarder, a railroad flat so cluttered that almost all the space was unusable. There were ceiling-high boxes of papers, stacks of books, paintings by his ex-wife, Irene

Rice Pereira, and the works of his artist friends (and Beckett's) Bram and Geer van Velde. There was one narrow pathway down the hallway leading from the entry to the front room, where the only uncluttered space was the sofa that became their bed at night. I could not believe my eyes the first time I walked in, but almost before I could adjust to the gloom caused by all the boxes blocking the dirty windows, George said we should repair down the street to Dorrian's Red Hand, where we could get a drink. What he meant, as I had ample opportunity to learn from that day on, was that he would drink scotch whiskey and I would pay for it. George was a falling-down drunk, an alcoholic who shrewdly dangled just enough documents to keep me coming back. But every time I became so frustrated over how much whiskey I had to buy that I threatened to have no further dealings with him, I stopped to tell myself that his contributions were priceless. The difficulty was getting him to dole them out, a nightmare that lasted throughout the seven years it took to write the book.

Whiskey drinking was a theme among Beckett's friends, as I discovered when I met Jack MacGowran in July. He was performing a one-man show at the Lenox Arts Center's Music Tent in Lenox, Massachusetts. Armed with Unterecker's introduction, my husband and I drove up to see the pastiche of Beckett's fictional characters that MacGowran had written for himself. It was an unseasonably cold and rainy night, so windy that the metal chains securing the tent cloth to the poles clanked eerily, enhancing the sound of the shuffling, sniffling MacGowran as he brought life to the characters from *Molloy, Malone Dies,* and *The Unnamable.* He wore a grungy overcoat several sizes too large, which dwarfed his small, thin frame, and his wretched boots, also too large, flapped loudly each time he took a step, adding another counterpoint to the wind and rain.

The audience howled with laughter when MacGowran performed the sixteen sucking stones episode from *Molloy.* Things grew quiet as he performed some of the darker passages from *Malone Dies,* and by the time he got to the last lines of *The Unnam-*

able, the audience was hushed in a mix of reverence and agony over the character's plight. When he said, "I can't go on. I'll go on," the memorable lines from *The Unnamable* that ended his performance, the only sound in the tent was the occasional clang of a chain until the audience caught enough of its collective breath to surround MacGowran with tumultuous applause. It remains to this day one of my most moving theatrical experiences.

Afterward I went to the tiny dressing room next to the tent, where MacGowran was taking off his makeup and pouring the first of his many post-performance whiskies. He was on a high, having had a full house and a receptive audience that called him back for repeated curtain calls. Gloria, his wife, popped in long enough to tell me not to rush, as he could take his time to talk at length. That was before she chided him to go easy on the whiskey. She might have been talking to the howling wind, for MacGowran was a dedicated alcoholic who made swift work of the bottle. I was enthralled watching him pour a glass whenever he paused to breathe while he gave me what amounted to a second, private performance. When I asked about when and how he first met Beckett, he launched into one story after another, until he stopped suddenly with a look of surprise on his face. "Do you know," he said, "I've never talked about Sam like this before. I have much to say that I think is important, but before you, no one ever asked."

He told me how awkward their first meeting had been, at the Royal Court Theatre shortly before the premiere of *Endgame,* when he asked the British director Donald McWhinnie to introduce them. Beckett told him to come before the dress rehearsal, after which he would leave immediately for Paris, because he never attended his opening nights. MacGowran said he "was reduced to pitiful silence" and Beckett "was equally silent because he was shy. It was like this until I understood that silences were common with him, in life as well as in his art. I blurted out something about rugby and he sprang to life, saying yes, there had just been a great match. Rugby, cricket, a six-day bicycle race—suddenly we were talking nonstop, and I was aware of the intonations and idioms of

Dublin speech. I asked about his Irish background, and we learned that we were born and raised three miles apart in the suburb of Foxrock. All of that, the nature of our natal rhythms, the terrain we both loved, the characters we had known—a deep friendship was formed, and this was only the first of many conversations."

Both men were Anglo-Irish Protestants and from families that we decided were slightly higher on the Irish social rung than upper middle class. Their fathers were both hail-fellows-well-met, the source of the fun in their lives; their mothers were the rigid disciplinarians who kept spotless houses, held elegantly formal (and boring) teas, and made sure they went to the Anglican church every Sunday, dressed in uncomfortable suits and shirts with itchy collars.

Foxrock was also the gateway to the Wicklow Hills, which both men explored as boys. As Jack described the landscape, citing the occasional marker, monument, or unusual road sign, I found myself jumping in to say, "But that's in . . ." and then naming one or another of Beckett's novels. "Yes, yes!" Jack would agree, bouncing on his hard wooden chair as he reached over to pat my hand in agreement. I was enthralled by his imitations of the Dublin characters, the real people who were so thinly disguised in *Murphy*, many of whom were so upset by Beckett's portrayal that they refused to speak to him for years after it was published. Jack told me to prepare myself for Beckett's spot-on imitations of them when I talked to him, for Beckett was a gifted mimic.

On and on he went, telling me what I could expect Beckett to be like, and what he told me left me with two conflicting emotions. On the one hand, I could not wait to get to Paris to talk to Beckett, but on the other hand, I was terrified that I was about to undertake a project that was way over my head and beyond my capabilities. Well before I wrote a single word, I worried about how I would incorporate the personal into what would become a public document that seemed destined to reveal much about a hitherto private life.

We could have gone on all night, I am sure, and we were well into our second hour when Gloria returned to tell us that we really had to bring the conversation to a close. It was the first of quite a few casual conversations and formal interviews that I had with Jack during the months before my first trip to Paris and several times afterward. When he died on January 30, 1973, I lost a dear friend, one to whom I am forever grateful for his introduction to the physical realities of Samuel Beckett's Ireland and for the way he guided me through Beckett's transmission of his memories into his writings.

Through Jack Unterecker, I met one more person in New York that summer of 1971 who was a friend of Beckett, the writer John Kobler. They had met when a magazine sent Kobler to Paris to write a profile of the "reclusive Irish writer," and they bonded over what Kobler believed was a shared love of Bushmills Irish whiskey. When Jack Unterecker told Kobler that I was on my way to Paris, he phoned to ask me to come to his apartment on West Eighty-Fifth Street, because he wanted me to carry a gift to Beckett. I had no idea what I was walking into, but I was eager to meet anyone who knew Beckett, so of course I went. I blanched when I saw the gift, two huge bottles of Bushmills Irish whiskey that Kobler expected me to put into my luggage. I resented his attitude that I was merely an errand girl but felt I had no choice but to take them, as Kobler had already sent Beckett a letter telling him to expect them.

That was the first of my meetings with Kobler, who had a significant correspondence with Beckett as well as photos, diary entries, and notes taken for the several writing projects he had envisioned but never brought to fruition. Kobler was then writing a biography of Al Capone, so it was always an adventure to be admitted to his apartment and watch him go through elaborate cloak-and-dagger security precautions, because he was certain that other gangsters were ready to commit heinous crimes against him should he write something they did not like. I wish I had paid more attention to what I then thought was silly behavior; I might have learned something useful for my own book about Al Capone many years later.

In the lead-up to my departure for Paris, Kobler contributed something I found important about Beckett's character when he revealed a crucial fact about his friendships—how he compartmentalized them. Kobler lived on West Eighty-Fifth Street and Reavey lived on East Eighty-Fifth Street. Each man knew of the other, and each wanted very much to meet the other. I evinced surprise when they told me they had never met, and I offered to introduce them. Oh no, each man said at once; if Sam had wanted them to meet, he would have made the introduction on the several occasions when they had been in Paris at the same time. They could not think of getting together without (as they called it) "Sam's blessing."

And so off I went, in late fall, 1971, for my first meeting with Samuel Beckett. I felt as much anxiety about the enormity of the undertaking as anticipation over wanting to get started on it. I was loaded down with my own supplies plus the two heavy bottles of Kobler's Bushmills, and grateful to be traveling with my friend Nancy MacKnight, who generously shouldered some of my baggage. We checked into the Hôtel du Danube on November 6, and immediately after, I tried to contact Beckett, who seemed to have disappeared.

Our scheduled November 7 meeting came and went with no word from him, and as the days passed I didn't know whether to be angry, upset, or just plain worried. Where was he, and what cruel joke was this, to get me to Paris on the promise of meeting him to discuss a biography, only to leave me stranded? After Nancy finished her work in Paris, she left for London and I was all alone. Time was passing and I was running out of American Express traveler's checks. If I did not hear from Beckett soon, it looked like my new career as a biographer would be over before it even started. However, I had things to do before I gave up entirely, so I got to work.

4

Those ten days I spent waiting for my first meeting with Beckett passed in a haze of agonizing slowness. I seem to remember never straying too far from the hotel desk, where the receptionist soon learned to ward me off by shaking her head. *No, Madame Bair, no telephone messages, no blue pneu, no letter.* This anxious waiting overshadows all other memories from those days, but in reality I did manage to do some important work gathering all kinds of information about Beckett when I set out to meet and interview his friends. Little did I know that his friends would also want all kinds of information, not only about me but also about Beckett.

Carl Brandt told me to meet Mary Kling of La Nouvelle Agence, and she became the French agent who helped me with European sales after the book was written. She also became a good friend who helped me navigate the trickiness as well as the niceties of all things French. Besides giving me important introductions to many people in the French publishing world who were interested in my project, she set up my first meeting with Jérôme Lindon, Beckett's longtime publisher at Les Éditions de Minuit. For that initial meeting I went to Lindon's office hoping for a formal interview, during which I planned to ask easy questions that would allow me to establish a rapport that would let me ask subsequent ones with more substance. I wanted to begin with things like how Lindon had become aware of Beckett's writings, what had happened at their first meeting—all sorts of generalities. But I never got to ask anything of the kind, because Lindon dominated the conversation with his own questions. Who was I, he wanted to know, and how did I have the temerity to expect that Beckett's friends would tell a total unknown everything they knew about a man I had yet to meet? I had not thought to bring the letter from Beckett inviting me to Paris with me, mainly because I had not imagined that anyone would demand that I prove my bona fides.

Lindon had been first on my list because I thought that if anyone could tell me where Beckett was and why he had so mysteriously disappeared, it would be he. But Lindon didn't even know Beckett was away, as their friendship had devolved to the point where they seldom met socially and communicated by telephone when they had business to discuss. My inquiry gave him the opportunity to press his point that he should not talk to me; if Beckett had been so willing to meet me, why had he gone away without telling me where? I had no answer except to say that I hoped Lindon and I could meet again after he spoke to Beckett and confirmed my scholarly legitimacy. In the end he accepted my answers and agreed that we should meet again, when he would provide access to his files and photos. We parted cordially, and I left feeling that I had accomplished something important.

Mary Kling also arranged for me to meet Denis Roche, the poet and editor then at Éditions du Seuil. Within minutes after I sat down in his office, Roche told me he could not publish my book because he was "so close to Sam" that he would be uncomfortable reading revelations about the life of his friend. I wondered why he had bothered to meet me if he felt this way, but I told him it was fine with me because I had appointments with two other publishers later in the week. I was gathering my things and preparing to leave when he began to talk, or rather to ask me questions. I could not decide whether he was trying to help me by suggesting persons to interview or he had quite another reason—that he wanted me to tell him everything I knew about his "close good friend Sam." I thought it unusual that he would need to ask me such basic questions, but I was able to say truthfully that I couldn't answer most of them, as I was just at the beginning of my research.

Roche asked if I had talked yet to A. J. "Con" Leventhal, the Irishman living in Paris who was another old and close friend of

"Sam's." I told him that Leventhal was high on my list of the friends of "Mr. Beckett." (Throughout all the years I knew him, he was always "Mr. Beckett" and I was "Mrs. Bair" when we were together, or just "Beckett" when I spoke of him to others. I never called him "Sam," and as I learned over the years, there were quite a few who did so without any right to claim such closeness.) Roche threw out other names I already knew of, including Man Ray and Maria Jolas, the widow of the publisher Eugene Jolas, who had known Beckett from his earliest days in Paris, when he was in James Joyce's circle. At a name I had not yet heard before, Georges Pelorson, I looked puzzled, before Roche added that I probably knew him as the publisher Georges Belmont, who had changed his name after the war because of his shady past during the Nazi occupation. Yes, Belmont was on my list, too. We continued discussing these names and others for well over an hour, but it took me some time to realize that I was being seriously pumped for information about my knowledge of Beckett's social circle. And when it ended, Roche asked to make a lunch date for later, saying it would be good to get together after I had talked to Beckett and all the people on my list so that he could "advise" me on what I had learned from them. He shook his head in sincere regret as he reiterated that he could not bring himself to edit the life of a friend, but he did hope I would tell him what others said about "Sam."

It was yet another example of Beckett's compartmentalizing people. Indeed, he had many friends, but most of them did not know each other and would not presume to initiate an acquaintance, let alone a friendship, unless he condoned it. And I found it increasingly distressing that all these people expected me to be the conduit for information about him that they would not otherwise have. By expecting me to be a go-between, I felt, they were putting me into the unsavory position of being the teller of tales, the relater of gossip. And I wanted no part of it. As a reporter, I had never revealed or betrayed a source, and as a burgeoning biographer, I was not about to start doing so.

Next I paid a visit to A. J. "Con" Leventhal, a critic and scholar who had moved to Paris from Dublin after he retired as lecturer in French at Trinity College. I had heard rumors that ranged from the positive ("He is an old and trusted friend who always offered support during the years of Beckett's Irish misery, when no one would publish his writings") to the unkind ("He is Beckett's charity case; Beckett takes pity on his poverty and allows him to describe himself as his secretary so that he can contribute financially to his support"). I did know that Leventhal's late wife had been Ethna MacCarthy, a striking and spirited woman on whom Beckett had had quite a crush when they were students at Trinity. However, that was all I knew, and again, it came from Dublin gossip and needed to be fact-checked.

I met Leventhal at the comfortable apartment on the boulevard du Montparnasse he shared with his partner, Marion Leigh. It was not the apartment of someone down on his luck but, rather, a spacious and comfortable home, one that I came to know well over the years as Leventhal assumed the role of the go-between who conveyed information to me from Beckett, telling me all the things Beckett wanted me to know but did not want to say directly. It would take me months to figure out that this was the game the two of them played.

I did not have to explain myself to Leventhal, because Beckett had alerted him that I was coming to Paris and said he should receive me if I asked to see him. Leventhal had a puckish sense of humor, and his tone was one of levity when he said he wanted to see for himself the American woman who thought she should be admitted to "Sam's inner sanctum." When he told me he was eager to learn what I hoped to accomplish, my reporter's instincts kicked in, and I became exceedingly cautious about what I said. I was not about to reveal anything without getting something in return, so I did what good reporters always do: I asked Con Leventhal straight out where Beckett had gone, and why. And he told me.

Beckett had contracted a virus, flu, bronchitis—Con didn't know which—but he couldn't shake it and Suzanne, his wife, was very worried. She liked to go to a little nontourist hotel in Tunisia, where they had been when Beckett received the phone call telling him he had won the Nobel Prize. She had taken charge of travel arrangements and they had left on the spur of the moment. Suzanne thought she had canceled all her husband's appointments; unfortunately, she forgot to cancel the one with me—if she had even been aware of it.

It was a great relief when Con told me where and why Beckett had gone—he wasn't playing some cruel game after all—but the truth raised a number of perplexing circumstances for me. He may have had every intention of meeting me after he returned, but when would that be? How long could I stay to wait for him? My mind started to race; I was running low on the money I had allocated for Paris, and I still needed to go to London and Dublin to fulfill the commitments I had arranged. I could not wait indefinitely.

Then my thoughts veered from these serious matters to a ridiculous one and I blurted out, "I have two bottles of Bushmills for Beckett. May I bring them to you to keep for him?" Con laughed so loudly that Marion came in from the kitchen to ask what was so funny. Without my having to tell him, he knew whose whiskey I was carrying.

"Deirdre has been commissioned by Kobler to carry Bushmills. Should I take it from her?" Marion was a forceful woman of firm convictions who did not hesitate to speak her mind, and she said at once, "Absolutely not." They knew it was an old trick of Kobler's to find someone to transport liquor, and they also knew that Beckett could not bring himself to tell him that he had all but given up drinking because of various physical maladies. Besides, Bushmills had never been one of his favorites, so he always gave it away.

Dumping the Bushmills became one of my major priorities. I knew I could not do something so impolitic as to leave it at the Hôtel du Danube and ask Beckett to call for it at his earliest convenience. Mary Kling had already told me she would have no part in helping me get it to him, and told me not to send it through the mail. She urged me strongly not to get myself involved in delivering any more favors—for anyone. I was stumped by Leventhal's refusal until he suggested that another of Beckett's friends, Avigdor Arikha, was certain to accept it.

I had not known of the Romanian-born Israeli artist until Con Leventhal told me to make an appointment with him while in the next breath casting doubt on Arikha's closeness to Beckett. He said not to ask beforehand if Arikha would take the whiskey but just to take it with me, because he knew Arikha would grasp at any opportunity to be in Beckett's company. This was one of my earliest indications of the kinds of snide backbiting Beckett's friends sometimes practiced as they jousted for favorable positions.

But Arikha was not so removed from Beckett's inner circle as Leventhal thought. He and his wife, Anne, were the only other people who knew I was in Paris specifically to meet Beckett, which they could have learned only directly from him. As I found out, they also knew where he was. Anne was a serene American woman, and Beckett was very fond of her. They shared a love of music and sometimes played piano duets. Surprisingly, because Beckett was not always comfortable with children, he liked Anne's and was relaxed when he visited and they played around him.

As for her husband, I got the impression that Avigdor thought I was calling on him as a way of paying homage or seeking his approval. I thought him self-important when he told me proudly that he called himself "Sam's policeman." He let me know that he was looking forward to reporting his impressions of me to Beckett the moment he returned. Coyly, he did not tell me what those impressions would be. Leventhal was right about the whiskey: when I revealed the two bottles of Bushmills, Avigdor said of course he would tell Beckett he had them, and Beckett would then put him in charge of deciding to whom they should be given, for, as he repeated once again, he was "Sam's policeman."

Anne helped to resolve my logistical dilemma when she told me she had just received a postcard from Beckett saying he would be staying in Tunisia for at least another week or ten days. It was November 8, and he was not expected to return to Paris until the sixteenth at the earliest. Finally I had something concrete to help me decide what to do. Although I was terribly disappointed to think that I would return home without having met Beckett, I decided to leave Paris and go to Dublin or London—still to be decided.

I sent a note just before my departure telling Beckett that I would be going on to London and Dublin and that I hoped to hear from him about the possibility of a future meeting. In the meantime I would continue to conduct interviews. I intended to incorporate some of what I had learned on this trip into the dissertation, as there was still time before its final submission in February 1972. I told him I would also try to persuade the Danforth Foundation to fund a return trip to Paris so that I could show it to him and ask him to confirm its accuracy.

When I think back to those years now, they seem the golden age of air travel, when reservations could be made and changed without penalty, and for $325 round trip one could have a travel agent call TWA and ask for a seat from New York to Paris on Flight 800, the number tragically retired when one of the planes fell from the sky some years later. Flyers to Europe were also entitled to one stopover in each direction, but my excellent travel agent had fixed it so that this time I could stop in both London and Dublin on the way home.

London became an extremely important stop for research, because I met two of Beckett's friends who became close friends of mine. The great Irish poet Brian Coffey had been Beckett's friend since their university days. He and his wife, Bridget, and quite a few of their nine children went out of their way to offer gracious and generous hospitality on that initial trip and then for years after, which I tried to return when any of the children were in the United States. Years later, when I wrote about C. G. Jung, how I wished I had known that Bridget was the eldest daughter of Jung's close confidante H. G. Baynes, but in my Beckett years I knew her only as an accomplished artist and beloved wife and mother. Brian, meanwhile, became one of my most trusted advisers. He was a loyal friend to both Beckett and me as well as a walking repository of Irish literary history and culture. If there is richness in the biography about Beckett's Irish years, much of it came from Brian.

James Stern was the other person I contacted on this first research trip to England. He had known Beckett from his earliest years in Paris, when he and Beckett were both members of Joyce's circle. Jimmy was a journalist and writer, and he and his wife, Tania, became close to Beckett when they were in Germany at the same time in the 1930s. Their friendship continued, and whenever Beckett was in England, he sent tickets to all his productions and dined privately with them. Their contribution to my book was as important as Brian Coffey's.

I knew I had to interview many other people in London who had figured in Beckett's life and work, but I had to let them wait until I was more knowledgeable about the roles they had played. An equally important reason for moving on was a matter of logistics: money was in short supply if I wanted to go to Dublin.

Looking back at some of the notes I took as I left Paris without having seen Beckett, I see that I was not in the best or most positive mood when I landed in Dublin. I worked hard and saw many different people whose memories and stories enriched the biography, but in retrospect I had more to say about the atmosphere in which I found myself than about the things I learned. Much of what people told me I eventually discovered was pure and unmitigated gossip. However, there was enough factual truth in the "good goss" that I was able to compile long lists of topics to investigate and people to interview on subsequent trips to Ireland and elsewhere.

On this brief first stay, I concentrated on those who I thought were the most important, and that meant starting with Beckett's family members. His niece, Caroline Beckett Murphy, was the first. In typical fashion, her uncle had told her to see me or not, as he would "neither help nor hinder" me. It was the first time I heard the expression that came to define the book I wrote, for Beckett repeated it to anyone who asked his permission to talk to me. I met Mrs. Murphy at The Shottery, the house she inherited from her parents, where she grew up and was now raising her children. She was gracious and forthcoming with family history, as were Beckett's cousins, Ann Beckett, who lived far out on windswept Howth, a part of Dublin I came to love, and her brother, John, who despite infirmities told me some fascinating tales. Hilary Heron Greene, a cousin who had been close to Beckett's mother in her declining years, showed me the glorious copper cauldrons Mary "May" Beckett bequeathed to her. They all loved "Sam," even though they all seemed to be looking to me to tell them how they should interpret his behavior as a boy and how to understand the man he later became.

With my head reeling, it was time to go home. I was leaving Ireland with piles of tape-recorded interviews, several notebooks filled with ideas for future research, and a huge stack of folders crammed with family photos and documents pertaining to Beckett's education, activities, and memberships in schoolboy organizations. I was returning content that I had made so much progress but sad that I had fulfilled everything but the main purpose I had gone for, to meet Samuel Beckett.

On my last day in Dublin, November 15, when I was so busy packing and so short of time, I decided on an impulse to go to the American Express office to ask if by chance any letters had come for me. To this day I don't know what made me do it. I had long since cashed my last traveler's check and had told no one to send letters to the Dublin office. My Jungian friends would call what happened synchronicity. There was just one, said the clerk, and he handed me a small notecard-sized envelope with a Paris postmark and the thin, spiky handwriting I recognized at once. It was from Samuel Beckett.

He was so sorry he had not been able to contact me before I arrived in Paris, but "something unexpected" (he did not specify illness) had happened and he had been "called away." He had sent a similar letter to the London American Express office, and he hoped that I would receive at least one of them. He would be so grateful if I could possibly return to Paris, where he would be happy to see me at my earliest convenience.

Naturally, I dropped everything and went.

5

After a quick phone call to my husband to sort out the logistics of wiring money to Paris and another to TWA to change flights, I was back in Paris on November 16, once again in the Hôtel du Danube and warned by the desk clerk that the boiler was malfunctioning so perhaps I should go elsewhere. I had to stay there, I told him, as I had a very important meeting the following afternoon. And so there I was, again waiting for my first meeting with Samuel Beckett. I have already described both my nervousness and the hilarity (only in retrospect) of the circumstances. Now, as I think back upon my awkwardness, I think Beckett was probably as nervous as I was, as we each tried hard to put the other at ease. Friends tell me that I often work too hard on social occasions to make others comfortable by chattering away, and that's exactly what I did. I thought he seemed to be smiling even though he said nothing and stared.

I was all set to launch into what I hoped would become the first of many interviews about his life, but faced with his silence I couldn't decide how to begin. After he called himself a charlatan and I replied that I was not sure I was "cut out for this biography business," I told him that perhaps I should just write a long article, a *New Yorker* sort of profile based on the information I had collected in London and Dublin. Suddenly he perked up. "Who have you spoken to, and what did you learn about me?" he asked. I grasped for a starting point, reaching all the way back to Jack MacGowran and how moved I had been by his performance. Somewhere later in my unfocused monologue I told him about the Bushmills that awaited him at Arikha's; he laughed out loud, and his entire visage was transformed. He relaxed and so did I.

He smiled when I told him about my visit to Caroline Beckett Murphy at her family home. That led to a discussion of how I had been drawn to his writing through my love of Joyce's *Ulysses* and how, after an extensive study of Irish literature and history, I recognized so many of the people and places he had incorporated into his fiction. This led to my interest in exploring the relationship between his art and his life and my surprise realization that the critical study I was trained for would not suffice.

That was what had initially intrigued him in my letter, he said, elaborating with an interesting revelation that I filed away carefully for further exploration. For years Beckett had made it known that he never read anything written about his work, but in fact I found that he was well informed and had strong opinions about almost every critical discussion of it. And despite all that ink spilled—all those interpretations of him as (and here he quoted my initial letter) "the poet of alienation, isolation, and despair"—I was the only one who recognized such things as his portrayals of some famous Dublin characters and the actual places in the Wicklow Hills, County Kildare, and Leixlip.

How then did I intend to go about writing his biography? Beckett asked. I was totally unprepared to answer. Off the top of my head, I spouted ideas for how we might work together, most of them drawn from my career as a journalist. Only much later, when I made friends with other biographers who described their anguished work situations, did I realize how naive I had been in asking for the most privileged arrangement any writer could wish. I told him I would conduct formal fact-finding interviews with others as well as with him, and I would expect him to answer my questions and provide clarification, correction, or enhancement. Also I would expect to receive whatever documentation I might ask for, such as letters, photos, and manuscripts. I would want to interview his family, friends, and professional associates, and I hoped he would tell them to cooperate. And, oh yes, I concluded, it would probably be best if he did not read what I wrote about him until it was published.

Without hesitating, he agreed. I didn't think much about his readiness to cooperate at the time. Having no idea how biographies got themselves written, I assumed that everything I asked for was the standard procedure. "My word is my bond," he told me, and I was ecstatic to think that all lights were green and all roads were open. It wasn't too long after that that I came to understand why he cooperated so blithely: he did not take me seriously.

I learned this one year later, when I was once again in Paris. I was shocked during a dinner at the home of the artist Stanley William Hayter and his wife, Désirée Moorhead, when Con Leventhal and Marion Leigh offered to tell the rest of us what Beckett had told them about me after our first meeting. Fueled by good wine, Con energetically quoted Beckett as waving his hands and saying, "Good God, the woman has striped hair!" He was referring to what was known in those days as a frosting and now as highlights. An overzealous hairdresser had made huge streaks of platinum blond in my normally light brown hair, which were indeed garish and which seemed to take forever to grow out. When Con told this story, I thought it was clear that Samuel Beckett found everything about me amusing. If he did not take me seriously as a person, he certainly felt the same about my project.

My astonishment slowly bloomed into anger. I sat through the rest of that dinner smiling as the others laughed at "the striped hair girl" or prodded me to tell them "whatever you and Sam talked about" in our meetings. Yes, I was smiling, but deep down I was upset and needed to digest this. I could not wait to leave the Hayters' and take the long walk down the rue de Vaugirard to my rented apartment. Perhaps Beckett did think the best I was capable of was a puff piece, a hagiography of "Saint Sam, the good and great," my private shorthand for the many such descriptions I was fed by people who figured in his life.

Nevertheless, he had told me that his word was his bond, and

I had no reason not to believe him, because our correspondence continued when we were apart, as did our meetings when I was in Paris. I thought back to how the meetings had progressed since that first one in 1971, but especially about how relaxed we had both become as I told him about my adventures in London and Dublin. I remembered how he had told me that he could stay only briefly, and what a surprise it was to us both when he looked at his watch and realized he had spent so much time with me that he was going to be late for everything else he had planned for that afternoon and evening. Our second meeting did take place then, on the following afternoon, November 18, again at my hotel, again at two o'clock sharp. I hope I hid my smile and stopped muttering to myself as I walked through the Luxembourg Gardens one year later after that dinner at the Hayters', probably frightening late-night strollers. I was thinking of several things Brian Coffey had told me to "always remember about Sam." First, "he is a stickler for punctuality." The second had particular relevance after I found out what Beckett had said about my striped hair. Brian told me that "Sam never does anything he does not want to do." He expanded on that statement, telling me that of all the young would-be poets and writers in their university days, none so wanted "to know what posterity would think of him while he was still alive to know it as Sam." I entered my building having decided that I would pay no attention to such frivolous commentary. I would continue to do the work I thought needed to be done; I would write the book I thought needed to be written. I remember that I slept very well that night.

6

To return to 1971 and our second meeting, we began again at two o'clock precisely, to continue talking about the ground rules for how I would work. Once again Beckett used the expression that had caught my attention the previous day. Recapping the plan I had laid out, the perfect situation I wanted, he interrupted to state that of course he would "neither help nor hinder" my independence. Through seven years of emotional ups and downs I clung to those words—I thought it such a striking phrase that I printed it on a file card and hung it over my desk. Truth be told, he did end up helping me throughout the writing process, but the unorthodox way in which we worked created a certain amount of hindering as well, as I was about to find out.

As I headed for the tiny table, Beckett suggested that we might repair instead to the *bar-tabac* next to the hotel, where he had spotted a secluded empty booth. While we were getting settled, I thought I should begin what I assumed was going to be a formal interview with some easy conversation. I asked about his years at Trinity College, Dublin, where between 1923 and 1928 he had been an undergraduate and graduate student and for a brief time a lecturer. I asked him for the various places in college where he had lived and he rattled off the names of the dormitories and the room numbers. Because I have severe math anxiety and numbers throw me, I fished madly in my purse for pen and notebook to write them down before I confused or forgot them.

Suddenly he jumped up and shouted, "What are you doing?" I tried to explain, but he broke in: "No pencils! No paper! We are just having conversations. We are two friends talking. You must never write anything that we say. And don't even think of a tape recorder." As if this were not unsettling enough, he added a seemingly bizarre non sequitur: "And you must not tell others that I meet with you. Ever!"

I was utterly stunned by this. I was used to keeping very careful records, everything from reporter's notebooks to tape recordings. Often I supplemented them with thoughts and impressions in different colored inks, even cross-referencing where appropriate. I was still unsure about how to go about writing biography, but I assumed from the first that the genre required even more careful documentation than I had applied to journalism. I knew that I had to figure out new ways to operate in such constricted circumstances. We were roaming far and wide on that dismal gray afternoon as he suggested people I would probably want to see, and I had to struggle to keep all those names in my head.

Time was passing and the *bar-tabac* was growing dark when suddenly the door burst open to admit a noisy gaggle of young men from the medical school across the street, and the sleepy bartender rose from his nap over a newspaper to turn on the lights and the radio at the same time. I was concentrating so hard on the details of our conversation that I didn't realize Beckett was trying to get my attention until I felt his hand on my sleeve. I looked up and saw that one of the young men was bent over our table, staring in utter disbelief and stammering both a question and an exclamation: "You—you—you are Beckett!?"

Beckett, ever the gentleman, handled the situation with aplomb. Turning first to me, he asked if I would permit the young man to sit down with us. What could I say but yes, even though I was irritated that Beckett wanted me to share my limited time with one of his fans. Beckett deftly turned the fellow's questions into his own: where did he come from, what year of his studies was he in, what kind of medical practice did he envision? But the student was indeed a true fan of Beckett's writing, and I heard him beg Beckett for his address so he could take his copies of the novels and plays around for signing. Beckett deflected the request by saying he was on his way to his publishers, where he would sign copies and have them sent to the young man's home if he would provide his address.

The break time was over, and with a great deal of fuss and confusion, the raucous group left the bar. The bartender turned down the radio, dimmed the lights, and returned to his newspaper while Beckett turned to me and said, "He was such a nice young man. I could not refuse him." I think I managed a thin smile, but this would hardly be the only time I was with Beckett when someone recognized him. Beckett was too polite to ever turn away his public. Usually these encounters were brief, but I still resented having to share my limited time with him, and I believe he knew it. Although I tried never to show it, I think there were times when he deliberately prolonged these encounters just to see if my composure would break. It was only one of the several games I thought Samuel Beckett played as he tried to test my resolve to write his biography.

It had been a long afternoon and I was mentally exhausted as darkness fell. Beckett was indeed on his way to Jérôme Lindon's office at Les Éditions du Minuit, not only to sign books for the medical student but also for an evening rendezvous to talk about rights and permissions for an upcoming production. He told me that Lindon was his "guardian of the gates," and he counted on the publisher to relay decisions (usually negative) for which he did not want to claim responsibility.

Watching him sway down the rue des Saints-Pères, I was actually relieved to see him go. Back at my hotel, the first thing I did was to pull out my tape recorder and speak into it everything I remembered, all the while jotting down detailed notes to complement or explain what I was saying. After several hours of feverish work I realized that it was very late and I was terribly hungry, so I walked down to the rue Saint Benoît and into the first bistro I found. As I ate, all I could think about was the challenge that lay before me: conducting extensive interviews without being able to write anything down. How was I even going to remember what questions I wanted to ask, let alone the order in which to ask them?

By the time I finished my late supper I thought I had the answer, and with slight refinements it became my modus operandi from then on.

I called it "playing intellectual solitaire." I wrote each question I wanted to ask on a small file card and laid them out on hotel room beds or apartment dining room tables—wherever I happened to be staying at the time. I committed them all to memory, and in the process I would shuffle them, rearrange and reshuffle them, sometimes rewrite them, always trying to make them more precise, more meaningful, and oftentimes to make them less likely to anger or offend Beckett. I never slept well on the nights before we met, as I would get up to fuss over the cards one more time. And after each interview I would rush back to the hotel or apartment, set up the notebook and tape recorder, and document everything I could remember that he had told me. As I spoke into the recorder, I would try to capture his exact remarks with all their inflections. For example, he might have called someone a "nice fellow," saying it sarcastically and meaning the exact opposite; I would write that down, too. Days later, I was still remembering things from previous interviews and conversations, and I took to carrying small pocket notebooks that were dedicated solely to things he said that kept coming back to me. I would write them down, giving the dates he said them and the context in which they occurred. Remembering and reconstructing was an ongoing process.

I later confided some of my difficulties about interviewing Beckett to two of his friends, the American director Alan Schneider and, on a separate occasion, Con Leventhal. Each shed some light on Beckett's request that I keep our meetings confidential, saying that he insisted on strict secrecy because so many others had asked to write his biography and he had refused them all. There was one candidate in particular he was adamantly against: Richard Ellmann. Ellmann's excellent biography of James Joyce, which I and many critics and scholars hail as one of the finest of our time, was originally published in 1959, when the lives of great men were written with usually oblique references to their sexual peccadilloes, and Ellman's book had deeply distressed Beckett because of its detailed personal revelations. In the 1960s and 1970s, Samuel Johnson's dictum that biography should include "all that is seemly to know" in a man's life reigned, and Beckett thought Ellmann had shockingly overstepped the boundaries of taste and discretion.

At our third and final meeting before I left Paris that November, again at 2 p.m. at the *bar-tabac* next to the hotel, Beckett's face twitched with irritation because I had to refer to the paper on which I had listed all the people whom we agreed that I should interview in Dublin, London, and North America (there were several Canadians), and I needed to make sure the list was complete.

As soon as we finished going over the list, I put the paper away, exhaustion and inexperience leaving me without anything further to discuss. However, instead of claiming he had other appointments to rush off to, as he had done at our first two meetings, Beckett suggested we have another coffee and wind up our "business," since I was going home the following day. He wanted to know how I intended to move forward with what he called "this business of my life"—an expression that became one of his favorite euphemisms for the biography, a word he seldom used.

I told him that the holidays were coming up and I would have to spend the next month or so taking care of my family, deliberately stressing the family obligations. Experiences from my newspaper days had taught me that this was a wise approach, and it seemed to jibe with how I thought I should present myself in my new incarnation as a scholar-writer and nascent biographer. I had usually been one of few—if any—women in the newsrooms where I worked, and I had learned early on how to create environments where I could either stop any sort of male passes before they started or else fend them off. I had had to use those tactics on my brief research trip to Dublin the week before meeting Beckett, and I wanted to make sure that if any sort of gossip about my behavior was relayed to him in Paris, he would have my version of the story for comparison. It is trite to say, I know, but like Caesar's wife, I believed the only way he would take me seriously was if I were above and beyond reproach.

I had already been propositioned by one person in Paris who knew Beckett, and during the following years there would be others. Frenchmen were always quite direct. "Are we going to bed?" one asked. "No," I replied. "Fine," he said, and that was the end of it. An Englishman who became a very good friend to me and my book, the entrepreneur Tony Johnson, was also direct. A denizen of swinging sixties London, he, too, asked if we were "going to get it on." No, I told him, as I rolled out a portrait of myself as the happily married mother of two young children who did not want to risk anything that would harm that happy *Leave It to Beaver* life. "Fine," he said, before offering me the use of whichever one of his several apartments he was not in at the time, either in London's posh Shepherd Market or Paris's rue de Vaugirard overlooking the Jardin du Luxembourg. These advances were never threatening and usually friendly, easily dispensed with in the moment. If I thought there was a possibility of harassment or danger, I found ways to extricate myself and make it clear that such behavior would not be tolerated. In several cases, strangely enough, some gentle invitations that I politely rebuffed opened the door to genuine friendships that lasted for years.

I presented that same portrait of myself to Beckett because I wanted him to understand clearly that I was there only to write a book. That was my work; my life was elsewhere. In retrospect, I was making a very important decision about how I would conduct my professional life, one that would prove crucial to my development as a biographer. I've heard stories of biographers who so identified with their subjects that they moved into their homes or affected the same styles of hair and makeup. A woman who called herself Anaïs Nin's biographer wore Nin's clothes and makeup after she died, and one Napoleon biographer claimed he could write only when he wore a hat purportedly belonging to the Little Corporal. I've also listened to biographers so determined to shoehorn a subject into a theory or thesis that they boast of manipulating materials to ensure that *they* and not their subject have the final say on how the life was lived. In one case two biographers tried to top each other with tales of how they created false personae, stopping just short of outright lying to coerce information out of people they were interviewing. From the first I knew that none of that was for me.

By making a grand show of my personal circumstances, I was deliberately framing my professional life as lily white and spotlessly clean. In other words, *Hands off me. All that matters is the work I am here to do.* And it worked—most of the time.

Beckett listened to me without interjection but with a slight hint of a smile on his face, and when I was finished, he made no comment. He realized what version of myself I was presenting. He said he would welcome me the following summer, when I planned to bring my family with me for a long research trip. In the meantime we would stay in touch through letters, and I would start on the several hundred interviews I wanted to conduct.

After the rocky start of our long-postponed first meeting and the detailed conversations that set up the ground rules during the two that followed, I flew home in deep contentment, relishing the work and envisioning the adventures that I hoped lay before me. After lunch and a little bottle of TWA's bad wine, I slept all the way to New York.

1

I returned to Paris for my second research trip in the spring of 1972, as I had told Beckett I would once I was a newly minted doctor of philosophy and had my dissertation in hand. I did not have a teaching job, nor did I want one. Several publishers were interested in offering book contracts, and that was where I focused my energies.

Beckett and I met again in the *tabac* next to the Hôtel du Danube, with me determined to show him everything I had written and then ask for his comments, corrections, suggestions—whatever he wanted to offer for the biography. As I worked my way through the dissertation, conversation was cordial until we arrived at the final third, what I was calling "Notes Toward a Possible Biography." He threw up his hands and said we had done enough for one day and perhaps we should save that topic for another time. In fact, he concluded, perhaps we should never discuss it at all; perhaps I should just proceed without any advice or input from him. I remember trying to lighten the mood by speaking of the role of the United States Senate when I said something like "and give no advice and no consent either." He not only did not reply, he gave me a withering look that I interpreted as my cue to end that afternoon's meeting.

I saw him one other time on that trip, again in the *tabac*. We discussed generalities over coffee and parted amicably. I went home content that everything was proceeding smoothly, and for the rest of that year I worked in libraries in the United States and conducted interviews. The rest of 1972 was a tranquil interlude as I educated myself to write biography, and I was glad to have had it.

———

There was not a happy start to 1973. Jack MacGowran died on January 30, in New York, at the age of fifty-four. The official cause of death was complications after a recent bout of the flu, but the friends in the Beckett world who loved him said the real complications were too many barbiturates and too much whiskey. I started out for his funeral in Manhattan on February 1 but could not get there because of massive car crashes and train delays caused by an ice storm. I was told he had a standing-room audience, which he would have loved.

I had come to think of MacGowran as the friend of Beckett's who was particularly insightful about aspects of his character and personality. We had met frequently throughout 1972, and I learned much about Beckett's ferocious intellect as well as his outlook on worldly things in general, what MacGowran called his "deep compassion for humankind." MacGowran told me that once Beckett and I got deeper into our "just two friends talking" conversations, I would find him retiring but with "a ruthless desire for the truth at any cost." He said that Beckett always insisted he was "a novelist who just happened to write some plays," and when he talked spontaneously about his work, he often said that "writing was an agony." Nevertheless, MacGowran believed that Beckett felt he had no choice but to "show things as they are, as he sees them, to tell everything with compassion, always with humor."

Beckett was famous for never interpreting, analyzing, or explaining anything about his writings, particularly the plays. Although he would discuss modes of interpretation, MacGowran said, Beckett always fell back on the same final comment when questions got too close to the one he hated most: "What did you mean when you wrote X?" He brought such discussions to a quick end with "I would feel superior to my own work if I tried to explain it."

In many of our conversations, MacGowran told me there was one question he had always wanted to ask Beckett directly but that he had never had the courage to ask. "Sam was the only man I ever met who has total womb recall," MacGowran said. "He could remember being in the womb and the exit thereof." The topic rose peripherally when they discussed some of the prose texts MacGowran wanted to use in his monologues, particularly when Beckett explained how he wanted certain lines from *Molloy* to be delivered. I've never forgotten how MacGowran jumped up and acted out those lines for me, and I've always been grateful for our many conversations, which so deeply enriched my thinking about the man who was the writer Samuel Beckett.

I stayed busy during the first six months of 1973 conducting interviews and preparing to spend the entire summer in Paris. I was still finding my way into the various kinds of research necessary for writing a biography. Some of what I did consisted of talking to people who figured in Beckett's life, but always with an eye toward how he interacted with them. One example was wanting to interview Andre Gregory about his production of *Endgame* in New York, because Alan Schneider, Beckett's foremost American director, was intent on stopping it. Beckett refused to grant Schneider's request that he cancel it, and I needed to know why.

I was always in search of historical background, and Cyril Cusack, then playing in Seán O'Casey's *Juno and the Paycock* at New Haven's Long Wharf Theatre, proved to be a walking repository of Irish theatrical history. He also gave me a long list of persons to see in Ireland who became crucial sources.

I spent many days consulting archives, roaming through Yale's Sterling Library in the good old days when the stacks were open, often finding books I would not otherwise have thought to consult. A chance sighting of *Wisden Cricketers' Almanack* told me that "Beckett ii, the younger brother of Becket i [Frank, the team captain and Beckett's older brother], has an awkward habit of walking across the wicket to all balls." Kenneth Nesheim at the Beinecke

Library alerted me to collections where I would not have thought to look, as did the formidable Lola Szladits at the New York Public Library's Berg Collection.

Mostly, however, I concentrated on talking to the two persons who had played major roles in bringing Beckett's work before the American public, the director Alan Schneider and the publisher Barney Rosset. They told me that in letters to them Beckett mentioned that he had met me in Paris, but he said nothing about my writing a biography, only that I would probably be contacting them. He did not say whether he approved or not or whether they should cooperate or not. I think both men initially agreed to see me because they were curious.

At least Alan was, for when I went to his home in Hastings-on-Hudson for the first time, he plied me with question after question about my relationship to Beckett. I recited my usual litany, the condensed, rote version of the nice Connecticut housewife-turned-scholar/writer, with almost-teenage children, a museum administrator husband, and two English bulldogs and two Persian cats. I felt silly saying all this, but Alan was a persistent inquisitor who was familiar with women who may have begun their relationship with Beckett professionally but which they often managed to turn personal. Alan was not going to tell me anything about a man he revered and also tried to protect until he decided whether I was "legit" (his word). In the years I knew Alan, I saw how quickly he assessed character and made decisions; he certainly made a quick one about me that day.

He took me into his office and showed me everything from photos to production notebooks. He pulled out files of correspondence between him and Beckett and also between him and everyone involved in his productions, from actors to stagehands. That day was the start of an important working relationship as well as a friendship that lasted after the biography was published and until his tragic death in 1984, when he stepped off the curb into heavy traffic on a London street and looked the wrong way.

Barney Rosset was not as curious about me as Alan had been.

He took me at face value, as just another writer who was simply writing a book about his beloved Sam. Barney told me I would have to go to Syracuse if I wanted to see documents and correspondence, because he had given most of his archives to that university's library. However, he was happy to tell me stories of his love and respect for Beckett, which included naming his son after his "most favorite author." Barney also told me something that stood me in good stead during all my meetings with Beckett: that he had a quick temper, which could turn vicious in an instant. His anger would come on suddenly, and then, just as suddenly, he would bring it under control. Barney told me that it took a great deal to make Beckett erupt and I would probably never see it, but he was wrong: I had the unfortunate ability to ask questions that provoked Beckett's temper far too often.

Apparently my presence in the world of Samuel Beckett had given rise to all sorts of machinations among people I did not yet know, particularly in the academic community. As I was still learning how to create a biography, one of the first things I did after returning from that first meeting in Paris in 1971 was to contact all those who had written about Beckett. By the summer of 1973, when word had gotten out that I was spending the summer in Paris, the idea of a Beckett biography was arousing all sorts of responses whenever I asked people for cooperation. Lawrence Harvey at Dartmouth College gave me photocopies of all the materials Beckett had given him in 1961, when Harvey was thinking of writing a critical biographical study. Later he gave them to the Dartmouth College Library, where they can be read by other scholars. Richard Ellmann, then at Yale, told me he would never grant me an interview because if he had anything to say about Beckett, he would write it himself. Ruby Cohn, who taught at the University of California, Davis, was disdainful, but she did have graduate students who were writing about Beckett and she expected me to share my findings with them. Hugh Kenner, at Johns Hopkins, did not answer my letter. James Knowlson, then on the faculty of the University of Reading in England and later a Beckett biographer, told me that any scholar was welcome to consult the Beckett archive he was instrumental in setting up there. He did not respond to a request for an interview. There were other so-called scholars, all of whom claimed close friendships with "Sam" and who boasted of spending booze-soaked evenings carousing around Montparnasse with him. When I checked the dates of their stories, they all unraveled, because Beckett was not even in Paris when most of these jaunts were supposed to have happened. And even if he had been there, he had all but given up drinking.

And then there were the publishers who claimed special connections to Beckett and who thought I should grant them the right to publish the book—for free, of course—because of the honor they would bestow upon me. When I said that I was already under contract, Jeannette and Richard Seaver, publishers at Arcade Press, were the first to be offended. Beckett's British publisher, John Calder, was the next. Richard Seaver had been one of Beckett's earliest champions in the 1950s, when he published short stories in the literary magazine *Merlin*. The Seavers were great friends of Calder's then-wife, the singer-dancer Bettina Jonic, who had never met me but who nevertheless came to New York and told the Seavers that everyone in London was boycotting my project, so they should tell everyone in New York to do the same. Curiously, her husband's partner at Calder and Boyars, Marion Boyars, was in New York at the same time, and she took me to lunch to implore me to break my contract with Larry Freundlich at Harper's Magazine Press and sign one with her firm. When I replied that I was content (thrilled, actually) to be where I was, she rushed back to London to tell John Calder that he needed to write a Beckett biography they could publish before mine. When I later met Calder, he laughed as he told this story, saying he didn't think I would ever write a biography, so neither would he. By the fall of 1973, however, he (like so many others) was taking the biography seriously, because what I called "the bandwagon effect" was well under way:

the train carrying those who cooperated was leaving the station, and suddenly all sorts of people wanted to jump on board.

It started before I went to Paris, in April, when I had personal business in San Diego. In one of life's little ironies, my mother and Samuel Beckett shared the same birthday, April 13, and I decided to visit her and make a side trip to San Francisco to talk to Kay Boyle. Her ties to Beckett began during his earliest years in Paris, and they continued with a friendship that lasted for the rest of their lives. She was high among those who wanted to be interviewed, because she did not want to be left out of the book. She wrote to Beckett, who replied with a letter she showed me, in which he said he was "very sympathetic [to me] as a person." For him to write that, she said, meant that he wanted her to cooperate.

Boyle was living in a house on Frederick Street in the hippie Upper Haight. She was dressed in the flowing peasant garments and heavy native jewelry so typical of the time and place. A formidable presence, she was tall, rail-thin, of regal bearing and strong views. Her version of Beckett was so overwhelmingly and powerfully opinionated that even as I took copious notes, I knew that everything she said had to be fact-checked to the nth degree—particularly when she kept insisting that I must not write one word about her archrival, Peggy Guggenheim, the first wife of Boyle's husband, Laurence Vail, and partner in a flaming affair with Beckett in the 1930s. Guggenheim, Boyle told me, "MUST" (her emphasis, in a strong voice then and all caps in a later letter) be left entirely out of the book. In the end, with the exception of her dislike of Guggenheim, almost everything Boyle told me turned out to be as close to the truth as any postmodern iteration of that word permits, and I considered her a reliable source.

I saw her several times after that first meeting, and for several years after, I called on her whenever I was in San Francisco. She would invite me for tea or a glass of wine (one small glass), obviously hoping for news of Beckett. Thus I found it curious when, forty-four years later, in 2017, I met the journalist Jan Herman, who had also written about her, and he told me how, when he interviewed her in 1987, shortly after the death of her friend and his, Nelson Algren, she insisted that she had refused to give me any assistance at all. She told him she had never spoken to me and had advised everyone she knew who was also a friend of Beckett's to do the same. I found it odd because of the letters we exchanged, especially the one she sent immediately after the biography was published in which she praised the book highly. I wish I had known about what she told Herman while she was still alive. I would have asked her what had happened to make her believe she had never met me, especially because so much of what I wrote about her role in Beckett's life could have come only directly from her.

I have thought about Kay Boyle ever since my conversation with Herman, because her shifting memory represented something that puzzles me and many other biographers. There is often a fairly significant contingent of people whose memories of their interactions become, as Boyle's were with me, far, far removed from reality. Some people I talked to exaggerated their roles, often in a direction far from their actual closeness to Beckett. Those who helped sometimes wanted to distance themselves from the written life, while some who put serious obstacles in my path lost no time in claiming that I could not have written the book without their constant guidance. I thought about this particular trick of memory, of deliberately forgetting, while writing this bio-memoir and reading Julian Barnes's *The Noise of Time*. He writes of how Shostakovich could not remember whether he had gone to the Finland Station when Lenin returned to Russia. "He no longer knew which version to trust," Barnes writes. "Had he really, truly, been at the Finland Station? Well, he lies like an eyewitness, as the saying goes."

April was almost over when I returned home, and I had only May to prepare for my first long research trip to Paris, where my family would be with me. My husband, Von, was beginning his career as a museum administrator and was able to arrange his schedule to be with us. It was an exciting time, and the month flew by. The kids, Vonn Scott and Katherine Tracy ("Katney"), needed new shoes and haircuts, and there were orthodontist appointments to keep. Many activities were connected with the end of the school year and required family attendance; passports had to be put in order and plane tickets picked up, house sitters lined up for the animals. And then there was my professional life as I ran back and forth to New York, trying to cram in as many interviews and as much background work as possible. I had to figure out a schedule for everything I needed to do on this trip and, most important, to let Beckett know when I was arriving, as I was hoping he would be there to see me. I don't remember getting much sleep that month, but somehow we all pitched in and managed to organize the details. I left first, to find an apartment, sort out what our daily life in France would require, and set up a work schedule that would somehow—magically—allow me to have fun with my family even as I tried to navigate through what was fast becoming a daily round of rather strange experiences. I was beginning to think of myself as Alice, up and down the rabbit hole, and my summer in Wonderland had not even begun.

8

I exchanged several letters with Samuel Beckett between January and May of 1973 that were mostly about my research and interviews and his work and travel. He told me he was going to London in January to work with the actress Billie Whitelaw on *Not I* and with actor Albert Finney on *Krapp's Last Tape*. Even though he would not be in the theater to see it, his plan was to stay through Whitelaw's opening night on January 16 and return to Paris the next day. Then he wanted to leave immediately for his country house, about forty miles northeast of Paris, in Ussy-sur-Marne, where he needed to take care of his voluminous correspondence before heading "south and sunward" to Morocco. He agreed that it would indeed be best if I waited until the summer before coming to Paris. Beckett did not tell me, but he did tell George Reavey, that he had had all his remaining teeth pulled before leaving Paris so that new dental prosthodontics would enable him to eat normally while in London. He had a sentimental fondness for his first novel, *Murphy*, and he also told Reavey that while walking in Kensington Gardens to the Round Pond, he had seen a man resembling his character "Mr. Kelly without his kite."

I wrote to Beckett that the reviews I had read of *Krapp's Last Tape* gave guarded praise to the production, but the few people I knew who saw it had mixed feelings about Finney's acting. Beckett replied that Finney was "miscast" and he was not pleased with his portrayal. When we talked about it in Paris some months later, he was vehement about his distaste for the actor. Holding his ubiquitous little brown cheroot in one hand and slapping the other down hard on the table, Beckett said, "Finney was the worst Krapp I ever had." I tried hard to stifle a giggle and was almost choking to hold back laughter when he realized his double entendre. He gave a little shrug and colored slightly—certain topics actually made him blush. "Oh well," he said as he laughed, too, and we moved on to other subjects.

In one of his replies to my several letters that spring asking when I should plan to be in Paris, Beckett told me he would spend the summer going back and forth between Ussy and his apartment on the boulevard Saint-Jacques and we could meet during that period at our mutual convenience. I arrived armed with introductions to people who knew someone who knew someone who might have a place to rent. My agent, Carl Brandt, sent me to one of his clients, the writer John Gerassi, whose parents had been close friends of the young Jean-Paul Sartre and Simone de Beauvoir and who was now writing Sartre's biography. If anyone could help me find my way around the "real Paris," Carl thought, it would be John. I went to see him at his apartment just off the boulevard Montparnasse but got no help in finding one of my own. Instead I got an invitation to lunch that day with Sartre and Beauvoir at the Select, their neighborhood bistro.

Gerassi told me he was inviting me only because he needed someone to keep Beauvoir occupied so that she "would not butt in" while he was talking to Sartre. He resented that she was "a nosy woman who always had to be part of the conversation," one who did not hesitate to make her views known. "She likes to talk to American *girls*, particularly if they have read *The Second Sex*," he said. And then he blanched in terror: "You did read it, didn't you?" *Yes, John,* I thought but did not say that, like every *woman* of my background and education, I had read *The Second Sex*. And even though he seemed not to have much respect for Beauvoir or her book, I had tremendous admiration for both.

In any other circumstance I would have crawled over hot coals to meet Simone de Beauvoir and Jean-Paul Sartre, but I had to turn down that invitation because lunch was at 1:30 and I was scheduled to meet Beckett at 2 p.m. and I didn't dare to be one second late. That was in June 1973, and I did not meet Simone de Beauvoir until almost a decade later. I never did meet Sartre, who was already dead by then.

Apartment hunting was not the only thing on my mind when I arrived in Paris in early June; I was also worried about connecting with Beckett. Alan Schneider told me he had found Beckett deeply depressed when they were together on May 10 and 11. He refused to dine out at one of his favorite locales, so they ate a simple meal in Beckett's apartment, during which he kept repeating, "What's the sense of living when all your friends have died?" He did not specify who was dead or why he was dwelling on his own mortality. Alan said I should prepare myself to take Beckett's mental state into consideration when I interviewed him, as his present sadness and gloom might color his recollection of past events. My career in journalism had made me aware of the nuances of memory and how they imposed themselves on accurate recall, so I made a careful note to keep in mind that Beckett might be recalling parts of his life through the lens of his present negativity rather than through an accurate picture of how he had experienced them.

Beckett had given me his telephone number and instructions about how and when to call. He had set up a code: I was to dial at precisely 1 p.m., let the phone ring twice, hang up, and call again, and he would then answer. But when I got to my hotel at the end of May, I found a note telling me that he was in Ussy and would stay there until sometime around June 19 or 20. With my list of apartment leads yielding no immediate results, I decided on the spur of the moment to rearrange some interviews and go to Geneva to see Beckett's cousin Maurice Sinclair and then on to Venice to see Peggy Guggenheim.

It was desperately hot when I arrived in Paris, and I packed only the most casual summer clothing for this short trip, which meant I was not dressed appropriately for anything. During my first stop, I froze in Geneva's constant cold rain. Maurice was the son of Beck-

ett's beloved aunt Cissy (Frances Beckett Sinclair) and her colorful husband, Henry Morris Sinclair, always called "the Boss," and
Beckett often sought comfort in the Sinclairs' home in Germany
during his unhappy years in the 1930s. Even though Maurice had
been just a boy then, I thought that collecting his memories would
be important, as it would help significantly, to use the expression
I liked, "to put flesh [color] upon the skeleton [biographical facts]."
I thought Maurice could be especially helpful regarding Peggy,
his older sister who had died tragically young of tuberculosis. Letters and photos given to me by Beckett's cousins in Ireland and his
niece, Caroline Beckett Murphy, showed that Beckett had been in
love with Peggy Sinclair. All these relatives were convinced that
the elderly Krapp's reminiscences of his lost love were an expression of Beckett's feelings about Peggy.

Maurice relayed fully to Beckett everything he told me during
that first meeting in Geneva, and he did the same after we met
several times later when he came to Paris on business. I suspect
this played no small part in Beckett's attitude toward me when I
finally saw him at the end of June. He was astonished at the depth
of my research and had very mixed feelings about it—further confirmation that he had not taken me or my work seriously when we
made our initial agreement. His attitude toward the book fluctuated repeatedly over time, but the first time I noticed the effect
the project had on him was after I returned from meeting Peggy
Guggenheim in Venice.

My wardrobe left me seriously underdressed in a light T-shirt
and trousers when I met Peggy Guggenheim at her glorious palazzo
on the Grand Canal. I had written in advance asking for an interview, which she had granted, telling me to phone when I arrived. In
the notes I made next to her phone number the first time I called,
I wrote: *"Voice bitchy as hell but she did say come right over."* When
I entered the courtyard, she was sitting in the garden, dressed in
an elegant silk caftan, gold slippers, and the most extravagant cat's-
eye sunglasses, the likes of which I had not seen since the 1950s.
She waved a hand vaguely in the direction of a chair next to a small

table, where she had a vile concoction already poured and waiting for me—Campari and brandy, or something equally potent. Hardly the most cooling drink for a hot afternoon, but I was thirsty, and two quick swigs made me extremely light-headed.

My daily visits to the palazzo for the next week overflowed with booze, so I was relieved not to have to rely on memory or notes, as Peggy let me tape all our conversations. She was pleasant that first afternoon, even if she did natter haphazardly, roaming unfocused through the details of her affair with Beckett. With every other sentence she would interject something about "what an Oblomov he was," comparing his passivity and her relentless pursuit to the hero's lethargy in Ivan Goncharov's novel. She produced three photos taken during the height of her affair with Beckett, at Yew Tree Cottage, her country house in England, and she told me to come back the next day, when she would have more photos, letters, and, most important of all, scrapbooks filled with everything from menus and playbills to love letters (mostly from her). I could not help but think of a warning I had received from Kay Boyle during my spring research, when she had insisted that "Peggy will try to take over your book." But so far Peggy had produced documentation that corroborated everything she told me. Even so, I did remain cautious on each of the afternoons when we met to talk.

On my penultimate day in Venice, Peggy invited me to a very special dinner that night. I was in a quandary, because she had two houseguests, two gay American expatriates, who told me they always dressed for dinner at the Palazzo Guggenheim, which was their way of telling me that I had been seriously underdressed all week. The closest thing I had to evening wear was a polyester dress, an imitation of Diane von Furstenberg's ubiquitous wraparound. It would have to do, as there was no time to shop and I had no money anyway.

When I returned to the palazzo that evening, I knew that something exciting was about to happen. Peggy was in a gold lamé Fortuny, one of those magnificent pleated dresses that had been all the rage in the 1930s. This one had seen better days, because it had been her favorite during the years of her affair with Beckett, and she had quite a few photos of them together while she was wearing it. Nearly forty years later it had become a museum-quality garment, and I was horrified to see her gaggle of pug dogs rubbing against it, snorting, drooling, and leaving traces of their scabrous skin diseases all over its beautiful fabric.

She had instructed me to get there early, before her other (unnamed) dinner guests arrived, as she wanted to show me the bed with the silver headboard that Alexander Calder had made for her. We were accompanied by the two houseguests, the wealthy American John Goodwin, who told me he lived in Ireland for "estate purposes," and another man I knew only as Hornsby, who lived in Rome and advised her on her art collection. As we walked to the bedroom, the two men squabbled in low voices that only I could hear over who would occupy the Calder bed with Peggy that night. Because she had bad dreams and fitful sleep if left alone, one of the duties of houseguests was to take turns sleeping there, too—no euphemisms meant here, or as one of my favorite Beckett sayings has it, "no symbols where none intended." Everything so far was Alice in Wonderland territory for me, and the evening became even more surreal when we returned to the living room and the other guests arrived.

In walked playwright Lillian Hellman, escorted by the young poet David Kalstone. I had read enough about Hellman to know that she could be bitingly cruel, and from one of my friends who thought he might write her biography I knew that at dinner parties she liked to pick on one person to ridicule, especially a young woman. As I was the only one, I expected the worst. Hellman was dressed in something long and formal that I thought looked like a bathrobe. It was half open down the front, revealing a hideously wrinkled décolletage made especially noticeable because of the collection of impressively large sapphire stones in the tight choker she wore.

When introductions were made and drinks served, I sat quietly as close to a corner as I could find in that grand salon. I tried to let the conversation flow over and around me, but there was not very much of it, because the hostess and her primary guest were meeting for the first time, and after sizing up one another, they seemed to find each other boring. Peggy paid attention to her dogs and Hellman spoke only to Kalstone. The two houseguests continued their grumpy squabbling about the Calder bed, and I just sat there grinning and probably looking foolish. Second drinks were not offered, Peggy seemed to have fallen asleep, and everyone else had fallen silent. The only noise came from the snorting pugs until we heard shuffling footsteps echoing along the marble floors of the hallway. It was such an eerie sound that we all sat there listening in mesmerized silence until in came a very old and stooped man, wearing what looked like broken-heeled bedroom slippers, telling us to adjourn to the Braque dining room for dinner.

Although I had seen most of the palazzo's rooms on previous visits, I had somehow missed this one. I was stunned by it. A sixteenth-century refectory table set with hand-painted pottery dishes representing the months of the year gleamed in the soft candlelight that lit the magnificent paintings on the walls. We were about to take our seats, me in the middle on one side of the table, Hellman directly opposite, when Hellman beckoned me to come over to her side. I feared that my session of verbal torture was about to begin, but all she did was whisper, "My mother's sapphires are choking me. Would you kindly take this damned thing off me?" And so, with shaking hands, I removed her choker before quickly returning to the other side of the table.

The little man came shuffling back into the room, this time carrying a huge black cast-iron pot tucked under his arm. With a wooden ladle, he reached in and plopped something down on each dinner plate. In retrospect, I think it must have been some version of tomato-beef stew, but what I remember most about the glop on our plates was Hellmann leaning over and whispering to me, "Now I know how the rich stay rich: look at the slop they eat."

I saw Peggy one last time the next day and returned to Paris loaded down with the papers and photos she had given me, my head reeling as I relived the bizarre and magical week in Venice. Once I was back, practical concerns reasserted themselves and the apartment search continued. I was fortunate to find one belonging to a British professor who taught at the Sorbonne and was returning to England for the summer. It was in a traditional turn-of-the-century building, formerly grand and now slightly shabby, on the rue d'Alésia in Montparnasse. With six spacious rooms, parquet floors, gracious moldings, and wide windows overlooking the trees that lined the street, it was perfect for us. I moved in on July 1 and prepared for my family's arrival the next day.

That night I had the fright of my life when the concierge brought a letter from my husband, Von. "Don't be alarmed when you see Katney," he wrote, without elaboration. So naturally I was worrying so much that I hardly slept. When the family stepped through customs at Orly the next morning, I saw Katney, then twelve, with a plastic mask covering most of her face, and I nearly fainted until she told me, sheepishly, why she was wearing it. She had been pestering her brother (almost fourteen) with a water pistol and he had swung his arm to avoid getting wet, accidentally hitting her nose and breaking it. Fortunately, she was well enough healed that she needed to wear the mask only for another week or so, and then just when doing something that might compromise her recovery.

The Alésia neighborhood was a family-friendly area, and ours settled in quite seamlessly. Because we all spoke French in varying degrees, we found warm welcomes everywhere. Both children were studying French at school, and Von knew enough of the language that they could all navigate quite well on their own while I was working. Vonn Scott went out every morning to bring back fresh croissants, along with the neighborhood news from Madame, who ran the local bakery and apologized for having to increase the price a few centimes every time the price of butter went up. Katney forgot to put a cake of soap in her basket one day when she did the shopping at the little grocery store across the street. When the clerks saw me coming home from an interview, they ran out with much chatter and arm-waving to give it to me, saying they had saved it until they saw one of us, their neighbors. All in all, we could not have been better situated.

It was good that the others could manage on their own, because my days were fully booked. Besides meeting with Beckett, I was lining up interviews with everyone I could think of who had ever known him, from his publisher, to people he had worked with in the theater, to his friends, and even to some relatives passing through on their way to Ireland or England. I had enough work to keep me busy for the rest of the year, let alone the summer. But first I had to determine how I would proceed with Beckett, and the most immediate decision I had to make was how to broach the subject of his meeting my family.

He was still in Ussy when they arrived, and so I decided to write a letter, for after all, a letter had worked when I had proposed writing his biography. It was a brief note, asking if he would like to come to the rue d'Alésia for tea, or perhaps to meet us for coffee at the large Café Zeyer on the corner by the Métro station. His reply was not unexpected: he declined, saying that he and I must stick strictly to the "business of his life" (his quotation marks). Frankly, it was a relief. Even though I wanted my children to be able to say in years to come that they had met Samuel Beckett, I was glad not to have to worry about where or how that meeting would take place. When he and I met the following week, in a café on the boulevard Raspail near his apartment building, he tried to offer an excuse about being "too busy" and not being good with "small children" (even though he knew mine were teenagers), and I responded at once to say that I quite understood. After that we never spoke of it, even though he came perilously close—literally—to running into them one week later.

Both children were excellent runners—Vonn Scott was a New England prep school champion long-distance runner, while Katney was managing the school's team and doing well in her own races. My husband ran marathons in Boston and New York, among other

prestigious races. All three ran every day in the glorious Parc Montsouris near our apartment, and whenever possible I jogged along
way behind them, after which, thoroughly winded, I plopped down
with books or newspapers while they did their serious workouts.

I generally sat among all the old men who took their afternoon
leisure in chairs along the running path. I called it my daily giggle
as I watched them nod approvingly when the kids roared past, then
ask each other concernedly, *"Où est le papa?"* until my slower husband appeared several minutes later. I was deep into a *Le Monde*
article about the unfolding Watergate break-in when I looked up
and saw the long thin figure of Samuel Beckett, who also liked to
walk in the park, sway into view. In a moment of confusion followed by panic, I slouched down in my chair and held up the paper
to hide my face. Beckett, lost in his own private world, crossed in
front of my little group of old men without seeing me and continued on his way. When he was almost out of my sight, my children
appeared from the other direction, not exactly crossing his path
but close enough that they could see each other. Naturally there
was no flash of recognition on either side. When I made a note of
this near-encounter later that day, I could not help but use the trite
expression of ships passing in the night.

As July continued the heat intensified, and as I ran around Paris
every day, I sometimes thought I'd never survive it to chase down
even one more interview. Theater people I saw ranged from the
famed actress Madeleine Renaud and her actor-director husband,
Jean-Louis Barrault, to the playwright-director Simone Benmussa,
to two of Beckett's favorite actors who had been in the original
Godot, Roger Blin and Jean Martin. Publishing people included
Mrs. Jenny Bradley, the legendary agent who seemed to have been
in Paris forever as the representative of every possible literary light,
and who had known Beckett since the 1930s. Von and I dined with
Bill Hayter and Désirée Moorhead in their atelier on the rue de
l'Observatoire. There I met the Irish poet John Montague, whom I

interviewed shortly after on the rue Daguerre in the studio of his first wife, Madeleine Montague. She worked in publishing and she, too, was a friend of Beckett's, so I interviewed her and the other people she led me to in publishing and journalism who played small but significant roles in Beckett's life. One person eluded me, not because she wanted to but because she was not in Paris: Maria Jolas. Her daughter, the composer Betsy Jolas, told me that her mother was looking forward to meeting me when she returned from a week in London.

As I began to write this bio-memoir, I dug out a box of old calendars and appointment books, hoping to establish chronology and verify dates. Until I reread them, I did not remember how much more they contained, filled with detailed observations about all the people I interviewed. I called them the *Daily Diaries*, or the *DD*. And I did not appreciate how valuable they would be until I heard Margo Jefferson speak about the various techniques she used in her memoir, *Negroland*. Jefferson said she wanted "to show the makings of a particular self at a particular time, at a particular moment in history." My *DD* permitted me to present myself as I was then, the young woman writer feeling her way toward a new kind of writing, even as the self who writes this now is using the perspective of time and distance. The older (and I hope wiser) me needed help to recall that brash young woman who became aware only gradually that she was upending a small slice of cultural history in a time of significant social change.

Madeleine Renaud was one of the first persons I wrote about in the *DD*. I noted that during our formal interview, "*She sat up and performed into the tape recorder, and when she was finished—that was it. She turned off as if a curtain had gone down and the performance was over. I had the feeling that I was getting the top layer of French cordiality in what she said about SB while underneath there was a packet of worms.*"

It was an accurate perception, because later that day, when I met Roger Blin, he confirmed how difficult Beckett found it to work with her: *"How do you tell the grande dame of French theater that she has to read the lines the way you wrote them? Eventually he had to give up and let her do what she wanted. Nobody benefited from her performance, neither author nor audience."*

My typical mood in those days was one of overheated frustration, as when I first tried to contact Blin. After several attempts, I finally got the phone in a *tabac* to accept my *jeton*, the token that one purchased to make a call on a public telephone. Blin answered on the first ring and said that he had nothing to do, so why didn't I come to his apartment right away, by 5 p.m.? He lived just off the rue de Rivoli in the heavily trafficked center of the city. It was then 4:30 and I was calling from far south, in the thirteenth arrondisement. Not knowing Blin and believing that everyone who knew Beckett was probably as great a stickler for punctuality as he was, I began a trek that started on the Métro, changed to a bus, and finally found me running as fast as I could to get there on time. As I approached Blin's building I looked up and saw a fellow leaning on the iron barrier at the bottom of his window, smiling down on the street scene below. It was Blin, taking his afternoon ease.

I was dripping with perspiration when I climbed up to the fourth or fifth floor—I forget which—where he offered me a beer, warm because he did not have a refrigerator. He said it was good I had not come in the morning, because I would have had to take my coffee black, as he couldn't keep milk or anything else that needed chilling, until winter came, when he could use the windowsill. I sipped the warm beer and sat for several hours while he enthralled me with stories of that first production of *Waiting for Godot*, often jumping up to act a particular scene or sequence, declaiming lines in such a magnificent voice that I was glad the tape recorder was purring away. To my horror, when I tried to play it back, I found that the purring was the result of the machine's malfunctioning, and it had to be replaced. Nothing of that first conversation was recorded, but as was my custom, I had taken copious notes to ensure that I could re-create it.

Over time Roger Blin gave me illuminating stories of how he and the other actors, especially Jean Martin, who played Lucky, approached their roles, and how Beckett interacted with them. Other insights came from Simone Benmussa, who gave me the most accurately detailed description of how Beckett worked on the technical aspects of his plays. She was ostensibly the assistant to Jean-Louis Barrault, who was by then old and ill but unwilling to retire. In reality she was running the company, and it was she upon whom I relied for insights into everything from how Beckett directed to how women were treated in France, not only in theater but in all aspects of public intellectual life. She was a feminist whose insights I relied upon, then and later, during the years when I was writing Simone de Beauvoir's biography. But it was Roger Blin to whom I turned time and again. In the beginning it was for every tale he could tell about staging the first production of *Waiting for Godot*, and then just because he became such good company for me and my family.

My first afternoon with Blin was on a Thursday, and on the following Sunday we were having a little dinner party on the rue d'Alésia to welcome Jean and George Reavey to Paris. Bill Hayter and Désirée Moorhead were coming, and they were bringing two of their friends, the Italian artist Lia Rondelli and her English partner, the artist Eddie Allen. Blin said he'd be delighted to come. He was not working, had not seen Beckett for quite a while, and seldom saw any of the old friends. And if I was a decent cook, he would be happy to eat my food.

That Sunday he was the first guest to arrive, looking spiffy in a blazing yellow Italian silk jacket and a black shirt with huge char-treuse polka dots—an outfit he was proud to say he had bought for the occasion at the Porte de Clignancourt flea market. That was when he told us he never wore underclothes and illustrated it with the story I included in the biography, of the ex-convict who vio-lated parole to come to January rehearsals of *Godot* in thin summer prison garb and who asked Blin for some of his old clothes, par-ticularly his underwear. When Beckett heard about it, he gave the man money to buy what he needed, especially the underwear. My children listened in wide-eyed wonder. The stories continued when the other guests arrived, and the party went on until 2:30 a.m. I think we were all dropping with exhaustion, but Blin kept going strong until he decided it was time to go home. He didn't even say goodbye; he just got up and walked out of the apartment. The other guests staggered after him, and my husband and I left all the dinner's detritus and fell into bed.

The next morning was a busy one for the three other Bairs, who made an early departure for Chartres. I was still lying abed around eight o'clock, as my first interview was not until lunchtime, when the bedside phone rang. The caller said in a loud and imperious voice, "This is Maria Jolas. Sam told me I am not to see you, but he did not say I was not to talk to you. So I am telephoning." I had to ask her to repeat what she had just said, because she had awakened me from a deep sleep. When I finally processed what she was saying, total panic took hold. "Sam" had told her not to see me, but she had decided that his decree did not include the prohibition to talk to me? What sort of mischief would she be creating for me with Beckett? I did not have time to digest my thoughts, because she launched into a monologue that went on for over two hours. I had a small notebook next to the bedside phone, and I filled every page of it. I actually wrote on the wall when I ran out of paper. I sat there with legs crossed, needing the bathroom badly, but the phone cord did not stretch that far and there was no way I could interrupt her.

She covered innumerable aspects of Beckett's life, from the first time he met James Joyce to his relationship with Joyce's daughter, Lucia, to how Beckett met his wife, to what he did in the war—on and on, and onward yet again. I have always described the conversation as "the Gospel According to Maria." Her authoritative declamation of all things literary and her dogmatic insistence that only she knew the truth were irresistible; her charisma was overwhelming—and it resulted in the only factual mistake I would make in the biography. But what I had to deal with immediately after that extraordinary telephone conversation was Beckett himself, for I was scheduled to meet him in the café at Raspail at two that afternoon, and I would have to tell him all about it. What had I done? I wondered—for that was how I thought in those prefeminist days. What sin had I committed, what heinous deed had I done to let her talk, which surely would bring Beckett's wrath down upon my head? I sort of found out that afternoon.

9

The "conversations" I had with Beckett between my other formal interviews took place mostly in cafés next to the Métro stops at Denfert-Rochereau and Raspail, and occasionally at the Falstaff, a restaurant and bar in Montparnasse where all the locals knew him and respected his privacy. Having done my "intellectual solitaire," I was always prepared with more questions than we could possibly answer in the hour and a half to two hours these encounters usually lasted. However, I was seldom able to get through even those at the top of my list, because Beckett always had his own questions. He was intensely curious about what other people were telling me, and because it was his life I was exploring, I thought he had a right to know what they said and to comment on it, so I generally told him what he wanted to know—at least most of it.

Every so often he would ask about something that I was hearing for the first time from him, something that had not come up in any of my interviews. I soon recognized that when he introduced such topics, it was because he thought they belonged in the biography. He would speak in a firm, louder-than-usual voice, all the while looking at me straight on and nodding his head vigorously. Sometimes, when I was mentally filing away his earlier comments, he seemed to think I was not paying close enough attention, so he would repeat his current comment once or twice, again with vigorous nodding. I found myself nodding back, as if to say, "Yes, I got it. Yes, yes, I'll definitely investigate this." I never said it out loud, but once he was sure that what he told me had sunk in, we would continue our "just two friends talking" conversation. These planted topics or pieces of information would go straight to the top of my to-do list for follow-up. And as soon as I had a basic grasp of the rules of the game we were playing, I found oblique ways to ask Beckett to tell me his version of whatever it was that he was so insistent I should investigate.

Once or twice, after I told him what I had discovered and he seemed reluctant to give me his side of the story, I'd say, "Perhaps you'd better give me your version, just to make sure I will get it right." There were certain subjects—his relationships with women high among them—for which this tactic proved essential. Beckett was not only smart, he was shrewd. He knew that sometimes I didn't know much—if anything at all—about the subject in question and that I was hearing about it from him first. He was also clever about guiding me toward the knowledge he wanted me to have by implying that I was to accept his version and go no further. I, in turn, would use what he told me, but only as the starting point for further research and for writing what I eventually concluded, which became the version that ended up in my book. What I wrote was frequently much more nuanced and complex than what he told me, as I sometimes relied upon what others told me as much as or more than what Beckett did.

What had happened between him and Lucia Joyce was one such example. I introduced the subject because at least a dozen people I interviewed insisted that it was the reason for a serious break in Beckett's relationship with Joyce. When I asked Beckett about it, I was unsure of his reaction, whether he was upset, angry, or a combination of both. He dismissed it in several sentences, saying that Lucia may have had "a brief schoolgirl infatuation that was over in a minute," and then he changed the subject. After sifting the testimony of so many people who had been there to observe both Lucia Joyce and Samuel Beckett, and then after reading what Beckett himself wrote in letters to friends (George Reavey and Thomas McGreevy among them), I knew this episode required much more explanation than Beckett's casual dismissal.

By the time I learned this, I had had enough meetings with Beckett to know that even though my questions occasionally led him to lash out in a fit of temper or pique, I sometimes felt free to prod him to answer some he did not like. On one tiring afternoon when he was less than forthcoming, I blurted something like "Well, you'd better tell me about this if you don't want Ellmann to write about it first." Instead of making him angry, it made him laugh, and he did something he often did when I asked about a particular person: he imitated Richard Ellmann. I never met the man, so I cannot vouch for the accuracy of Beckett's imitation, but I think it must have been good. Every time he imitated someone I came to know personally, he was (to use one of his expressions) "spot on." I would sit in wide-eyed wonder at the accuracy of his mimicry, often thinking that he could have acted in anything he wrote because he was so gifted at portraying someone else's character and personality. Some of his imitations were simply funny, but there were others that I thought verged on cruelty and ridicule. To this day, I always describe him as a courtly Old World gentleman with impeccable manners who sometimes shocked me with his sharp, accurate, and devastating portrayals.

All this came up on an afternoon when he was reluctant to talk about his admiration (if not his love) for Ethna MacCarthy, medical doctor and poet, who rejected him to marry Con Leventhal. In exasperation, I made the remark about Richard Ellmann. That was when he launched into the imitation that literally took my breath away. Ellmann's name became a sort of code word during the next several years, when all I had to do was mention it to get Beckett to tell me grudgingly what I wanted to know.

Sometimes, when he wanted to know who was on my list of persons to interview, I would read off names and Beckett would offer capsule biographies, imitate voices, or convey mannerisms. Later, when I met some of these people for the first time, I was struck by how accurately and perceptively he had conveyed their reality. As he ran through each imitation, his face would soften, but curiously, his eyes never met mine and he usually turned his head away. I wondered, was he embarrassed? Was he perhaps ashamed of these moments when he was so open with me? Did he wonder how much of himself he was revealing, and did he worry about how I would interpret his imitations, or if I would write about them? In all the years since then, I have never arrived at a definitive conclusion. Perhaps all these random and unfocused speculations were valid; perhaps none were. When people ask me what it was like to be in the presence of Samuel Beckett, they usually do so with reverence, as if he were a deity. I generally respond as briefly as possible with something respectful but dismissive that will let me turn the conversation to other things. Sometimes I say it was like putting together a difficult jigsaw puzzle; other times I say it was like punching my way out of the proverbial paper bag. Until now, I have told only one or two of my most trusted confidantes how I really felt: most often, like a marionette whose strings he was pulling, because I never knew where I stood with him. In the beginning he was friendly, open, and eager to hear of my interviewing adventures. And for most of that summer of 1973, I was a dutiful reporter, in the sense that I did report back to him much of what he wanted to know about the work I was doing, in library archives (hunting down book and theater reviews) and in personal interviews (when people often gave me correspondence, photographs, and other personal souvenirs). But sometimes things changed and I saw another side of him. Whenever he felt that I was getting too close to something he was reluctant to make known, he could become clipped in his speech, cutting in his comments, and dismissive of my work.

I thought a lot about this while in Paris that summer, because I was still in the process of learning how to become a biographer. Before I made this research trip, I had been invited by the late distinguished scholar and biographer Professor Aileen Ward to join her biography seminar at New York University. There I met other biographers who became my friends, and from them I learned a great deal about technique, method, and content as I struggled to determine what the book I was trying to write should be and to define the task I was undertaking. Mine was unusual, in that I was writing about a living person, while most of my seminar colleagues were writing about people who were long dead. I was often asked by those who worked solely in archives on letters, diaries, and other documents what it was like to conduct research with "talking heads," a common expression for those I was interviewing. Even more, they wanted to know what it was like to interview Samuel Beckett.

All these thoughts coalesced that summer in Paris, particularly when I remembered Con Leventhal's story of how Beckett described me as "the woman with striped hair." Every time I thought about it, I concluded that Beckett considered me an intellectual lightweight whom he was merely tolerating. It was upsetting, because it raised memories of my early days as a journalist, when women were mostly "girl" reporters cordoned off from the men, either doomed to be researchers (as I had been at *Newsweek*) or exiled to the so-called society pages to write about recipes and clothes, bridge clubs and social circles (where my newspaper editors tried to place me before they gave up and let me write news and features). To think that Beckett might be slotting me into this category was depressing. Often I had to remind myself of the two things he had told me when we were setting the ground rules for how I would operate: "My word is my bond," he said, and he would "neither help nor hinder" my work. I clung to this, particularly after Maria Jolas's telephone call, which I felt obliged to tell him about.

I was still trying to sort out how to deal with her bizarre monologue, to determine what—or how much—of what she said I should tell him. Would he become so upset that he would withdraw his cooperation? Eventually I concluded that even after I told him most (but not all) of it, he would keep his word. And if he could find a way to bolster his version of events, he would do so. I hesitate to describe his efforts by using the contemporary word "spin," but sometimes I thought he came perilously close to Brian Coffey's contention that he was trying to shape what posterity would think of him while he was still alive to enjoy it.

I interviewed hundreds of people in the years it took to write Beckett's biography, and in all that time I felt most like a manipulated marionette when he told Maria Jolas not to see me. She was the only person he asked not to cooperate, and when I asked why he had forbidden her, he did another of his imitations, one that portrayed her as the epitome of a nattering, chattering old gossip.

Maria Jolas's phone call presented other, longer-term problems for me, rooted in the fact that much of what she told me touched on sensitive areas. One hard-and-fast rule for what I would use while writing the book came from my career as a journalist: I would need multiple sources for every single story. I knew that much of what I wrote about Beckett was new and unknown to the world at large, and that every sentence I wrote would have to be fact-checked to a fare-thee-well.

Considering Beckett's opinion of Ellmann's Joyce biography and how he compartmentalized his own life, leaving even his closest friends and family members to ask me to tell them things I was astonished to learn they did not know, I became skilled in deflecting such questions so as not to risk Beckett's displeasure. Also, as a researcher, I did not want to dispense information that amounted to mere rumor and might later be proven untrue. With this as my most basic premise, I decided that I would have to have three separate sources for any information I included in the book; three disparate individuals would have to tell me the same story, describe the same situation, reveal the same hitherto unknown fact, all independently and without any prompting from me. And for some of the most sensitive information, I wanted more than three, sometimes as many as five sources, or I would not use it.

Yet even such a rigorous system proved not to be foolproof, and it was Maria Jolas who led me astray with the story of how Beckett met his wife, Suzanne, a topic about which I found it difficult to ask Beckett for the truth. Suzanne was high on the list of subjects Beckett was reluctant to talk about. Although he introduced her name easily into almost every conversation, and he always gave her credit for the struggles she endured to bring his work to publication, her name invariably brought on that deep red blush, a prelude to a quick flash of anger, so I took care to change the subject quickly when these occasions arose.

I must have had more than a hundred people tell me the story of how Beckett and Suzanne met. Half said he met her on a night in the 1930s when he was gratuitously stabbed by a disturbed person as he walked down a street, and Suzanne came to his rescue while he was lying on the ground. The other half said no, he and she were already involved in a relationship well before the stabbing. Maria sided with those who said the two had met when Suzanne happened to be passing by and saw Beckett being stabbed. Because everything else Maria told me checked out, and because most of the sources I trusted the most—many more than five—agreed with her version, that is what I wrote. Unfortunately, it was not true.

After the book was in print and I learned of my mistake, I contacted many of those who had agreed with Maria to tell me again why they believed what they did and where they had obtained their information. Originally they had said things like "Sam told me" or "I was in Paris at the time and visited him in the hospital." Later, while I pressed them for more detail, they would say that actually, upon further reflection, they knew "someone close to Sam who was there" and who told them about it. And that someone always turned out to be Maria Jolas, who was indeed in Paris at that time but who had not been close to Beckett then and had no firsthand knowledge of his private life. I did fact-check—I just didn't check far enough.

One sensitive relationship that I did verify but did not include in the biography concerned the translator Barbara Bray, with whom Beckett had a long-standing affair. It was common enough knowledge, and almost everyone I spoke to in London and Paris knew about it and took it for granted. Furthermore, consensus held that it was nothing untoward; if Suzanne Beckett accepted it, they did, too. It was different in Dublin, where many people snickered as they tried to introduce salacious topics into conversations. The affair came up time and again in many of my interviews, and I struggled over what I should do when—if—I wrote about it. During my research, I made it a point to talk to everyone I could find who had known Beckett, regardless of their opinion of him because I did not want to risk being accused of selecting only the positive and ignoring any of the negative. I had had enough experience to know that, as reporters often said, unless you were writing a puff piece, the operative mode for any story was CYA: cover your ass. If there were unseemly aspects of Beckett's behavior, I had at the very least to consider them, and most probably I would have to write something about them. And in the 1970s, such affairs may not have been thought of as morally reprehensible, but they were certainly something to be kept private.

With this in mind, I telephoned Barbara Bray to ask for an interview, not about her relationship with Beckett but about how she worked alone or with him on translations. I planned to let the conversation unfold naturally and take its own direction. But she did not give me a chance to explain why I wanted to talk to her. She screamed that she knew why I was calling, and if I wrote one word about her relationship with Beckett, one of her children would commit suicide and she would tell the world that I was responsible. I tried to stammer some kind of denial, for I was too shocked to think coherently, while she continued to vilify me before slamming down the receiver. I never wrote a word about her affair with Beckett and only made a discreet reference to her as a translator.

The tenor of the times had much to do with the decisions I made about what to include and what to leave out, and content considered suitable for publication was limited to fairly discreet information. But more than that, my position as a woman biographer (and an untested one at that) placed me in some very large crosshairs. The 1970s were the early days of women writing and publishing novels and memoirs about their own lives and biographies of other women. Although feminist theory was on the upswing, women were told (mostly by men) that they could never achieve success because their subjects were not worthy of study, and besides, when they did write, they approached their topics with too much timidity to make them authoritative. They were accused of "writing differently," and this difference meant that what they wrote was second-rate. Women largely accepted what the men decreed and excused themselves by saying they had too few role models, which perhaps did indeed result in a genuine fear of creativity.

Some pundits called it "the anxiety of authorship," a term I actually found soothing. I confess, I had the anxiety of authorship. I, the bold reporter who had had no fear of asking tough questions for an article, was the victim of some serious mental shaking once the biographer took over and had to decide what to do with personal information.

My family spent the rest of that summer on wonderful excursions, to Chantilly, Versailles, Fontainbleau. Vonn Scott played chess in the Luxembourg Gardens and came home with a sketch of himself bent over the board, a gift from an artist who marveled at the skill of the skinny kid with the blooming blond Afro. Katney was thrilled when she went alone to the big shoe store on avenue du Général Leclerc and bought what became known in family lore as "the French disasters," a pair of bilious yellow plastic shoes that hurt her feet and ended up at our local Goodwill store.

As for me, my feet were hurting, too, as I trudged all over Paris with my heavy tape recorder and notebook, conducting daily rounds of interviews that often left me reeling. After several people spoke to me, they told me they wondered if Beckett knew what he was in for when the biography appeared. I found this a particularly curious way to describe his participation, and I tried to read between the lines of their comment. Perhaps there were negative, painful, hurtful secrets I had yet to uncover, and if so, I had no idea how I would write about them.

Often I found myself sitting in our apartment in the late afternoon, shades drawn to keep out the summer heat, waiting for my family to come home and fill the dinner hour with stories of their adventures, stories that would delight me because of how they relieved the pressure of the unfolding drama of my daily discoveries. More than once I found myself sitting in the dark at night, holding my head in my hands, wondering what I was trying to do. That early sentence—"Oh dear, I don't know if I'm cut out for this biography business"—came back to me over and over. But I was in the thick of it, a process in which I was inventing myself, too, as I went along. I had to follow it at least long enough to determine whether it was worthwhile, and so I continued.

10

Each interview I conducted was different from all others. This was true not only for those to whom I spoke only once, but also for people whose conduct differed over multiple interviews. Someone who was friendly and outgoing, informative and chatty in one conversation could turn stone-cold nasty in the next one. Jérôme Lindon was a prime example. In one of our first interviews, he let me tape for two solid hours while he imparted everything from detailed information to wild gossip about the people Beckett worked with in the theater, and he chuckled through tales about those in publishing who now regretted that they had not published his work when Suzanne Beckett approached them after the war. Lindon showed me all his correspondence with or about Beckett and gave me copies of some of it. He opened his photo archive and gave me a substantial pile, those of the first French *Fin de partie (Endgame)* production among them. He showed me overflowing files of clippings and told me to come back in a few days, when he would have them all ready for my perusal. He was quite different several days later when I phoned to make an appointment, saying that it would not be possible for me to see the clippings because they were "too precious." It was a strange reversal, for they were merely a collection of articles and reviews. Reading them in his office in those pre-Internet days would have saved me a great deal of time that I could have put to better use than having to look them up in archives. When I told Geneviève Serreau, the actress-playwright wife of theater director Jean-Marie Serreau, about Lindon's abrupt about-face, she stepped into the breach and made her own extensive clip files available. She saved me days, if not weeks, of exploring French theater history.

Georges Belmont was another curious interviewee. He was known as a writer and translator when I met him. He first met Beckett in 1928, when he was known by his birth name, Georges Pelorson, and was the only student in his class at the École normale Supérieure studying English; Beckett was the exchange lecturer in English assigned to be his tutor. Their friendship began then and deepened over the years, but it became seriously strained after the war. Pelorson's wartime behavior was less than circumspect but not compromised to the point that he was among those punished in the postwar purge of intellectuals who had collaborated openly. He changed his name to Belmont quietly, lived modestly, and found a minor position in publishing, where he suggested English-language books for French publication and sometimes translated them. It was a life very different from the one he led before the war, when Beckett introduced him to James Joyce and his circle, all of whom welcomed him warmly. Afterward, those who survived, Maria Jolas prime among them, would have nothing to do with him. Beckett was the only one who continued to see him and, on a few occasions, to give him personal recommendations or help him financially.

At my first meeting with Belmont in his office, he was clearly uncomfortable, and so as I always did, I chattered away to put him at his ease. I told him I had made one research trip to Ireland already, and without referring to his name change, I said I was interested in when he first met Beckett in France and then how the friendship deepened when they were both at Trinity College, Dublin. He grew animated as he told me story after story of their collegiate escapades and pranks. His face took on a healthy glow, and his entire body straightened and relaxed. It was clear that he was having a fine time, and so was I, but then it was time to move on. Everything changed when I skipped over the war years and asked simply if he remembered when he and Beckett had met the first time after it ended. Before he could answer, the door to his office opened and in came one of his colleagues, a slight, stern-faced woman who glared at me. I could see fear in Belmont's face, for it was drained of color, and his hands, which had been so expressive, now began to tremble as he tried to light a pipe, a cigarette—I don't remember. I remember only the shaking.

Mary Kling, who had arranged the meeting with Belmont, had warned me of this woman, whom she called his "guard dog" and who had apparently been just outside the closed door for more than an hour, listening to everything we said. The moment I might have turned my questions from pre- to postwar, she was there to protect him.

I told Beckett about this meeting, and my doing so strengthened another impression I was gaining about him. Although he did not like to discuss women—any women, either those he worked with professionally or those with whom he had personal relationships (whether friendly or sexual)—he never hesitated to talk about men, and often in great detail. My ultimate impression of how he felt about Pelorson/Belmont was one of sadness, that here was a man who had begun his professional life with such promise and was now merely living out his days, lonely and suffused with shame.

John Montague presented another different encounter. He wrote from Cork, Ireland, where he was then teaching, to say that he had heard from Beckett that I was writing his biography. Montague was coming to Paris and was sure I would want to talk to him, because he was "so close to Sam." He expected me to accommodate his schedule, and he set the date, time, and place for us to meet: in front of the large church on the avenue du Maine, Saint-Pierre-de-Montrouge, at precisely 11 a.m., after which I would go with him to the Willy shoe store across the street, where he would buy the only shoes that did not hurt his feet, of which there were none to be had in Ireland. Then we would proceed to the home of his ex-wife, Madeleine, on the rue Daguerre, where he would finally allow me to interview him. I had a habit of silently saying "Okaaaay . . ." when I was given such orders, and I certainly said it a time or two before the great day dawned.

When we arrived at Madeleine Montague's, I met a charming Frenchwoman who spoke excellent English and who cheerfully forgave her ex-husband for the philandering that had led to their divorce and his remarriage and fatherhood. She excused herself and left. Montague then directed me to a seat while he positioned himself to stand in front of me at a table where he amassed the materials he wished to present. I felt like a student in a classroom as he began a lucid, professional lecture, clearly thought-out and obviously prepared beforehand, all about how important a player he was in the life of Samuel Beckett. He stopped several times to make sure that my tape recorder was working and that I was also taking careful notes, telling me to be sure to write it exactly as he spoke it and to be sure to cite him effusively in my endnotes and acknowledgments. To reinforce his importance in Irish literature, he presented me with copies of various publications, among them the prestigious *Dolman* magazine.

After several hours of lecturing and marking passages in various publications where he was mentioned, he said he was tired and had to stop for the day, but he instructed me to return to Madeleine's at precisely 11 a.m. the following day so he could give me copies of his correspondence with Beckett. He had kept the best for last, just to make sure that he could reinforce his importance, not only in Beckett's life but also as a major poet in his own right, and also to ensure that he could grill me the next day to see if I had recorded all that he told me. And, oh yes: that evening he was "having a drink with Sam." He dangled another carrot before my little pony nose (for it was clear that to him I wasn't even a mature mare): he said he would be sure to tell Beckett what a "responsible scholar" he thought I was.

Just as suddenly as it had begun, the interview was over and I found myself ushered out onto the street. I reeled my way down the rue Daguerre and through a warren of streets until I got to rue d'Alésia and our apartment. I had to sit quietly for a long time to digest the events of my day, all the while silently saying "Okaaaay . . ."

Writing about Montague made me think of other writers I interviewed who claimed close friendships with Beckett. Their attitude can be described only with the Yiddish word "chutzpah," defined in English dictionaries as "shamelessness" or "gall." I think of Israel Horovitz in this category. His interview took place at his home in New York after he telephoned me in the last frantic May days of 1973 as I tried to organize myself and my family for our Paris sojourn. He had heard of me through Jean and George Reavey and their New York theater grapevine, and because he, too, was "so close to Sam," he said it was imperative that he "enlighten" me before I left. I had not heard of a Horovitz-Beckett friendship before this, but because I followed up every possibility, I dutifully showed up at his house on Eleventh Street at the time he specified. There were no social preliminaries before he ushered me into a chair. With an elaborate ceremonial flourish, he held out a file folder with a cover that he had obviously hand-decorated himself. He opened it reverently to show me a typed series of questions and answers.

"These are the questions you must address in a biography, and to do so, you will need my answers," he said. "You may not use any of your own words or opinions, and you will quote me exactly as I have written here, and you must reproduce this book exactly as it is here. It must be inserted into the middle of your book, so that it opens naturally to these pages, which will be the most important in it." I was too stunned to open my mouth. I just sat there holding this object in front of me, all the while wondering how fast I could get out of there. Horovitz was undeterred, beaming as he told me, "You will not only have the biography of Beckett; you will have the authentic record of his greatest friendship with another great playwright." It was another "okaaaay" moment, and needless to say, none of it found its way into the biography.

The Reaveys came to Paris in early July 1973, and as usual, they created all sorts of dramatic scenarios that ended up causing trouble one way or another, but more for Beckett than for me. Because my family and I were spending the summer in Paris, the Reaveys wanted to be there, too, and they expected me to cater to their whims. At least I was not alone in bearing the burden, which I ungraciously called their "cashing in" on Beckett's generosity. Even though Beckett had already repaid the debt many times over, all these years later, George still laid it on thick with "you owe me" because of all he had done to steer *Murphy* to publication. On this trip, Beckett paid for their hotel, took them to dinner repeatedly, and made an even greater personal sacrifice when, at Jean's insistence, he introduced them to Jean-Marie Serreau and Roger Blin. Jean Reavey fancied herself a playwright and was friendly with the actors at the Mabou Mines company in New York. She had managed to set up meetings with Beckett for the founder-director, Lee Breuer, and some of the actors when they went to Paris, including David Warrilow, who became one of Beckett's finest interpreters and one of his good friends.

The first thing Jean did upon meeting Beckett on that trip was to hand over a huge stack of her writings. When he saw me the next day, he mimed himself staggering under the weight of her scripts and wailed plaintively, "She gifted me with a stack of plays and now what on earth am I to do with them?" I didn't know what to say, so I just shrugged my shoulders. I changed the subject by asking him about Blin and Serreau, and he told me that Jean Reavey had come prepared to give them similar stacks but they had refused to take them, saying they could read only French so she would need to have them translated. Jean immediately looked for help to Beckett, who was embarrassed and horrified by her request but who nevertheless engaged a young translator he knew and liked. Jean's several meetings with him got off to a rocky start, and they ended when the translator left for his August holiday two weeks early to get away from both Reaveys.

Once my family's happy Paris summer was over and we were all back home, the Reaveys thought nothing of phoning at inappropriate hours, whenever the whim hit them, to give me what I called my "marching orders." These consisted mostly of my driving into New York to meet George at Dorrian's Red Hand and buy him drinks while he ever so slowly drew out an "important" letter or two that Beckett had written in the 1930s. I usually managed to drop everything and meet him, because indeed the letters were important, and I needed them. Sometimes, when he could sense my irritation at how he upended my life, he would reach into his pockets and slowly—as if he could not bear to part with them— pull out pages of a diary he had kept during the years when he was trying to sell *Murphy* to publishers; other times he showed me letters with drawings on their pages that were sent to him by his and Beckett's beloved friends Geer and Bram van Velde. George had the only copy of the rotogravure illustration of chess-playing monkeys that Beckett wanted to use for the cover of *Murphy* (the publisher refused, but I used it in the biography); even the newspaper that originally published it did not have one. His pack-rat apartment was loaded with materials that were historically important, not only for the life of Samuel Beckett, but also for the history of midcentury European arts and letters.

George had been a Zelig who knew everyone in the early years of the twentieth century, and he had the goods to prove it. Getting him to part with them was like having to tear out my hair and pull my own teeth at the same time. But I was also very sympathetic to the old and poor man, sadly neglected by the contemporary cultural scene, who felt he had gained a new lease on life by speaking with me. He expected me to put him front and center for anything related to Beckett, and I consoled myself by thinking of it as a mitzvah, my good deed. But oh, it was hard!

Even worse than the afternoons I spent dutifully buying him drinks were the weekends when he and Jean "simply had to get out of New York" and invited themselves to my home in Woodbridge, then just a village abutting New Haven. We lived in a house my husband had designed, out in the woods on a steep hillside, with a wraparound deck that had a large oak tree growing up through it and that overlooked a stream and a pond. It was a magical house with plenty of bedrooms, and we always welcomed houseguests, but the Reaveys trampled all the boundaries. I usually found out they were inviting themselves when they phoned to tell me what time their train would arrive in New Haven so I could be there promptly to pick them up. They played the poverty card expertly, even though I had my suspicions, considering that Jean's maiden name was Bullowa and she was of the Bulova watch family. But if I wanted the documents, I had to take care of both of them.

While we were in Paris, my children were wildly excited about the upcoming Bastille Day, with its parade and fireworks. The Reaveys thought that would be a fine day for me to give a dinner party in their honor, and they presented me with their guest list. Beckett was at the top, but after the incident with Jean's plays, he told me he had wisely decided to depart for Ussy and would stay there until just before the Reaveys were to fly home to New York. They wanted me to invite their old friend Bill Hayter and the charming (and sensible) Désirée Moorhead. As Bill and Désirée were once again hosting the artists Eddie Allen and Lia Rondelli, we were delighted to invite them. Con Leventhal and Marion Leigh could come only for drinks, as they had a dinner engagement. Hayter told Montague about the party, and so he phoned and invited himself. What could we say but yes? We invited Roger Blin, and he asked if he could bring Jean Martin. We were thrilled to meet him.

Suddenly we had thirteen people invited for drinks with ten staying for dinner. Montague ostentatiously let us all know that he had a dinner engagement, hinting that it was with Beckett. I exchanged looks with Con and Marion, for we knew that Beckett was not even in Paris. By now I was used to dealing with all the

"Becketteers" who claimed they had had drinks and dinners with "Sam" at times when he was nowhere near town; I just smiled and wished Montague well.

Fortunately, the dining table in the apartment was a large one that ten people could crowd around. But what to serve them? We decided to be very American and make hamburgers and potato salad, served along with some excellent cheeses, and for dessert I would make a tarte Tatin that could pass for an American apple pie. Everyone loved the menu and ate heartily, and when Beckett returned from Ussy the following week, he knew all about the party, because he had interrogated most of the guests. He knew that we had served American food, and that my children had come late from the parade, gobbled their dinner, and left abruptly to get to Parc Montsouris in time for the fireworks. He asked many questions about the hamburgers, especially about the bread I served with them, saying that he had not much liked the bread (bun) when he had had one in New York in 1964, the only time he was in the United States. He knew that Blin and Martin had "performed," as they entranced with stories of what it was like to appear in a Beckett play, even acting out a few parts. Everyone stayed until well after the Métro shut down for the night, and my husband and I took turns escorting them to the taxi rank down the street, where it seemed we waited forever for cars to come. We were exhausted, and it was growing light when we could finally go to bed. I told Beckett it had been a wonderful evening, to have so many of his friends there, and all of them celebrating him. At that point things changed radically.

Our conversation had begun cordially, but I sensed Beckett's questions were becoming sharper, carrying a definite aura of disapproval. He did not appreciate that so many of his friends had become my friends. Even more, I think he was horrified that I had ruptured his compartmentalization by bringing them all together where they could compare notes and exchange information about him. My mind flashed back to New York, with Reavey living on East Eighty-Fifth Street and Kobler on West Eighty-Fifth and the

two of them not daring to meet each other until I brashly introduced them. I realized that the same thing had just happened in
my apartment on Bastille Day. With the exception of the Hayters
and the Leventhals, none of Beckett's friends had known each
other before then.

My impression was strengthened when Avigdor Arikha telephoned several days after my meeting with Beckett to say that he
had run into the Reaveys on the boulevard du Montparnasse as
they were all gathering to walk to dinner with Beckett, and George
had told him about the party. The conversation had resumed at the
dinner table, when Avigdor asked the Reaveys why I had not invited
him, which he could see made Beckett upset. What did Beckett
say? I asked. Avigdor mumbled something I could not understand,
but it was pretty clear that Beckett did not like it at all, neither the
party nor the various conversations and questions that followed.

I related all this to Mary Kling, who had done so much that
summer to make my way smooth, and Mary said that perhaps it
was time for me to leave Paris so that things could "quiet down."
Mary's contacts in the publishing world were extensive, and the
signals from within the smaller Beckett world indicated uproar.
She reported that feedback ranged from curiosity (who was I, what
was I doing, and why was Beckett allowing me to do it) to pique
(mainly, why had I contacted X and not Y?). Most stunning of all
was when Mary told me that Lindon had told her that Beckett was
upset over having allowed himself to be drawn into the "excitement" that my presence and my project had created.

Mary was amazed by what I had accomplished in such a
short time, and when I added up all I had done, I realized that it
really was an amazing amount of work. I also realized that I was
exhausted. My family had had a glorious time exploring the city
and its environs, and I decided that it was time for me to have a
little fun myself. We made farewell visits to favorite restaurants,
museums, and stores. We visited our favorite markets and bought
exotic cheeses and fruits. We sat in the Luxembourg Gardens and

watched children sailing little boats, and I watched my own as they made farewell runs through the Parc Montsouris.

By then it was almost mid-August and I had two kids I needed to get ready for school. I needed to get myself ready also, as I was about to begin the pattern that would persist until the book was written and in production: I would teach for one semester as a part-time professor anywhere I could find a job, save as much money as I could, and return to Paris as soon as the semester ended for the next research trip.

It was time to go home. We were sad to leave the rue d'Alésia, and we had to buy an extra-large suitcase to carry all the materials I had collected. We made our farewells and off we went, with me planning, plotting, and worrying all across the Atlantic. Once I was back in my office in Connecticut and I opened that suitcase, what then? I was nowhere near ready to start writing, but at some point I would have to sit down quietly and figure out how one actually went about writing a biography.

11

On November 17, 1973, I noted in my DD that "two years ago today I met Samuel Beckett for the first time. If I had only known!" On the same page, I also wrote: "This year is almost ended and I really haven't written a word. Disgusting." I couldn't be too depressed about not writing, though, because I had been given several important collections of documents, which took time to read and study, including Professor Laurence Wylie's archive about Rousillon, where Beckett hid during the war after his Resistance cell was exposed.

And yet, even though I was buoyed by the generosity of Wylie and several American academics, it was disheartening to think that the only real writing I had done since returning from Paris was in numerous grant applications, desperately searching for research money while I kept busy teaching two difficult and overenrolled courses at Trinity College in Hartford during my one-semester appointment as a sabbatical replacement. Trying to raise funds for the necessary research while balancing responsibilities to my family would nearly consume the next four years of my life. I had friends on the faculties at several Connecticut state universities, and when someone at Southern or Central was on leave, they arranged for me to fill in. I was at the bottom of the state's academic totem pole, where it was customary for professors to teach three or four courses, so I was usually assigned four sections of composition, with enrollments in each class always between thirty and forty students who resented having to fulfill this requirement.

Thinking about their weekly essays, I am still reluctant to add up the amount of red ink I used to correct them. And for all this

I was paid an adjunct's pitiful salary. Small wonder, then, that the year was ending and I had not written a word; nor was it a surprise that I blamed myself for my lack of progress, for my inability "to have it all" and to be the amazingly "together" creature all the women's magazines were telling me I should be.

On top of all the teaching, the grant-writing process consumed me, from the sheer physical exhaustion of filling out forms to the emotional tension of waiting to hear the results. I was truly a nobody, a PhD without a full-time job who was writing a biography—anathema to the literature scholars who would be judging my applications. Still, several of the most revered fellowship organizations were sufficiently intrigued by my project to ask for detailed descriptions and samples of my writing. Having raised my hopes, they then went on to dash them.

I did not secure any of the lucrative fellowships that would have let me spend a year doing writing and research, but I did end up getting grants-in-aid totaling several thousand dollars from the American Council of Learned Societies and the American Philosophical Society. It was a great relief, because they were enough to let me arrange for a winter research trip to London and Dublin at the start of 1974 that would end with a brief sojourn in Paris. But they were not enough to let me contribute anything toward household expenses, particularly the children's tuition at the local private school.

This was a circumstance not born of parental vanity, because our local public schools were excellent. However, the public schoolday would have begun with a 7:30 a.m. bus pickup and would have brought them home at 12:45. I worked at home, and it would have been difficult to have two adolescents doing all the loud and noisy things teenagers liked to do during my most productive writing hours. Also, when I was traveling for research, I did not want them to have so much unsupervised time until their father came home. They were good, trustworthy kids, but it was still too much alone time. While they were at the Hopkins School, they left the house at 8 a.m., were in classes until 4, and had compulsory sports afterward. They returned home at 6, along with their father, and we all had dinner together shortly after. It was a much better schedule for everyone. I may have been away from home a lot during the next several years, but I was determined that when we were together, we would observe family traditions, and having dinner together was important to us all.

By then my husband, Von, was a museum administrator at the Wadsworth Atheneum in Hartford, the celebrated museum that was then under the visionary direction of James Elliott. Von oversaw day-to-day operations, freeing Jim to concentrate on filling the museum with vanguard contemporary art. Peter Marlow was the curator who worked with Jim, and he gave both Von and me an education in what was cutting-edge, while another colleague, Charles Edwards, helped Von steer the financial ship. Serendipity played a large role in my book research, and Charlie Edwards was one of the foremost examples. His father-in-law, General Pierre Reynauld, happened to be a prominent officer in the French Army who secured my entry to the military archives at Vincennes, where I discovered the citation for the médaille de la Résistance that Beckett earned for his heroic work in World War II.

The Atheneum brought other serendipitous contacts, such as Alexander "Sandy" Calder, and his wife, Louisa. Both Calders knew Beckett slightly, having met him during what they called his "Joyce years," and they gave me a useful list of people in France, including Gabrielle Buffet-Picabia, the ex-wife of the painter Francis Picabia, and their daughter Jeanine, who had been two of Beckett's primary Resistance associates. Louisa described the heavy, bulky stamp machine the Nazis had used for identity cards that Jeanine Picabia had stolen from an office where she was being interrogated. When I met the Picabias, mother and daughter took great delight in acting out how they had hidden it under Gabrielle's voluminous skirt and how she had had to shuffle out of the building with her legs held together while Jeanine waved off several solicitous young soldiers who wanted to help the two ladies.

Another Atheneum boon of tremendous importance came

through the network of museum donors. I used to call myself "the hired help's wife" because of all the black-tie events I had to attend, where I was expected to help charm wives who might have otherwise been neglected while their wealthy husbands were being courted for donations. At one of them, someone told me that the Connecticut Commission on the Arts was dispensing grants-in-aid to scholars and writers. I thought I had nothing to lose, so I applied for one. That little $1,000 grant took more of my time than all the others combined, because no one on the staff knew quite what to make of it. The program was relatively new and no firm procedures had been set up, and because my request was fairly unusual, I had to submit to a number of steps that were afterward streamlined. Not only did I have to submit budgets and detailed statements of how the grant would be used, I had to go in person to be interviewed by several members of the board. I also had to submit a "personal" section of the file, where I wrote of my two children and my need to contribute to their education. Eventually I did get the grant, which meant that, coupled with the other two, both my personal and professional responsibilities for 1974 were covered.

Many years later, the arts commission's then-director, Anthony Keller, told me that within the organization there had been hesitation about whether to award what became known thereafter as "the first baby-sitting grant." In subsequent years, when feminism was both pushing women to work and permitting them to take part in public life, mine became the model the board always cited when debating whether to fund women with unusual requests. I was so pleased and proud when Tony told me of the small role I played in helping this to happen.

And so, with the money in place, it was time to get the family ready to function for the month or so I planned to be away. We had an enormous chest freezer in our basement, and even though my husband was a talented cook—certainly more than I was—I thought it was my obligation to fill it. After dinner, as I graded papers, vats of spaghetti sauce simmered on the stove. On several autumn Saturdays the other three Bairs peeled apples from the backyard tree while I made crusts for fifteen pies. I made meat-loaves, prepared stews, and made cookies and casseroles. My husband kept telling me I didn't have to do all this work, but at the time I felt I had to be and do everything, especially on the domestic front; if I wanted a life of my own, I had to make sure that my family came first. I did all this as much out of guilt for leaving them as in the hope that the food would remind them of my love while I was gone.

Katney recently told me a story I had not heard before, of the neighbor across the street, a stay-at-home wife and mother, who always prepared a gigantic hot lunch for her husband and two daughters. "You poor little thing," she would say to my daughter, "so neglected by your mother, who goes away and leaves you. You had better come and eat with us." Katney said she was always puzzled by this. She missed me, certainly, but she loved the way I always returned with wonderful souvenirs from wherever I went. Vonn Scott told me that he didn't remember anything at all "bad" about my being away, because I always found a way to stay in touch. Transatlantic phone calls were expensive, but mail was relatively cheap, so we exchanged weekly voice tapes. He still remembers one he made with third-grader Katney, who was just starting school music lessons, on which he acted as an announcer to tell me that she would now entertain me with her "plucking viola." Besides the weekly tapes, I always inserted something interesting into my frequent letters, usually clips from local papers about rock bands or chess tournaments. Even more important to a growing boy, there was always something tasty for dinner, so it didn't matter that much if I was not there to eat it with them.

Because the grant money came in the fall of 1973 and I was not able to leave for Europe until January of 1974, I decided to use a small part of it in October to make a quick overnight visit to Ottawa to interview the Polish playwright and critic Adam Tarn. He had been instrumental in presenting the avant-garde French theater to his country as editor of *Dialog*, and he had worked directly with Beckett on a Polish translation of *Godot* that he helped to stage. I found Tarn to be a personable and fascinating conversationalist despite his poor health (he died a little over a year later), but his condition may have been why he was so eager to talk freely about Beckett. For every interaction they had had, or for every theatrical event concerning one of Beckett's plays in which Tarn was involved, he produced reams of documentation. That was why I was so flummoxed when he produced letters and other notes telling me something puzzling and, from my standpoint as biographer, problematic about Beckett's sexuality—exactly the kind of thing I hoped I would not find out. Tarn showed me letters in which Beckett hinted vaguely at sexual encounters that he seemed to be saying were initiated not by him but by other men. When I met Tarn again the following day and asked to reread the letters and make notes, he seemed amused by my "American sexual puritanism." He presented the letters matter-of-factly, but frankly, I was too embarrassed and nonplussed to ask about them in detail, because I really did not want to have to deal with this information. I had no idea how I would handle it in the biography, so I just accepted his explanation that such encounters were unexceptional and did not originate with Beckett but with others. I thought I could file the information away for future reference and count on other interviews either to verify or discount what he told me.

That night on the short flight to LaGuardia Airport, I struggled with what to do about this knowledge. In 1973, the word "gay" was still relatively new, and most public figures who were gay or bisexual kept that fact deeply private. To "out" someone did not exist in the lexicon, and "closet" had only one meaning. For me to out a man of Samuel Beckett's stature would have been simply unthinkable. Still, I had to find a way to deal with whatever information came my way—I could not ignore what Tarn so casually insisted was fact—but I would have to find a discreet, tactful way to ask others about it. I could not show my cards, and I certainly did not want to alert or alarm anyone, especially Samuel Beckett.

During the flight I thought back to the previous summer, when John Montague and I were chatting in Bill Hayter's atelier. Montague could not conceal his glee as he told me, "You are making Sam very nervous, because he is sure you are going to write about his sex life." At the time I thought Montague was merely hinting at Beckett's Dublin romances or his ongoing liaison with Barbara Bray. I had turned to Bill Hayter with a question on my face: could what Montague just said about Beckett possibly be true? Montague had proven himself to be "the Great Exaggerator" in my notes, and I considered him an unreliable witness. However, Hayter was not smiling, and his face was stern as he nodded his head in agreement. I had filed that away for future thought and had not pursued it, but as the plane touched down, I could not help but wonder if it had been this aspect of Beckett's sexuality, so offhandedly divulged by Tarn, that made him so uneasy during several of our less successful conversations.

I thought I had an opportunity to begin the process of unraveling Beckett's sexuality in December, when something extraordinary happened. I received a letter from Con Leventhal telling me that he and Marion were planning to be in New York and they would like nothing better than to visit me in Connecticut. This was an astonishing development on several fronts. Con and Marion were not in the most robust health, and they did not have American contacts or family ties that I knew of. Also, they were poor pensioners who lived so modestly in France that such an extravagant vacation seemed beyond their means. George Reavey was quick to tell me that it was a gift from Beckett, who paid for their plane fare and posh midtown hotel. And of course when Con and Marion came to Connecticut, George and Jean would come, too, having appointed themselves their escorts.

Fortunately, the semester I taught at Trinity College had just ended, so I was free to invite them for a day. I met the four of them at New Haven's Union Station and we drove directly to Hartford and the Atheneum, where we had lunch in the restaurant and then toured the galleries. Afterward, Von joined us to crowd into my big old Ford Country Squire and drive to our home. My terrific kids had set the dinner table, put the huge roast beef into the oven, and lit a match to the fire I had laid that morning. We had just put up a few Christmas lights, and I lit some candles. The house gleamed and glittered, and I saw Con and Marion exchange looks that showed they were impressed. As soon as we arrived, George headed straight for the liquor cabinet and the scotch, and soon everyone was in a jolly mood. There was no opportunity to ask Con anything of substance, so the talk remained genial and superficial.

Von and I drove the four to a late train, and after we got them safely onboard and it was pulling away, we turned to each other and asked, "Now what was that all about?" We both knew the answer: Beckett was curious, and they would report their experiences back to him.

12

In so many ways 1974 was the most extraordinary year of the biography's genesis. When I look back now, I wonder how I survived it. I needed to begin the 1974 research trip in Dublin and London because there were still so many people in each city whom I had not yet interviewed, but because of the unexpected visit by Leventhal and Leigh, I thought it wise to begin with a week in Paris in case I needed to do damage control with Beckett. I wrote early in December and received his reply several days later, one of the tiny calling cards on which he wrote a sentence or two before sending it off in an airmail envelope. All it said was to telephone upon arrival.

I landed on Saturday, January 6, and phoned as instructed, but he did not answer, so I sent a little blue pneu and started immediately to confirm my other appointments. I had budgeted for only one week and needed to hit the ground running. I phoned him again on Sunday, and again there was no answer. I was uneasy but kept busy seeing friends over the weekend, including Mary Kling, who took me to Sunday lunch and encouraged me to start writing the book so she would have something to show the several interested French publishers. I didn't want to tell her how little writing I had done, so I said I still needed to do more research before I could show anything with confidence. That explanation was sadly true.

Madame and Général Reynauld invited me to dinner, and he volunteered to consult documents in the Vincennes archives, which were not scheduled to be open to researchers until 1975. Since I did not expect my book to be written and published for at least a year after that, we agreed that we were not breaking any laws.

I met John Gerassi at the Select because he told me he was expecting Simone de Beauvoir to be there. He said he had told her about me, and she wanted to meet because she had a lot to say about Beckett, particularly how much she disliked him. I already knew from Beckett how much he disliked *her*, so I was eager to get her side of the story. I waited for her until shortly before I had to leave for my next appointment, when it was clear that she was not coming. I did not meet her then, but I often thought of this near-encounter years later, when I began to write about her, wondering if knowing her beforehand would have made me hesitate, if not actually decline, to write her biography.

On Monday I called Beckett again, and again there was no answer. When I returned to the hotel after a day of interviewing, I found that I had missed a call from him, from Ussy. The message said that Monsieur Beckett had called from there but nothing else, and he had not left a number. I wasn't alarmed, because I assumed it meant that within the next day or two he'd be back in Paris and would call again. So I kept on with my appointments, including those with a number of people who had known him during the war, when they were in the Resistance together.

Madame Marie Péron, the widow of Alfred, Beckett's friend and Resistance colleague, gave me a deeply moving account of the tension and terror endured by the families of Resistance fighters. She also told me of the kindness and generosity Beckett showed to her and her children after her husband, who had been in a concentration camp, died in 1945. I met the Picabias during this time, in their studio full of Francis Picabia's paintings and too many cats to count, all of them clawing their owners, climbing up the walls and onto the paintings, and hissing and screaming at each other. It was a wild but colorful setting for the Picabias' uproarious tales of dangerous Resistance exploits, leaving me in awe of their bravery. When I talked about them later with Beckett, he could only say admiringly that "they were fearless. Amazing."

I took a day to go to La Ferté-sous-Jouarre, the tiny commune near Ussy where the elderly Josette Hayden lived. Madame Hayden was the widow of the artist Henri Hayden, and both of them had lived in Roussillon when Beckett was hiding there. Like her husband, she had spent many boring days learning English to pass the time. She had things to show me, she said, but first we had to drink some "Aig"—Haig & Haig, her favorite scotch whiskey (it was 11 a.m.). After that she had to treat me to lunch. She had the driver who met me at the train station take us to the restaurant where she habitually took her noonday meal. There I had to meet the chef, who had once worked in "Quins" (Queens, New York). Josette (as she asked me to call her) ordered wine and said we must start with the excellent soup. I didn't need the wine, but a big bowl of hot soup on a cold day was just what I was after. She would order for me, she said, because she knew the menu and it was particularly good on Thursdays. The next course was a huge filet of fish in a cream sauce with potatoes and several vegetables, and it was certainly delicious. We both ate heartily and drank several glasses of wine to wash it down. I thought we were finished and only waiting for coffee when along came the next course, an enormous slice of roast lamb with more potatoes and vegetables. That tiny little woman tucked right in and expected me to do the same. Somehow I ate most of it, and also the crème caramel that followed. How I managed to function for the rest of the afternoon when we returned to her home and she poured more "Aig" still remains a mysterious blur. I was grateful for the tape recorder when she shared her Roussillon memories and materials, because my notes that day were not the most legible.

Madame Hayden's driver took me back to the train along with a carful of his fellow workers, who were going to begin their shift working on the railroad. They all told him he was a terrible braggart. I didn't look like a very important person, they said; I just looked like an ordinary American girl who might have had too much to drink.

Every now and again I did meet someone whose views on Beckett departed from the hagiographic "Saint Sam, the good and great"—usually another Irish writer. Such was the case with Aidan Higgins, whom I met at Bill Hayter's workshop. Higgins promoted what he called the "official" verdict of the Irish literati, but I could not decide if his snideness accurately reflected what other Irish writers thought about their countryman's writings or if he was simply jealous.

A negative view still surprised me, especially when it came from someone like Jenny Bradley, the famed literary agent, who spoke of Beckett with open hostility. She told me that she despised him because he had been "Joyce's sycophant" and advised me to "look deeply into his deadly serious desire for fame and fortune." She said I would be especially wise to dig for the truth about his "affair" with Lucia Joyce. No one before Mrs. Bradley had spoken so severely of Beckett, and because of who she was, I had to take what she said seriously. Her reputation for honesty and perceptiveness preceded her, and her judgments were trusted implicitly by the Paris literary community.

By the time I met Mrs. Bradley, I had already interviewed enough people—around sixty, and increasing every day—to realize that I had taken on the formidable task of writing the life of an incredibly complex man and there would have to be much serious discerning, sifting, and interpreting of both information and opinion before I could write a single word. The monumentality of the undertaking kept me up nights. There were times when I would wake up with what I called "the 4 a.m. galloping anxieties," wondering if I could find a face-saving way not to write the book.

The week was flying by, and suddenly it was Friday and I still had not seen Beckett, nor had I had further communication from him. Yet he managed to be an unseen presence hovering over me everywhere I went, and in so doing he made me terribly uneasy. Madame Péron told me he had phoned just before I arrived to make sure she would be there to receive me; the Picabias said the same as they thanked me for bringing him—or at least his voice—back into their lives after so many years. Désirée Moorhead dropped into Hayter's studio when I was talking to Aidan Higgins, and she also said that "Sam" had called to ask if she and her husband were going to see me on this trip. When she told Beckett that I was seeing Higgins that very day, he asked her to be sure to let him know how it went. It was maddening: if he was so intent on monitoring my progress, why wasn't he in town to see me?

One of my 4 a.m. galloping-anxiety sessions came early Saturday morning, probably because I was so worried about sleeping through the early alarm that would let me get to Gare Montparnasse in time for the first train to Mantes-la-Jolie and from there to the artist Joan Mitchell's house in Vétheuil.

I arrived shortly before 10 a.m. and looked around the station for Joan. Instead I was approached by a local fellow who asked if I was "Joan's American." He said he worked for her and that I should get into his car and he would take me to her. I opened my car window on that very cold day because the man reeked of booze and cigarettes. He was either baiting me or laughing at Joan on the short drive from the train station, not to her house but to a local bar. I could not tell which, because he spoke swiftly with an accent I could not decipher, and his vocabulary consisted almost entirely of outdated slang I could not understand.

Joan was at a table just inside the bar, a full glass of Pernod next to several empty ones. She asked what I would drink, and as it was 10 a.m. and I had not had breakfast, I said I would like coffee. She sneered at me as she made some crack about Americans who obviously could not hold their liquor. I had been warned that she could be sharp and nasty, particularly when she was drinking, so I knew I had to tread carefully. Joan was the American publisher Barney Rosset's first wife, and she had known Beckett almost as long as Barney had. She kept a small studio in Paris on the rue Frémicourt, but mostly she lived in the Vétheuil house she liked to insist was formerly owned by the artist Claude Monet. She shared it with the French-Canadian painter Jean-Paul Riopelle, or at least she had previously lived there with him. By noon, after numerous glasses of the potent yellow liquor had gotten her rather sloppy and her voice slurred, I learned that most of Riopelle's things were still there although he was living elsewhere with another woman.

By one o'clock Joan was still drinking and I was starving. I had nursed two or three cups of coffee and moved on at her insistence to the most harmless drink I could think of, a wine spritzer that I pretended to sip. A stress headache had been building over the last several frenetic days, and hunger was not easing it. Other patrons, mostly workingmen, came and went throughout the morning, and they all knew her. "Joan!" they would shout, followed up with comments I could not understand but assumed were ribald jokes and salacious teasing, because the only word I recognized in her reply was *foutre,* as she told them what they could do to themselves. The atmosphere was both menacing and testy. I really wanted to get out of there, and fortunately, at just about that time, the man who had brought me from the station returned. He picked up Joan by her elbow and said it was time to go home, as her cook (his wife) had prepared lunch and we had to eat it.

And oh, did I eat! It was one of the best home-cooked meals I have had in all my years of going to France. Consommé, lamb chops, potatoes, vegetables, salad, cheese, and molten chocolate cake with a bitter orange-chocolate sauce. I ate more than my share while Joan didn't touch her plate; she just continued with Pernod and cigarettes, leading me to wonder how she stayed alive. She spent the meal staring at me across the table and telling me repeatedly either that I was "all fucked up and needed a shrink" or that she liked me so much and we were going to be good friends.

After lunch we went to her studio, where she showed me several of her huge and extraordinary canvases, all done in vibrant shades of orange and red with an occasional smash of turquoise or blue. Those paintings astonished me, as I wondered how someone so slight and frail could expend so much energy on such hard physical work. While she talked, she studied what she had already done and occasionally picked up a brush to make frantic stabs and jabs at one of the works in progress. She told me story after story about Beckett, all in cold, clear prose and with absolute clarity. She was one of those drunks who could appear to be stone-cold sober, totally lucid, and mentally well organized. But she staggered at times, and I was afraid that the full glass of red wine or the point of the burning cigarette she held most of the time might end up ruining one of those glorious canvases.

Considering how my visit was unfolding, it should not have surprised me that some of Joan's stories couldn't make it into the biography for lack of corroborating sources. One of the more salacious involved a Bastille Day afternoon in Paris when she ran into Beckett as she was returning to her studio. They decided to go for a drink, and after a great many drinks, Joan said, "Oh what the hell, Sam, why don't we just go fuck?" He said, "Yes, why not," so they found a nearby fleabag hotel. "Did you?" I asked Joan, nodding my head to indicate that I meant the f-word while not saying it. "Fuck, you mean? Fuck?" she replied. "What the hell is wrong with you, woman? Why don't you just say what you mean!" I had no response, and let the question pass.

"Hell no," she said eventually. "We spent all night on our hands and knees on the goddamn floor looking for some of his false teeth that fell out." When I finally stifled my giggles and thought I could trust myself to reply, I asked if they had ever fucked, deliberately saying with heavy emphasis the word that I still don't like to say, even though I otherwise can and do curse with the best. "Nah, not really," she said. "I don't think he was ever much into that"— offering up yet another opinion to factor into Beckett's sexuality when I wrote about it.

I yearned to use this story in the biography but did not, because she was the only source and I was too embarrassed at the time to ask Beckett. It turned out to be true, however, as I was able to confirm from Beckett himself in 1983, almost five years after I had published his biography and when I was working with Simone de Beauvoir. Our paths just happened to cross as I was on my way to see her and he was walking down the boulevard Raspail toward his home. By this time our encounters were easy and cordial, and during the course of a meandering conversation, I thought I had nothing to lose, so I asked him if what Joan had told me had actually happened. He said quite simply yes, and we moved on to other topics.

But on that late winter afternoon it was becoming quite dark, literally and personally, as I asked repeatedly if Joan would call the man to drive me back to the station and she declined to answer. I had a dinner date that night with Leventhal and Leigh, and if I left her then, I could arrive back in Paris only slightly late for the 8:30 engagement. By that time Joan was in a very bad way, and she did not want me to go. She had a deep fear of being alone at night, and she decided not only that I was going to stay with her but that she was going to see to it that I caught up with her and drank myself into the same oblivion she was fast approaching.

I thought I was saved when another visitor arrived quite unexpectedly from Paris. He was the husband of a woman who had known Beckett since childhood, a woman whom I had interviewed that very week. I soon realized that he had come to spend the night with Joan and to join her in drinking, which was as good an excuse as any to renew my demand for a ride to the station. Her visitor said there was no need, for he had just that moment changed his plans and would happily drive me back to Paris, where we could then spend the night together in my apartment. Alas, I said, what a pity that I could not accept his kind invitation, as I already had a dinner date. He accepted the refusal and, as he had already been drinking heavily, retired shortly thereafter to one of Joan's bedrooms to sleep alone. But I was still stuck without a ride to the station.

That was when the phone rang for the first time all afternoon. I could hear Joan speaking in English and saying, "Yeah, yeah . . . okay . . . all right." When she hung up, she said, "That was Sam. He wants me to put you on the train so you can get to your dinner." And then, like a naughty child, she reached for her drink, snickered, and said, "But I'm not going to!" Another half hour passed and the phone rang again, and again it was Beckett. The same exchange ensued. Fifteen minutes after that it rang again, but this time it was the art historian Pierre Schneider, who said that "Sam" had phoned and asked him to drive to Vétheuil to take me on the forty-mile trip back to Paris. I had not yet met Schneider then, but I did have him on my list of people to see, as I knew that he and his wife were Beckett's friends.

Joan was on the phone with Pierre for a very long time, crying and not making much sense, until finally she agreed to let me speak to him. He told me that he had spoken to her driver, who was on his way to the studio and would take me to the train. He also said he wanted to talk to me about his friendship with Beckett and asked if I could meet him on Monday. Of course I said yes, which meant I had to change my Sunday flight to Dublin so I could stay in Paris an extra day. When we ended our phone conversation, he told me he would call "Sam" and tell him it was all sorted out and I was on my way to Leventhal's. It was not until I was safely on the train that I wondered, how did Pierre Schneider, a total stranger to me, know that I was going to Leventhal and Leigh's? And for that matter, how did Beckett?

I arrived for my 8:30 dinner date at 10:30 p.m. Marion Leigh handed me a glass of whiskey the moment I walked in the door and said we were going to eat a roast beef dinner that was so overcooked it was cremated, "and then we will be even when it comes to roast beef dinners." I was dropping with fatigue but still alert enough to wonder why she felt the need to remark so bitingly on the hospitality my family and I had so genuinely offered. I could hardly open my mouth to chew, let alone talk, but I didn't need to say much, because they already knew about my day chez Joan. Marion said "Sam" had kindly phoned to let them know I was on my way and asked them not to be upset with me.

At that point it was going on midnight, and in something between nervous exhaustion, panic, and sheer frustration, I broke down in a kind of outburst, shaking and nearly sobbing. "What in the hell is going on?" I demanded once I had calmed down. "What kind of stupid silly game is Samuel Beckett playing with me?"

Con and Marion looked at each other, and then he reached

across the table and put his hand over mine. It was not a game, he told me. Beckett had been felled by an outbreak of the cysts and boils that had troubled him when he was a very young man at Trinity College. He had several on his face and around his mouth that were particularly disfiguring, and he didn't want me to see them for fear that I would write about them.

I already knew of those that had plagued him during his university years, having been told by some of his Irish classmates at Trinity, who were most eager to go into the gory details of his unhappy time there, confirmed by his cousins and his two best friends at Trinity, Drs. Alan and Geoffrey Thompson. Beckett's niece, Caroline Beckett Murphy, offered further corroboration as she remembered hearing these family stories as a young girl. I hesitated a long time before including details about the boils and cysts when writing about Beckett's earlier years, but because they were woven throughout his fiction, I decided I had to include such embarrassingly personal information. But I certainly didn't mention this recurrence.

What a relief Con's explanation was! To learn that I had not crossed some red line gave me the best night's sleep since I had landed in Paris. Late Sunday morning, when I could finally rouse my aching head and bones from the lumpy bed, I wrote a letter to Beckett, giving him my account of the week's research and mentioning that I was staying an extra day to meet Pierre Schneider at the Closerie des Lilas—a place I liked because it made me feel steeped in literary history. But I omitted everything personal, particularly that I was keeping that afternoon free to buy presents for my children and planned to have dinner with an old college friend who happened to be in Paris at the time.

I had been at it for well over a year by this point, and I still struggled to find the right words to describe how Beckett and I related to one another. Working relationship? Mutual undertaking? The project we were embarked upon? But one thing was clear, which was that I had to remain "all business," as the expression goes. The last thing I wanted from Samuel Beckett was a friendship, especially a personal one. I knew that I would be revealing a great deal of his personal history to the world, history that he would surely prefer to keep private, and the notion troubled me deeply. Back in my reporting days, I had undertaken similar digs into subjects' pasts, but in those cases I had no regrets, because the stories concerned public figures whose private deeds bore on their professional conduct and needed to be made public. Now, as a biographer, the rules seemed different, leaving me to struggle with myself. I had come so far since the research that began with my dissertation in early 1971, and here it was 1974 and ink was finally hitting paper. How could I abandon almost four years of work because I was so reluctant to reveal ugly or embarrassing personal matters? Thankfully, the immediate, pressing needs of the research took precedence over worries about content. Right now I had to finish up in Paris and get myself to Dublin and London to keep to my appointed rounds.

13

I trod warily when I landed in Dublin. I went to Ireland many times during the seven years I worked on the Beckett biography, and every time I had mixed feelings about working there. On the one hand, people were so friendly, generous, and kind to me; on the other hand, I was always dealing with unpleasant behavior from men who, if they were not actual gropers or wannabe bed partners, took delight in slyly bombarding me with sexual innuendo. To them, a woman on her own was a prime target, but one who was also a married mother was almost incomprehensible and therefore the object of all sorts of objectionable behavior. I grew used to ignoring suggestions about my being in a "free marriage" that allowed me to "abandon" my children.

But I also remember lovely dinner parties in the homes of Sean and Mary White, where Seamus and Marie Heaney became my friends, and at Paddy and Monica Henchy's, where they and their friends took delight in watching me sputter as they introduced me to poitín, the potent Irish moonshine. I made friends among women journalists and others who were, surprisingly to me, well represented in the professions and public life. I enjoyed their company at rowdy drinks-and-dinners in their homes, where I learned a lot about how to navigate among "the ould fellers."

This particular trip was an exhausting week of evenings at the bar at Buswells Hotel on Molesworth Street, then a grungy dump where I was staying, during which I had to buy far too many drinks far too late into the night for assorted Dublin characters, all of whom told me stories of "Sam's escapades" during the years he had lived there. And many of them hinted at how much more they could tell me if I would just leave their hands where they put them on my knees, or, in one or two of the most egregious cases, if I might want to invite them for a private drink in my room. I spent many exhausting evenings sitting on a bar stool, trying to move out of the reach of one after another drunken Irish poet, actor, play-wright, journalist, or professor.

I related these "adventures" to my women friends, and they agreed with me that most Irish men found an American woman on her own an oddity, particularly one writing about Beckett. When I interviewed some of these women for background on Irish his-tory and culture, the topic of how Irish men treated them usually arose. They just laughed and said they had learned after the first pass how to keep things light and breezy, to reject the propositions and still keep the fellow as a friend. I learned a lot from them and followed suit.

This trip also offered me the chance to run down a signifi-cant lead regarding Beckett's sexuality. Several of my previous interviewees had stressed the importance of Beckett's deep friend-ship with the Irish poet Denis Devlin. Discussing the subject with Brian Coffey, who guardedly told me of Devlin's "importance" to Beckett, I asked if he was referring to Beckett's sexuality. By way of response, he told me to "look to McGreevy" for a full and accurate understanding of, as he put it euphemistically, "Beckett's life and work." Now that I was in Dublin, I set out to learn more about the deep and lasting friendship between Beckett and the late Thomas McGreevy, one that had begun during Beckett's Joyce years in Paris and lasted until McGreevy's death in 1967.

McGreevy was another Dublin character, which meant he was a man with an outsized personality and one about whom every-one, regardless of class or position, had a story. He had retired as the director of the National Gallery of Ireland and was a well-known and well-loved member of both the local intelligentsia and the ordinary drinking establishment. McGreevy was also honored by the French government as a chevalier of the Legion of Honor, which in Dublin parlance became his nickname, the "Shoveler." He was a lifelong bachelor devoted to his late sister and her two adult daughters.

Brian had told me of the voluminous correspondence Beckett had exchanged with McGreevy, all of which the Shoveler talked about fairly openly to any drinking companions who would listen. A great many people knew how McGreevy boasted of what he could reveal should he ever decide to publish the letters. Brian told me they would probably be the most important documents for a true understanding of Beckett and that I should make every possible effort to read them.

And therein lay the most important tale of my biography, what I called "the McGreevy Letters."

By the time I was conducting research, McGreevy and his sister were both dead and the two adult nieces were the inheritors of his estate. I interviewed them first together and then separately. They were both educated and cultured women, middle-class wives and mothers who tended to good-sized families while enjoying satisfying careers. One of them was a devoted scholar of the Irish language who did much to promote it in schools and other language programs. It was she whom I saw most of the time after I began to have repeated separate interviews with each of them.

Throughout the next three years, every time I went to Dublin (which was usually twice a year, or more if I could scrounge up the research money) I would take the McGreevy nieces to very nice teas and lunches, where I would ask politely but repeatedly to see the letters. Each time they told me the same thing: they were surely inclined to cooperate and they would certainly think about it, but they could not make the decision just then. Perhaps by the time I made my next trip they would have decided. I had a nickname for them, too: *"The Godot Sisters. Not today, but surely tomorrow . . ."* The day eventually did come, but it took a while.

When I asked Con Leventhal and Brian Coffey for the names of people who had known Beckett in his youth and the name of Mary Manning Howe came up, both would sigh deeply and roll their eyes in resignation and regret—resignation that she was indeed an important source and regret that I would be subjected to her possibly whimsical memories. The Manning family were neighbors of the Becketts and the two matriarchs had been close friends. Samuel was the brother closest to two (of three) of the Manning children, John and Mary, because they had similar interests in literature and theater. Mary became an actress-playwright in Dublin and later married the prominent Boston lawyer and Harvard professor Mark De Wolfe Howe. She and Beckett maintained a mostly epistolary friendship for the rest of her life.

Con and Brian acknowledged Mary's propensity to exaggerate and make herself the center of a story, but they both agreed that she was definitely someone I needed to interview. Her brother, John Manning, they concurred, would be a far more reliable witness than his colorful sister. They sighed deeply again when they spoke of Arland Ussher, an ancient man of letters, but agreed that he, too, had been close to Beckett and I should at least talk to him and see for myself how useful his memories might be.

My time in Ireland was not unmarked by the political conflict roiling the country. I had gone to Northern Ireland for interviews at the Portora Royal School in Enniskillen, where Beckett had been a student. I was on an early morning bus back to Dublin so that I could keep a lunch appointment with the Manning siblings and was both frantic and furious when we stopped in Cavan for no apparent reason. A policeman entered the bus and told us to remain seated. After almost an hour, exhausted and frustrated and worried that after I had gone to so much trouble to arrange the luncheon, I would not be able to keep it, I went to the bus door and behaved badly. I demanded that the two members of the Irish constabulary who were guarding it tell me what was going on. As they turned their backs on me without replying, the elderly passengers in the front seats whispered that I should sit down and be quiet. A long while later, when we were finally under way, they told me that there had been a shootout and two men were dead. They were very matter-of-fact about it, saying it was "all political" and nothing to be bothered about. When I read the Dublin papers that night, I learned there had been a bombing as well. Clearly there were many situations in Ireland when it was best to be the mousy girl hanging back rather than the brash American pushing her way forward.

That afternoon, when I met Mary (always called Molly) Manning Howe and John Manning, I was in a fairly sorry state after the episode in Cavan. Lunch proceeded smoothly, with ordinary conversation about Dublin people who knew Beckett, the state of Irish arts and letters, and the current theater scene. John left immediately after the meal, saying that he and I could meet again. Molly suggested we stay for another cup of tea, which led to all sorts of intimate details about Beckett's sexuality.

Her version was of a rousing, rip-roaring affair she and Beckett had carried on in the mid-1930s—before and after her 1935 marriage and just before Beckett moved permanently to Paris— much to the consternation of their mothers, who knew all about it. Everyone I interviewed who knew about it referred to it as a "brief encounter" and generally thought it had probably occurred "one time and [been] initiated by her." Molly's descriptions of Beckett's sexual passivity in Ireland resembled those I heard from Peggy Guggenheim and Joan Mitchell. Molly Howe went into far more detail about herself and Beckett than I wanted to hear, but of course I sat there and listened to it all. Despite my exhaustion, I came to fully alert attention when she hinted that her eldest daughter (of three) "could have been" Samuel Beckett's.

With this nugget of new information under my belt, I moved on to speak with others, putting the topic of Beckett's alleged parentage in abeyance for the moment. I thought it was so sensitive that I needed to discuss it with Brian Coffey and Con Leventhal first, and I thought it best not to discuss it with anyone else in Ireland. Molly Howe, meanwhile, was busy wringing her hands and fluttering about all over Dublin, telling anyone who would listen how terribly worried she was that "the American biographer" would "reveal [her] long-kept secret," the one she either described in detail or hinted at coyly. In the end, it was she who "revealed" it to Beckett and created a brief blowup that caused me all sorts of trouble with him, but that came later.

I traipsed all over Dublin conducting my prearranged interviews, and one in particular offered a chance to gather information about Beckett's romantic life. A grand old man of Irish letters, the essayist and translator Arland Ussher had just sold his Beckett letters, a collection that Molly Howe assured me was "second in importance only to Beckett's with McGreevy." We met in the Davy Byrnes pub, where I found myself sitting opposite a very old and very nervous man intent on pumping me for information about Beckett's views on the sale. I was not about to put myself into the middle of any contretemps that might unfold, so I told Ussher I had no idea what Beckett thought, even though I did—he was furious that the letters had become public, because he had written most of them during the desperately drunk and unhappy years he lived in London and after he returned to his mother's house, broke, depressed, and unsuccessful as a writer. He felt Ussher had no right to make them public, and went so far as to say he "preferred" that I not use them.

Beckett did not yet know that I had already read them when a prospective buyer asked me to evaluate whether they were worthwhile, and I thought it best not to rile him until I was actually writing the biography. I wanted to wait until I could determine what, if anything, they might contribute: if little or nothing, I would not use them; if they contained something that mattered, I would fight the good fight then. I would worry about this when the time came.

Molly Howe kept embellishing her version of what the Ussher letters contained whenever I saw her on that trip, hinting at the "scandal" they could reveal about Beckett's "peccadilloes." I tried to act the role of naive innocent every time, asking her to elaborate on what she meant, but she would just wave her hand dismissively and say "his unusual sexual proclivities." I was not about to raise the specter of homosexual encounters myself for fear that she would tell everyone in Dublin that I was snooping into Beckett's sexuality for a sensational book.

More hints at a relationship with Beckett arose when I returned to Buswells after a busy day of interviewing to find Con Leventhal and Marion Leigh sitting in the lobby having afternoon tea. They claimed to have family business in Dublin and on the spur of the moment had decided it would be good to do it while I was there. As they asked me to tell them whom I had seen and what they had told me—only as a way to help me, of course, just to see if they could verify the statements—it struck me as strange that everywhere I went, they also turned up. I drank the tea they offered and I told them what I wanted them—and Beckett—to know. Nothing more.

I had an engagement that evening, but I agreed to join them for dinner the next night. Marion had started drinking before dinner, and at the table she made snide comments that I chose to respond to as I did when difficult interview subjects were boorish: to go into what I called "cheerful and stupid" mode; to smile and deflect the conversation. She got very drunk, and as she did, her remarks became both shocking and upsetting, a rambling and convoluted monologue about how she had discussed me with Beckett after the New York trip. She told him "everything," from a description of my home and family to what George Reavey said about me, that I was independently wealthy and lived on a private income and that everyone in New York knew that I had received a huge advance from a publisher to "spill the goods" on Samuel Beckett. Not a word of this was true.

Her mean-spirited attack came, thankfully, at the end of the meal, which allowed me, still being cheerful and stupid, to hide my astonishment, feign exhaustion, and make a quick exit. In reality I was fuming. All the way to my room I alternated between two thoughts. The first was about Reavey: *"I'll fix that lying bastard."*

The second was about Marion Leigh: *"She and her 'Sam' have been getting their good goss in. Should I laugh it off or be worried?"*

The next morning I began my last day in Dublin. Marion phoned the room as if nothing untoward had happened, to invite me to join them for breakfast. I did, and the conversation was very general and superficially pleasant. I didn't stay long, needing to complete some last-minute interviews before rushing to the airport for the midafternoon flight to London. On the way back to my hotel to pack up my things, I saw Leventhal and Leigh walking languidly down Molesworth Street with Désirée Moorhead, all three chatting cheerfully away. Con and Marion had not told me that Désirée was also in Dublin, and as they didn't see me, I did not reveal myself. When I recorded it in the *DD,* I wrote that *"the enormous secrecy and double dealing of these people never ceases to amaze me. What possible game can they be playing?"* But there was little time to think about it; I had to get to the airport because my days in London were booked solid.

I was a basket case of nerves and anxiety as I headed for the airport, where I had another encounter with the Garda Síochána, the Irish national police, that reinforced just how tense the political situation was. I was seated on the small commuter plane when I became aware of nervous whispering around me. The passengers on my side of the plane were looking anxiously out their windows at the single piece of luggage on the tarmac that had not been loaded onto the plane. Two uniformed policemen were talking to someone who looked like a baggage handler. In his hands he held an object about the size of a football that he was trying to foist off on the officers, who refused to take it. Suddenly I realized: that was my suitcase, and the object he held was the clay teapot I had bought from a local potter! I jumped out of my seat and off the plane, down the few steps to the tarmac, yelling, "Don't hurt my teapot!" as the baggage handler was about to drop it. I snatched it from his hands just in time.

After I unwrapped it, the policemen opened my suitcase so that I could put the teapot back inside, displaying my dirty clothing to everyone on the left side of the plane. The suitcase was stowed and I reboarded, blushing violently and avoiding all eye contact, and the plane took off. I never drink hard liquor on planes, but on this short flight to Heathrow, I gratefully accepted a whiskey and would have had another if the flight were not so short. London was going to be crazy busy, but I was so glad to get away from Ireland that I looked forward to whatever lay ahead.

14

My budget for this research trip allowed for one week in each of the three cities. That meant spending the several months before departure trying to confirm interviews so that I would not waste a moment. Even so, they often had to be changed, which sometimes meant longer stays in one or more place, which then threw everything out of whack. It also meant trying to find ways to conserve money, and that often included finding friends whose apartments would be available for little or no rent. I was able to keep my prior frenetic pace going in London, thanks to Tony Johnson, who let me use his apartment in Shepherd Market as my home base. There was only one problem with it: he stored his fine wines there, and the temperature had to be fifty degrees at all times. The first thing I did after a cold night and a hasty lukewarm shower was to find a hairdresser to wash and dry my hair, for I already had a bad head cold and would have risked pneumonia had I done it in the apartment.

I had a full schedule of interviews, the first with my British agent, Mark Hamilton, who arranged meetings with British publishers who were interested in the biography. One of them was with John Calder, whom I described in the *DD* as *"in a feisty mood. I sensed that he regrets not having this book even as he berated me for having the chutzpah to write it. He kept saying he would 'guide me in the right direction,' but I knew he was guiding me toward non-important topics and non-valid sources. I wondered if he was all there because he muttered and mumbled to himself as he paced around his desk. A strange meeting, from start to finish."*

Tom Maschler at Jonathan Cape was my next stop. He, in the

DD, was *"dynamic, hard charging, very excited about the book. I'm thrilled that he will publish it."* Tom suggested lunch, but I had to decline because I needed to rest up before a late-afternoon meeting with Beckett's nephew, Edward. The cold I had caught in Dublin became a disorienting flu in London, and I was in such gastric distress I could not risk eating or drinking. Instead I went back to the apartment and huddled under blankets until Edward arrived.

When he rang the bell, I was both anxious about meeting him and befuddled from all I had done in the past several weeks as I went to the building's front door to let him in. The apartment was on the ground floor and close to the front door, and as soon as I greeted him, I realized that the apartment door had shut behind me and I had not brought the keys. Edward was shocked at my first words to him: "Oh shit! I've locked myself out." We stood in the hallway for a few minutes before I had the presence of mind to go down the street to the greengrocer, who called a locksmith. Edward was clearly confused by the situation he had wandered into, but he was game to stick by me as long as he could, and he trotted along beside me. He played the flute in the London Philharmonic Orchestra, and when we had arranged the time to meet, he had told me he could give me half an hour, forty minutes at the most, before he had to leave for rehearsal. We went back to stand outside the apartment building to wait for the locksmith. I was wearing only a sweater—heavy, to be sure, but not heavy enough for a January day on a London street.

The locksmith never came and Edward had to leave. We set a date for another meeting several days later, but on neutral territory, in a tearoom. I went back to the greengrocer, who related a great phone fuss with the locksmith, a "bloke from the neighborhood," who said he could not come until the next day. The greengrocer went back to the apartment with me, broke the pane on the front window, raised it, crawled in, and came to the main door to let me in. It was probably the only time I was grateful to have an apartment at the front of a building on the ground floor. Once inside, we called a glass man, who said he could come the next day at 9 a.m.

It was so cold and I was so sick that I had to spend the evening sitting doing nothing but trying to breathe, and the next day I spent the entire morning pacing, waiting for the glass man, who never showed up. More phone calls via the greengrocer got "this bloke's promise" that he would certainly be there "tomorrow." I never did see Edward again on that trip, but we did meet on a later one, when I was not so obviously flustered.

I spent the next afternoon interviewing very old Irish people who had known Beckett in the 1930s, listening entranced as they read entries from crumbling diaries or pulling from disintegrating envelopes letters Beckett had written after he returned to Ireland. The daylight was fading and the fire was dying, but the light in the old eyes and the lilt in the shaky voices was mesmerizing. I could hardly take notes, which induced horror afterward, when the interview was over and my euphoria became panic: *"My damn tape recorder is dead! Crapped out! I am so glad I am going home."*

I was frazzled when I arrived for dinner at the home of American friends who were longtime London residents. They immediately offered to let me borrow their recorder until mine could be fixed, so I was able to spend a much-needed evening relaxing and forgetting about work. The house was filled with the sounds of their preteen children joshing, chattering, and playing loud music. Good smells came from the kitchen and conversation flowed lazily. Back at the apartment, I told the *DD "that was the world of my life. Beckett's world is my work. I must remember this if I want to hold on to who I am and what I am doing while I am here."*

Despite my trials with the still-unrepaired window and the tape recorder, Sunday, January 27, 1974, was by far the most difficult day of all on this trip. I left early in the morning to get from Mayfair to Hampstead for a nine o'clock meeting with Dr. Geoffrey Thompson. He and his late brother, Alan, were physicians and friends of Beckett's, particularly during his Trinity years and just after. Geoffrey had been training to become a psychiatrist, and it was he who had first suggested that Beckett go into psychoanalysis and then persuaded him to do so. I had met him briefly on an earlier trip to London, when he had hinted at all that he might be willing to tell me, and now we were about to embark on a long and intense morning interview.

I arrived promptly at nine, as Dr. Thompson had firmly instructed, only to be told that it was "too early" and I should "walk about the Heath" for at least half an hour until he was ready to receive me. It was bitter cold that morning, and not a single place was open where I could have warmed up with a cup of tea. I spent the half hour walking the streets with my gloved hands under my armpits to warm them, stamping my feet to get the blood circulating.

When Dr. Thompson finally deigned to admit me, we spoke for three hours, even though he was exceedingly reluctant at first to talk. Instead he made me defend myself and my project: As a woman and an American at that, how could I possibly think I could write about an Irishman? How could I possibly understand his mental acuity? Here I got the distinct impression that he either planned to or was already writing a psychobiography: *"Then he started to spout all the crap and rumors I had already heard count-less times and discounted. Only after two hours did he finally start to talk in earnest about Bion and Jung as he kept saying 'I'm going to write to Sam to see if I should say more. To see how much I should tell you.'"*

He showed me the chess set he and Beckett had played on, and he demonstrated the game from *Murphy*, which I (not being a player) did not understand. I made a note to ask my son (who as a teenager was about to become a chess master) to explain it so I could write about it. Dr. Thompson also kept opening and shutting the center drawer of his desk, as if he could not decide whether to show me something. He handled a pile of letters and ruffled the pages of what appeared to be a typed manuscript, but he did not read from them, nor did he let me have a proper look. Several times he repeated in a mumble that I had to strain to hear, "I'll see if I should say more; I'll see how much I should tell you."

Unwittingly—or was it on purpose? I could not decide—

Dr. Thompson was confirming what I had suspected and what others, who could not provide confirmation, had told me: that Beckett had been in psychoanalysis in the mid-1930s with Dr. Wilfred Ruprecht Bion, and that Dr. Bion had taken him to hear C. G. Jung's Tavistock Lectures. But I still needed proof before I could ask Beckett if it was true, and that proof did not come until almost the end of the year, when I was making my second research trip to Europe in 1974.

My head was reeling when I left Hampstead. I took the tube down to Piccadilly hoping to find a restaurant where I could get a good Sunday lunch and find a store where I could buy some little things for my children. I was unsuccessful on both fronts: *"No shops open, no decent restaurants. How I hate Sundays abroad and alone. So I bought all the papers and saw front-page stories that Yale's Vineland map is a forgery. Shades of home. Tomorrow is my last day. I just hope the damn trains don't go on strike so I don't waste my last day."*

I was in Waterloo Station early the next morning to go to Compton, Surrey, and the home of two Beckett cousins, Mollie Roe and her sister Sheila Roe Page, who had lived in the Foxrock home when he was a boy. Fortunately, there was not a strike, only slowdowns that seemed to take forever. It was still a rewarding day, for the house was full of gifts from Beckett. I saw the Seán O'Sullivan drawing of him as a young man, four paintings by Henri Hayden done in Roussillon while they hid from the Nazis, and a small statue of a man that Beckett told his cousins had been his inspiration for the character of Pozzo in *Waiting for Godot*. The cousins told me that Beckett "did not like to own possessions" and said that they were often the grateful recipients of his largesse. I read the inscriptions he had written in his first editions; I saw books signed to him by other writers; I read his letters to the cousins and was able to copy photos of him taken during his visits to their house. My book's skeleton was growing nicely fat with such good flesh upon it.

Once back in London, I had time before leaving for Heathrow to post a letter to Tony Johnson, to tell him that the keys were with the greengrocer and apologize again about the broken window: "*I leave here with one unresolved situation: that damn window is still not fixed.*" Otherwise I left with few complaints and one very large nagging fear: few people had told me anything new, and many were telling me stories I'd heard before. It was time to start writing the book. The big question now was how and where to begin.

15

It took a while for reentry into real life to take hold, but the weather helped. It was winter in New England, snow was thick, school was canceled, and the kids were home. I sat in my office staring at a mountain of tapes that needed transcribing and notes that needed to be typed and put into order, while the smell of cookies baking and the sounds of conflicting music (his and her differing rock favorites) blasted. There were museum openings for which I had to dig out my finery and play my usual role as the hired help's wife, and there were dinners to cook for visiting scholar friends who were working in various Yale libraries. Suddenly it was Monday, February 25, 1974, and I noted, *"I haven't done any work since Thursday and I am in a sustained state of block and panic. Just an observation in general."*

On the financial front, I nervously awaited news of fellowships, but the decisions were disappointingly negative. Trinity College in Hartford dangled the possibility of a job before withdrawing it because there was no funding. I went down to Westport several nights each week to give a "great books" course at a community center, and that was the only income I brought in during the winter, which made me worry about how I was going to pay for my next research trip. I knew that once I digested everything I had just collected, I would need to return to Paris to ask Beckett to confirm, correct, or even discount much that I had learned. However, the main thing I wanted to do was to write a first draft of the book so that I could have at least some idea of how it would convey the facts and events of his life. Content was primary, but how to structure it became another major concern. Just then Beckett's circle tracked me down, and so many interruptions cropped up that sustained writing was out of the question.

Joan Mitchell came to New York in early spring to prepare for a major exhibition at the Whitney Museum of American Art. The show consisted of a prodigious amount of work, twenty-two new paintings done in Vétheuil between 1969 and 1973. She asked me to come to her studio on St. Mark's Place, not because she had anything new to tell me about Beckett but just because she "liked" me and thought I "might be worth saving." It was another "okaaaay" moment, but I genuinely liked her, so I went.

I arrived at her studio to find her busily working the phone to set up appointments with Barney Rosset, her ex-husband and lifelong friend. She wanted the three of us to get together to talk about Beckett, which we did, and which sent me off to explore some interesting aspects of his work.

Joan's exhibition opening was a gala affair. She was radiant and looked beautiful in a French designer's pantsuit in lush beige Ultrasuede (all the rage then), over which I promptly spilled a large glass of white wine when one of the well-wishers crowding her jostled my elbow. She was in such a good mood that she laughed it off, thus relieving me of my humiliation. The art world turned out to celebrate Joan, and I was able to chat with artists and museum people I knew from all the parties and openings at the Wadsworth Atheneum. It was quite the love-in, and Joan reveled in it.

Barney Rosset was enjoying Joan's moment as much as she was, and he took me aside to tell me he had "lots of new stuff" to show me and suggested that we meet, without Joan, in his office two days later. She would be busy doing publicity in connection with her show, and he did not want to wait, because "Sam" had told him to "show [me] correspondence and anything else" I wanted to see. That was the first sign I had received since the January research trip that all was well between Beckett and me. It was an incredible relief to learn that none of the people I had seen in London and Dublin had carried negative tales back to him, or if they did, that he chose not to believe them.

Snow continued to fall in record amounts, but I did not let it stop me from getting in to Barney's office, where I worked for the next several days. Mostly I concentrated on correspondence that he and Beckett had exchanged in the early years, starting around 1953. There were various typescripts of novels and plays, photographs of various productions, and occasional souvenirs (mainly postcards) sent by Beckett when he was on holidays and far away from his work.

New York was teeming with French people just then. The novelist Nathalie Sarraute was speaking at the 92nd Street Y, and the publisher Maurice Girodias was still in residence, although busy preparing to move permanently to France. Unfortunately, neither could see me then, as their schedules were too full. I saw them both in Paris on a later trip and was rewarded with stories of their involvement with Beckett that I used in the book.

Girodias told me to talk to Iris Owens, who had written novels on command for him under the name of Harriet Daimler in the 1950s. She had rollicking stories about the writers she called "the *Merlin* gang," the young writers who had been associated with the magazine, and especially Richard Seaver, who was the first publisher of Beckett's *Watt*, in a partnership with Girodias's Olympia Press. Richard was then an editor at Barney Rosset's Grove Press, and he, too, was one of Beckett's most trusted friends in the publishing world. Richard and his wife (and later copublisher), Jeannette, gave me long lists of names and addresses of all the "young Turks" (their expression) who had written for *Merlin* and Olympia. They saved me months in those pre-Internet days by telling me where I could find Austryn Wainhouse, Jane Lougee, Alexander Trocchi, Christopher Logue, and others.

I mention all these names because of another one that gave me a strange feeling some years later about how small and interconnected the intellectual and artistic world is. Girodias was the son of Jack Kahane, whose Obelisk Press had published Henry Miller in Paris in the 1930s, thanks to the generosity of Anaïs Nin's banker husband, Hugh Guiler, who paid all the printing bills for his two

Tropic books. It was one of those curious correspondences that had no meaning for me until I began to write about Anaïs Nin in 1990. By then I had forgotten entirely that in 1974 she sent me one of her signature purple postcards asking me to put her in touch with Samuel Beckett. Because Beckett had ordered me never to divulge his address, I suggested that she ask Barney Rosset to forward her request, so I never knew if she did manage to contact him. I had one other letter from her, responding to mine that asked if she had ever met him during her Paris years. She replied that she had not, but she had seen Alan Schneider's production of *Godot* and she wanted to contact Beckett because she wanted to write about him and it in her famous *Diary*.

While I was in Barney Rosset's office busily copying and transcribing almost everything in his Beckett files, letters and phone messages were piling up at home. George Reavey was feeling neglected because I had no time to meet him at his favorite bar, so he dangled a letter or two that he had "miraculously just found." Jean Reavey expected me to write to Beckett and ask him to help her find French producers for her plays, and it took all my tact and discretion to divert her. I almost did not take the call from George that came late one night in March, telling me that John Montague was in New York and wanted to see me. We could meet at Martell's, he suggested, for lunch. And I should plan to spend a long afternoon with them and, although this was unspoken, to pay for everything as well. Gritting my teeth, I told George I could manage only an hour and I could not arrive until midafternoon. He didn't like it, but *tant pis,* I said to myself, using one of the French expressions I was trying to use so that I would not curse in English.

I did end up lunching with Montague and Reavey, but I managed my exit after I paid for my meal and left them to pay for theirs while they were still drinking. The reason I accepted in the first place was that Montague told me he had been in Paris and had "had a long conversation with Sam" about me and the biography, but that turned out to be a ruse. Montague had the mistaken idea that I had enough clout at various colleges and universities to get him a teaching position and, if not an actual job, at least a lucrative speaking engagement. I could not find a permanent position for myself, so I certainly could not drop one magically into his lap.

Joan Mitchell phoned every day, to my home and to Barney's office, asking me to come to her studio to keep her company. Most days I did drop in, and fortunately, she let me leave when I had to go. There was only one repeat of what I was calling my *"kidnap by Joan,"* when she refused to let me leave her studio. Luckily, her gallerist, Xavier Fourcade, phoned and volunteered to come and stay with her, so she let me go home in time for dinner with my family. When she left for Paris, I saw her off with great tenderness and the genuine promise that I would see her on my next research trip.

There were other strange happenings that spring. Marion Leigh wrote a chatty letter asking when I planned to return to Paris. She admired a blouse I had worn on my last trip, one that I liked so much myself that I had bought it in several colors. Could I buy two and send them to her? I did, in the size and colors she requested, and I sent them via airmail. Several weeks later I got her reply: the colors were not exactly right and neither was the size, so she had given them to a charity. Nothing was said about payment. I fumed but said nothing.

And then Israel Horovitz returned. I had seen him in the Grove Press offices on several occasions when I was working on Barney's archives, but we had not spoken. He sent me a letter saying he was now ready once again "to consider answering any questions put to him in writing." I replied, saying that he knew the kind of questions I would ask and if he wanted to answer them, it would be fine. And if not, that was fine, too.

Obviously, with all this activity I did very little writing between the end of January and the middle of April, when I arranged to consult archives pertaining to Beckett in Austin at the University of Texas's Humanities Research Center. I was overjoyed to learn that Jack Unterecker was a visiting professor that term, and over lunch I talked nonstop as I caught him up on everything I had done since we had last seen each other at Columbia. Jack spoke seldom but, as always, wisely. He pointed me in directions I had not thought to go and helped me to rank people I had not yet contacted in terms of their importance to Beckett and the book. It was the last time I saw him before his too-early death in 1989.

One of the persons Jack thought would be not only a great resource for Beckett's Irish heritage but also a thoughtful scholarly editor was the critic Vivian Mercier. He lived in Ireland, and I wrote to him as soon as I left Austin. He asked me to phone him, since we would not be on the same continent anytime soon. I did, and we spoke for almost two hours. I consoled myself that the phone bill was still cheaper than a plane ticket.

Mercier was a fount of information about all things Irish, and he followed through on his offer to send me reams of information he had collected for his own writings about Beckett. But in the conversation he said something that I immediately confided to the *DD* and puzzled over for a long time: *"The proper person to do Samuel Beckett's biography is a young American girl who gives the impression of great naiveté."*

I didn't know what to make of that remark except to be upset by it. I thought I was presenting myself as a scholar-writer who was working earnestly to educate herself in every positive professional manner, and yet despite my best efforts, people who should have known better still thought of me as a naive girl. It was distressing then, and it still rankles now. However, it did have one positive effect: it gave me a tremendous burst of energy and put me into an "I'll show them" mode. I had done enough research, I had the basic outline for a biography, and it was time to settle down and start writing. I had said it before, but this time I meant it.

16

"The yawn factor" was a term I invented for what happened during interviews when I was stifling yawns of boredom because people were telling me things I already knew. Even though there were parts of Beckett's life for which I needed more information before I could write a consistent narrative, by the spring of 1974, I knew it was time to start.

As I began, I read other biographies carefully, studying style and technique as much as content. All I had read to that date seemed to start at the beginning—birth—and end at the end—death. He (for they were still predominantly about men) was born, and then he grew up and did, went, saw, became, and then he declined and died. Full stop and the end of the book.

By April the frenetic activity of the past several months was slowing down enough for me to concentrate more on where to begin than on how. At this point in my brief but ever-growing career as an accidental biographer, I had read fairly extensively in the genre, enough so that I taught with confidence a course at Trinity College entitled "Literary Biography." In the crash program I created to educate myself to teach others, I began with a survey of the classics: Plutarch, Suetonius, Vasari. I was entranced with the two lives of Charlemagne by Notker and Einhard and enjoyed biographies of Walter Scott, Thomas Carlyle, Charles Dickens, and John Keats. I read psychobiographies of Freud and Jung, and for reasons I was not then educated enough in that field to understand was dissatisfied with both. However, I did like the economist W. W. Rostow's psychobiography of James Forrestal for the judicious insights into how Forrestal's character influenced his public life. I felt I learned from it some interesting methods for crucial insights into Beckett's writings.

Talking to other biographers was as important as reading. I never missed a meeting of Aileen Ward's biography seminar, where I profited from discussions of works in progress about Nathaniel Hawthorne (Gloria Erlich), Doris Lessing (Carole Klein), Lillian Hellman (Joan Mellen), Dorothy Parker (Marion Meade), and Victorine Meurent (Eunice Lipton). That was when I first realized the impact that women writers were having on the genre, and I began to read Virginia Woolf's nonfiction writing with an entirely different eye, as the practitioner rather than the critic. Elizabeth Hardwick's essays about other writers and their lives and letters broadened my thoughts on how the boundaries of fiction and nonfiction were evolving in ways that I thought might have resonances for the genre of biography. I found myself gravitating to the women writers who were exploring the lives of women through nonfiction as well as biography, among them Nancy Milford (Edna St. Vincent Millay) and Susan Brownmiller, then writing her influential study *Against Our Will: Men, Women, and Rape.* Alix Kates Schulman had created a literary tsunami when *Memoirs of an Ex-Prom Queen* appeared, and Kate Millett's *Sexual Politics* was inspiring dialogue across every sociopolitical spectrum. In retrospect, I believe they were all subtle, unconscious influences on everything I wrote about Samuel Beckett.

I must have internalized something from every woman's methods and techniques, but I did not realize I had done so until 2016, when I read Paula Backscheider's 1991 study of biography, in which she wrote that "feminism permeates" my biography of Samuel Beckett. Initially I was astonished by her assessment, because I was not aware that feminism had been an active concern during the writing. Overall, I am pleased that such an eminent scholar discerned this quality, for as I began the writing, I really had no idea of what I was doing, let alone that I had instinctively created a way of thinking and writing about biography that became the foundation for all my subsequent work.

Having read widely and deeply, I thought I did not want to write one of those traditional biographies. I wanted to do something different, to begin with something exciting, just as Douglas Day had done in his biography of Malcolm Lowry. Day began Lowry's written life with his death, when he fell up (not down) the stairs in a drunken stupor. In Beckett's case, I wanted to begin with a fact or event that was the first thing anyone who knew anything about him would think of when they heard his name. Therefore, what better place to start than with *Waiting for Godot*?

This was an unusual first step for me, because I almost never knew what the first sentence of a piece of writing would be until I arrived at the end (which is still the case). This time I thought I knew exactly how I would begin, with the first sentence Suzanne Beckett said to her husband after he won the Nobel Prize: *"Quelle catastrophe!"* Then I would proceed to write about the play's first performance. I was about a page and a half into the first draft when questions and doubts surfaced. I confided all my questions to the *DD*, starting with how I should insert something about the circumstances of the play's creation, but before I could do this, how I had to set the scene by telling the reader where Beckett was at the time of inspiration. Or, I pondered, perhaps I needed to stop long enough to explain where he got the name Godot, or address the occasional lines that he borrowed from other writers and what he intended them to convey. And how about letting the reader know the part his wife, Suzanne, had played in all this? Suddenly it was May; a month had gone by and I was nowhere near a cohesive beginning. Starting the life of Beckett at the moment of his great fame was not going to work.

I reluctantly conceded that, novice as I was, perhaps others had the correct approach when they began at the beginning of a subject's life, so I decided to try it. One week later I had a very rough draft of a first chapter that carried Beckett from his birth to his teen years at the Portora Royal School. When I say "rough," it does not begin to describe those awkward and fragmented first pages. I may have created a skeleton, but I had very little flesh worth putting upon it.

I knew I needed to return to Ireland to get more information about Beckett's early life, but the problem was the usual one I faced throughout the writing: where to find the money to pay for the trip. I was officially under contract to Harper's Magazine Press, but the tiny advance had already been spent. My agent, Carl Brandt, said that the publisher, Larry Freundlich, would not advance more money until I had a significant chunk of writing to show him. Frustrated that I had to stop writing in order to fill out more grant proposals, I counted myself fortunate when the American Council of Learned Societies gave me the small stipend that would let me return to Europe that fall. With relief, I went back to writing.

My most immediate task was the mammoth one of organizing all the information I already had about the Irish years so that I could fill in what I didn't know when I got to Ireland. I realized that I needed a detailed chronology that would allow me to trace Beckett's movements and writings day by day, even hour by hour in some instances. But how to lay it all out in some useful form in those pre-spreadsheet days? I was a great fan of small file cards and I had written out chronologies separated by category—education, health, familial relationships, etc. However, I did not have enough space to lay them out and see them all at once; what I needed was a visual calendar, an outline that would enable me to integrate all the topics into a master timeline.

I found the solution in a local five-and-dime store that was going out of business. In a bin I spotted rolls and rolls of white paper that thrifty housewives who kept spotlessly clean homes used to line the shelves in their kitchen cabinets. Since I had never been such a model of midcentury domesticity, my first thought when I saw them was of how Jack Kerouac wrote *On the Road*: he used one continuous roll of paper that he typed on without having to stop to change the page. I would use mine to write a nonstop chronology of Beckett's daily existence.

The world knew very little about Samuel Beckett when I began to write about him. Academic writers claimed him as the recluse poet of alienation, isolation, and despair, while cultural critics assigned philosophical debts and resonances to Arthur Schopenhauer and Bishop George Berkeley, among others. Theatrical scholars and dramaturges settled for allegiances to Irish antecedents or alliances to the continental theater of the absurd. There was truth in them all, but none was the entire truth. I saw my task as to provide the biographical information that would allow all forms of critical writing to flourish in new and hitherto unknown or unthought-of directions. I was beginning to see the genre of biography as the tool that was the entry into deeper and more detailed inquiries into aspects of a writer's work.

However, when it came to methodology, I had none. I was intent on simply allowing the written life to unfold exactly as Beckett had lived—and was living—his own. I would not try to create a structure that would impose arbitrary boundaries on content, nor would I try to carve the life story into neat and tidy categories. Sitting in the quiet of my office, pondering the overwhelming task before me and trying to create a theory or thesis through random notes in the *DD,* I formulated what I called my "non-methodology," one I have followed ever since. I wrote that every life is messy and varied, subject to the vagaries of external events and outrageous fortunes. A biography was a living, breathing entity that had to be free to meander down its own particular paths and byways, which was quite unlike everything I had been taught in my academic life, where peer-reviewed journals expected subjects to be presented within rigidly proscribed parameters.

I found myself telling all this to Leon Edel when we met accidentally in the National Gallery of Art. We were both in Washington for a biography conference, he as a distinguished speaker and I as a rapt novice in the audience. We sat for well over an hour as I explained my method, posed my questions, and asked for his advice. He seemed to relish the conversation and was generous with examples from his own experience. I still honor the tips he gave, and I follow many of his techniques to this day.

When it came to my own process, allowing the writing itself to unfold freely often required ruthless pruning later. This was most apparent in my beginnings, the first paragraphs, which fell somewhere between overblown and florid. In my journalism career I had strived for the pithy first sentence, the "catchy lede" that would draw the reader into the story, but I rarely got there on my first try. I remember how my favorite editor would stand over my shoulder when I was writing on a deadline, peering at my typewriter through his little granny glasses. "Get up," he would say before he sat down in my chair, ripped out my story, and wrote his own simple and direct first sentence, which he would then paste over my gloriously inflated prose before sending everything off to the copy desk. You would think I had learned something about simplicity and directness in the several years I worked with him, but when I started to write Beckett's life, I began with my usual grandiosity. It would seem I had learned nothing.

Even though I knew that the "three p's," the "passionate purple prose" I was writing, would probably never see the pages of a finished book, it did serve a purpose. I sometimes needed to write ten or fifteen pages about a minor critical essay of Beckett's to be able to understand which several sentences, a paragraph at most, really expressed what was important. I had to leave the cutting-room floor awash in discarded pages before I knew what I needed to keep.

It took time to create my hybrid calendar-chronology that summer, but it was well worth it. This was a busy and productive period; I wrote steadily, watching the book take form in bits and pieces as I wrote those sections for which I had significant information and multiple sources to confirm it. I was still conducting interviews as I wrote, concentrating now on people in the theater who had worked on American productions of Beckett's plays, so that when I returned to Ireland and England, I could compare their approaches to various continental ones. I spoke to several psychologists and psychiatrists who had written about Beckett, all of whom were convinced that he had serious mental problems. I listened carefully, collected everything they gave me, and put it into a file for careful consideration. Vivian Mercier sent me his correspondence with Beckett and a chapter of the book he was then writing; I was relieved to find that nothing in it impinged upon mine.

And then Mary Manning Howe arrived to spend the summer with her daughter, the poet Susan Howe, in Guilford. There were many lunches and dinners, lots of fun and happy conversation at my house and Susan's, and even more when another of Mary's daughters, the writer Fanny Howe, arrived with her children. Soon it would be October and time for me to leave for Paris. As was my custom, I wrote to Beckett to give him my dates in Paris. I was stunned to receive his reply, in which he told me he "deplored the trouble you have caused with Mrs. Howe and her daughter Susan," ending with "I prefer not to see you."

Now what?

17

To say I was in shock when I read Beckett's letter does not begin to describe my reaction. Trying to fathom what had provoked it brings back the memory of one particular evening, August 8, the night Richard Nixon resigned the presidency. There were all sorts of rumors, but we didn't know what Nixon would do when I invited Molly, Susan, and Fanny to my house for dinner—only that he would be making a televised announcement. When I opened the door to let them in, I found Fanny and Susan wrestling a large television set between them. Fearful that I did not have one or that it might not work, they had brought their own. We set up theirs and mine side by side in the dining room and all of us sat in a row at the table, staring at them as if in a theater while our dinners went untouched.

In every conversation we had that summer, Molly had raised the possibility of Beckett's parentage of Susan, trying very hard to persuade me that it was the truth and should be written as such. Fortunately, I had Beckett's detailed calendar for the year in question and, to back it up, a great deal of corroborating evidence in his letters and postcards. He could not possibly have fathered her child, because she and he were not in Ireland at the same time. I knew I would not put rumor, innuendo, or unmitigated gossip in the biography, so I simply dismissed it and never bothered to ask Beckett about Molly's spurious contention. I certainly never raised the subject with Susan, and every time Molly raised it in our one-on-one talks, I always told her as firmly and as politely as I could that I would not write about it in any form whatsoever. I thought that those conversations had put it to rest forever.

At our last meeting in Connecticut at the end of August, I told Molly that I would be seeing her in October, as I planned to make Dublin my first stop before going to London, where I still had many interviews and much archival research to do. I had given Beckett my itinerary, but whether I went on to Paris afterward would depend on how long my grant money lasted. If I did go, it would be for only a brief catch-up, on the off chance that something had arisen to upset him, and to calm Beckett's anger if necessary.

Between August and the end of September, I kept on writing and was pleased with how steadily I was moving the book along. I had only bits and pieces of Beckett's later life written, but chronologically I was well into the 1930s and about to start on his permanent move to Paris. I was stunned to receive his reply to the letter that gave him my dates, when he told me how he "deplored the trouble you have caused with Mrs. Howe and her daughter Susan . . . on the strength of one of [his] letters to Mr. Ussher." He told me not to reproduce any correspondence, photos, or drawings in the book, ending with "I prefer not to see you." I could not understand what this mess was about and why Molly Howe had created it.

Even though I remembered Brian Coffey warning me that Molly Howe was "dramatic" and would use any situation for her own purposes, I could not fathom why, as Beckett said in his letter to me, she had told him that I was going to name him as Susan's father, or what made her ask him to denounce me, stop cooperating, and not see me ever again, especially after she kissed me goodbye and handed me a very special family treasure to cement our friendship, a piece of lace embroidered by her mother. Although it was she who had introduced me to Arland Ussher and she who had gone with me to his house to insist that he show me his letters, she had also told Beckett that I had browbeaten the poor man into submission before he agreed. She also insisted that she had had nothing to do with my discovering the story of Susan's possible parentage and that I had learned of it only after I read the

Ussher letters. I could not decide whether I was more stunned by her audacity or appalled by her lies.

Immediately after I received Beckett's letter, I went to see Susan. She was embarrassed and upset and asked me if she should write to Beckett, even though she had no idea how she would explain her mother's outburst. After I told her the truth of my role in this unpleasant brouhaha, she said, "That's just Mummy being Mummy," and we agreed not to speak of it again. I was relieved that the friendship we had formed over the summer remained intact.

And then I had to deal with Beckett, but how to go about that was entirely unclear. Luckily, something fortuitous happened that helped. Alan Schneider called to say that he had found some director's notes pertaining to *Godot* and he thought they might be useful. He was planning to be in New York the next week, and we agreed to meet in Barney Rosset's office, where we could compare notes on which theater people in London were the most important for me to interview.

Without going into the details, I told Alan and Barney that Mary Manning Howe had set off a firestorm between me and Beckett and I didn't know what to do about it. Both men listened attentively, and as I talked, I could see them exchanging meaningful looks. Barney spoke first, asking if this was the first time I had experienced one of "Sam's rare flashes of anger." As I thought about it, I realized that flashes of his anger were not rare with me, for my questions usually provoked at least one per meeting.

Alan offered a solution and I did take it, but only in part. He said I should reply to Beckett's letter at once, apologizing for any inadvertent part I might have played in "Mrs. Howe's fantasy," and then leave it at that—a very brief note and nothing else. "Fantasy" was what he told me to call it, and that was exactly what I wrote and what I intended to send, until stewing on the matter a bit longer made me very angry. After years of our in-person conversations and numerous letters explaining who I was seeing and what sort of questions I was asking, Beckett's accusations in his letter struck me as outrageous. As was my custom, I unloaded all these emotions into the *DD*: "*MMH has queered the ballgame. He is furious over all the Ussher crap and he blames me for everything. I thought about it all day and couldn't sleep most of the night but finally composed a very dignified letter that I hope will show him I am pissed off by his arrogance.*" I could not let things go without comment, because I knew his charges would fester and eventually cause me to erupt, and I didn't want the eruption to happen when I was with him. I went on to explain that the "fuss"—another of Alan's words—was all Mrs. Howe's creation.

Not satisfied with that and still seething, I could not resist concluding with an impassioned paragraph telling him that after all this time, I deeply regretted that he might still doubt the seriousness and honesty of my endeavor. I hoped he would change his mind, because I was too far along with the writing of the book, and too many people to whom I was contractually obligated were depending on me, that I had no option but to keep on with my work. I said I would be in Dublin and London, where he could reach me via my publishers, and I would go to Paris afterward only if he changed his mind and wanted to see me.

If he replied to this letter and sent it to one of the places where mail was being held for me, I never got it. But I suspect he did not reply. His flash of anger had dissipated, and by writing it, so had my righteous indignation. The next letter I received was not directly from him but from his cousin Mollie Roe, who said I should make a point to see her on my next visit to England, because she wanted to give me copies of letters and drawings she had earlier refused. When she asked Beckett about them, he told her I should have them. It seemed as though our correspondence and other kinds of contact would resume as if nothing untoward had happened.

The Molly Howe fiasco was not my only tribulation during this period. As I worked away, I was benefiting—or so I thought—from a constant correspondence and several long and expensive transatlantic telephone conversations with Vivian Mercier in Ireland. Up to that point in my writing life, I had often discussed my work with colleagues or friends, but I never showed anything written until I had a full draft, no matter whether it was a short news article or a long profile. I broke this hard-and-fast rule with Mercier to show him parts of the biography because I was worried about accurately capturing Beckett's Anglo-Irish heritage and social milieu and I wanted confirmation that I was not making any egregious factual blunders. "Naive American girl," he had called me, and although I resented the word "naive," in this instance that is exactly what I was.

I sent the better part of the manuscript to Mercier and he did help me with various "things Irish," as I called them, but his primary response was astonishment at the material I had discovered and how it was going to change Beckett scholarship. He told me time and again that no one knew any of what I was writing and that my book would become an extremely important contribution to "the academic Beckett cottage industry." It was as if he knew my innermost thoughts and dreams for the book's reception, as that was exactly what I wanted it to be, a genuine contribution to scholarship. I cheerfully kept on sending chapters as I wrote them.

I had been sending chapters for the better part of a year when Mercier sent me a letter telling me that he had written his own book, and because I was a total unknown "novice" and he was an "established scholar," he thought "it would be best" if he were to incorporate all the biographical information in my book into his own critical study. If it appeared there first, he argued, the public would be far more likely to take my book seriously. He was doing this only as "a great favor" to me. My so-called naiveté quickly took the form of action: I contacted my agent, who contacted my various publishers, whose lawyers all contacted Mercier's publisher. His publisher then submitted a revised manuscript to me to ensure that all of my research had been removed, and Mercier's book went to press as the critical study he had originally written.

Looking back on myself at that time, I see how I was gaining self-confidence. I had stood up to Beckett in self-defense, and it would appear that he had backed down. And I was standing up to the Reaveys time after time, refusing to be at their beck and call while focusing on my work, telling George that he could no longer dangle information but must either give it to me or not, and telling Jean that no, I had no clout with any of the theater people I had befriended and therefore I could not get them to produce her plays. Best of all, I had defanged Mercier's blatant attempt to steal my intellectual property. Thus empowered, I was confident that my upcoming research trip to Ireland would be very different from the last one. Various interviews I had conducted in the interim all pointed to the McGreevy letters as an essential piece of the Beckett puzzle, and I was determined not to come home without them.

When I made my flight reservations, almost two months had passed since I had sent the letter defending myself to Beckett, and I thought I should probably send another note to him with my itinerary. Before I could write it, I received one from him, telling me that he was in Tangier and would be there for the entire month, resting before attending rehearsals of *Happy Days* in London. Then he would be in Berlin throughout December and January to rehearse *Waiting for Godot*. My family, my agent, and my publisher all found it hard to believe I was so relieved that I would not be seeing him on this trip, but it was true. Being in his physical presence and directly subjected to his possible volatility and usual gamesmanship surely would be a distraction, one that would disrupt my focus on the task at hand: finishing *his* book so that I could return to *my* life.

Instinctively I felt that if my reading Beckett's correspondence with Arland Ussher had so upset him, reading those to McGreevy would almost certainly set off another of his flashes of temper, one that might prevent me from perusing those crucial letters. I knew that he had already asked several of his correspondents (who all had disobeyed his wishes) to destroy his letters, but I did not want even to hint about McGreevy's until I had safely read them. I was afraid that if I saw Beckett in person, I might slip up and reveal that I knew they existed. So I sent him a happy, chatty little note saying oh what a shame that I would not be able to see him and wishing him well in his work and travels. Then off I went to Dublin.

18

I checked into Buswells and found a message waiting for me. Mrs. M. M. Howe would like to invite me to dinner tomorrow at her home to meet Eileen O'Casey, the widow of playwright Seán, who had much to tell me about her friendship with Mr. Beckett. If Molly Howe wanted to act as if nothing untoward had happened, then so did I. I accepted her invitation.

Then I phoned Arland Ussher to see whether I needed to offer any amends or explanations. His housekeeper answered and said I should hold for just a moment and she would get him. There was a longish wait before she returned to say, "Do you know, I believe he has just gone away for a few days." That made for two "okaaaay" moments in half an hour, and I had a feeling I was in for an interesting week. I was not disappointed.

The bandwagon was becoming crowded, as all sorts of people wanted to climb on board. Every day for the next week my appointments began early in the morning and did not end until almost midnight. Curators at Trinity and University College were eager to show me archives that until now had been mysteriously unavailable. John Manning, Molly Howe's brother, took me to lunch at the posh Kildare Street Club to show me an album of childhood photos that included Sam and his brother, Frank. A boozy dinner at the home of a leading Catholic academic administrator revealed a shocking contempt for Beckett's work, while another evening of drinks with a nun and educator illustrated the Church's reach in Ireland and clarified the Catholic antagonism toward his writing. Beckett's cousin Hilary Heron Greene, an artist who lived on a cliff above the Irish Sea in Dalkey and who had been exceptionally close to Beckett's mother, invited me to lunch and spent the next four hours showing me more of the many things Mae Beckett had given her, all the while laying out Mrs. Beckett's version of how and why her son had left Ireland for France, a topic that would feature prominently in the McGreevy letters. After keeping such an exhausting pace, I concluded that it had been worthwhile, if only to know I was not leaving anything or anyone out. By Friday night, November 2, while summing it up for the *DD*, I just wanted to crawl into bed, sleep late, and buy a bucket of fruit the next day. I wanted a day to myself and no full English breakfast. I could not face another egg.

I did sleep late, but there was no slowing down. That night I had dinner at the home of the aforementioned leading Catholic academic administrator, who wanted me to meet others who represented the Catholic rebuttal to Beckett's Anglo-Irish sensibilities. It was a most unusual evening, wherein Beckett was not really the subject: I was. Most of the conversation consisted of questions about my personal situation, most about how I had "abandoned" my husband and children to go off on my own to a foreign country and whether this was common among American "women's libbers." But then came the question that left me speechless: why had I left my family to write about a man like "Thomas à Beckett"? Surely this had to be sarcasm on purpose, for no one had drunk enough wine to make such a mistake. I learned that there were two worlds in modern Ireland, and one of them did not approve of Samuel Beckett.

Another busy day followed on Sunday, and by the evening I wanted nothing more than to fall into bed when I returned to the hotel. As I headed for the elevator, the desk clerk came running after me with several messages. One of the McGreevy nieces had phoned to say that she would come to the hotel the next morning at 9:30 and asked me to call her before 11 p.m. to confirm that I would be there. It was just after eleven, so I took a chance, dialed her number, and with great relief heard her voice. She rambled and equivocated at length before she got around to saying that she and her sister had been talking and they were still unsure of what to do about the letters.

It was the same story I had been hearing for the past several years, but this time there was a slight difference. They had been reading some of the letters for the first time, and based on what I had told them about my book, they thought I should have them. But then again, perhaps not. Perhaps they were too private and should instead be destroyed. For the next forty-five minutes we went over it again and again: they wanted to show me the letters, and they did want to show me all their photos, but they just didn't know if they should. Also, if they did agree to let me read the letters, they estimated that it would take at least three or four days, if not longer, for me to get through them, and as they would not let them leave the sister's house where they were stored, they would have to figure out the logistics of where and when I could read them, because someone would have to be there to "watch" me at all times. I bit my tongue so as not to blurt out something sarcastic to assure them that I was trustworthy. I had no interest in stealing Samuel Beckett's letters; I only wanted to read them to ensure that what I wrote was accurate.

Monday was supposed to be my last full day in Dublin. I planned to leave Tuesday afternoon for London, where I had a non-stop schedule of appointments, so there was no way I could extend my stay. I was both frantic and frazzled, because it did seem that I would get my chance, but at significant logistical—and financial—cost. I would obviously have to return to Dublin and stay until I finished reading the letters, and to do so left going on to Paris to be decided.

The elder McGreevy niece came to Buswells the next morning, and by this time, after so many previous meetings with her, I could tell from her distressed face that all uncertainty had yet to be banished. She told me again how she and her sister had spent most of the previous weekend trying to decide what to do, until finally "we threw up our hands and decided to let you read them before we changed our minds." When she said this, the rush of relief made me light-headed. But the euphoria was short-lived, for once again she began to equivocate about whether it was the right thing to do. As she sat there literally wringing her hands, something in me snapped, and for the first time in all the years I had made polite conversation with her and her sister, I lost control of myself.

Fortunately, my blowup was not a loud and angry one but rather a cold, quiet, and reasoned speech. I think she was mesmerized by such a soft voice as I launched into an explanation of my personal circumstances. I leaned on the slightly overblown version, speaking of the book as a mission, a gift to the world of scholarship (an overinflated assertion that still makes me blush). But I also wove in the practicalities—how I was funding the book through whatever jobs or grants-in-aid I could scrounge; how I resented having to live under such financial stress; how I regretted that it took me away from my "real life," my husband and children, and how we all suffered because of the strain it put them under. I went off on an impassioned emotional monologue, telling her how I worried that I would not do justice to the life of this great man by producing the book I felt he deserved if I were not allowed to include the all-important McGreevy letters.

By the time I finished this diatribe, I was exhausted, slightly nauseated, and utterly resigned to never seeing the letters. This back-and-forth had gone on for so long and I was so tired that I almost didn't care anymore. I concluded by telling her that this was the last time I could come to Dublin, that I was almost finished with the full draft of the biography, and that I had to go home and finish it before the publisher became fed up with my delays and canceled my contract. It was now or never.

I think my frankness stunned her. We both sat there quietly, probably because neither of us knew how to bring the meeting to a congenial close. Suddenly I had an idea: we should ask Beckett if he would let me read the letters. I thought our newfound détente might extend to whatever new archival material I found, because after the fuss over the Ussher letters, Beckett had ultimately agreed to let me use them, and he had also told Mollie Roe to give me material he had originally refused. It was at least worth asking. I suggested that the niece and her sister should write to Beckett. She thought it was a fine idea and went to the hotel's phone booth to ask her sister what she thought of it. When she returned, she was smiling. A letter would be fine, but they did not consider themselves eloquent enough to write it, so they wanted me to write it for them.

And so I did. I went to my room to get the tiny Smith Corona typewriter I traveled with, and we sat in Buswells' lobby composing a letter to Beckett. There was a postal strike in France and no mail was being delivered from Ireland or England. This offered at least one possible resolution of my constantly changing plans: if he was still in Paris, I would probably have to find the time and money to go there and deliver the letter; if he was already in London for theater rehearsals, I could deliver it there and would not have to go to Paris. One way or another, my main problem concerning the book's content would be resolved: either I would have to finish writing it based on the information I already had, which meant I could probably give it to my publisher as early as the following spring, 1975, or I could tell him of this important new addition and beg for more time.

Beckett was not in London when I arrived, and my time there was the whirlwind I expected it to be, highlighted by tea at the Ritz with Harold Pinter (Beckett had told him I was "an engaging charming woman" whom he should "definitely see"). I was so engrossed as Pinter talked of his indebtedness to the clarity of Beckett's vision and the freedom it gave him to exercise his own that I left the scrumptious goodies untouched. We both let our tea grow cold as Pinter recounted some of the adventurous evenings he and Beckett had spent after they forged a deep friendship.

There were certain logistics to take care of as soon as I arrived, starting with picking up mail sent by my family to Mark Hamilton's office. He also kept a record of my friends and people in publishing who wanted to see me. At Jonathan Cape, the genius publisher

Tom Maschler took me for drinks while probing, not entirely gently, about when I was going to deliver the manuscript. Editor Anne Chisholm, then writing the biography of Nancy Cunard, soothed us both. Anne's husband, the distinguished journalist Michael Davie, took great delight in regaling me with Beckett's cricket statistics even as he despaired of making me understand the game. My friends Jimmy and Tania Stern took me to dinner to meet V. S. Pritchett, and my head flew back and forth as if at a tennis match while conversation sparkled around me. Tony Johnson convened a group for dinner at Wheeler's that included the political journalist Patrick Seale and his young wife, Lamorna.

In and around these meetings and on a hunch, I went to Somerset House to pick up a copy of Samuel Beckett's marriage license. I still remember the joy when a clerk told me it was there but would not be ready for several days. I was so buoyed to find that my hunch was correct, that like James Joyce, Beckett had married quietly in London late in his life so that Suzanne could inherit his estate in France. I walked all the way across London to Paultons Square and Gertrude Street, the World's End district where Beckett had lived while writing *Murphy*. I had to sit on the curb until my breathlessness subsided and I could favor my blisters as I walked to the nearest bus stop.

The next day was devoted to people Beckett worked with in the theater, including the actors Billie Whitelaw and Siobhan O'Casey and the stage designer Jocelyn Herbert. I also phoned Kenneth Tynan, who told me he gave only paid interviews and asked how much I was offering. I said I was a journalist who did not pay, to which he replied that he commanded serious sums of money and thus had nothing to tell me. And then he hung up. As I was walking out the door, he called back and told me what he thought I should know about how *Oh! Calcutta!* came to be. And then he hung up once more, never to call again.

The next adventure was with the writers who called themselves "the *Merlin* gang," who had been affiliated with the magazine in Paris during the publication of *Watt*. Most of them were now liv-

ing in London, and Christopher Logue had given me vague warn-
ings of what I would find when I saw Alexander Trocchi and Jane
Lougee. I wish he had been more direct. That night I recapped it
in the *DD*: *"Jane was so high she was incoherent, flaked out. House
a shambles. Hopheads lying around all over it. Alex had runny nose
and shaky hands. Tried to foist several tired and worn copies of* Merlin *on me for $38 because he needed a fix. Had a hard time getting out
of there and hailing cab for quick getaway."*

Bettina Jonic Calder was next on my list. The ex-wife of John
Calder, she requested an interview to tell me of the "flaming affair"
she had had with Beckett. I listened politely but filed away almost
all that she told me under "unreliable sources."

My next stop was the office of Calder & Boyars, because the
French postal strike was still on and I wanted to see if I could leave
the letter from the McGreevy sisters there for Beckett. John Calder
said I was welcome to leave it but he had no idea when Beckett
would be in London. Phone calls to his Paris apartment were unanswered and the likelihood was that he was still in Tangier, where
phone service was spotty and he often did not respond to messages.
I did not want to create any situation that might reveal the existence of the McGreevy letters, so I told Calder I would keep the
letter, as I would probably have to go to Paris, where I would leave
it directly in Beckett's mailbox.

The undelivered letter continued to plague me. Would I really
have to go to Paris if I could not find anyone who was going there?
I was running out of money and I was exhausted. I felt so removed
from what I called my "real" (as opposed to my "work") self that I
just wanted to go home and hug my cats, pet my dogs, and most of
all sit at the dinner table laughing and joking with my husband and
children. Still, there was the urgency of access to the McGreevy
letters, and everything else would have to wait.

Urgency became an imperative after an interview with the
literary critic A. Alvarez. I sensed it would be a dramatic event,
because I knew that his wife was a respected psychotherapist who
knew a lot about Beckett's therapeutic history and I wanted to talk

to her as well. I had learned about her during one of my earlier interviews with Beckett's friend Dr. Geoffrey Thompson, the psychiatrist who had granted Beckett access to the mental hospital where he worked when Beckett was writing *Murphy*. Thompson had hinted broadly about Beckett's psychoanalysis by W. R. Bion, but even after I asked him directly if Beckett had been analyzed and by whom, he refused to confirm or deny. I knew I needed to write about it if it was true, and with the tantalizing McGreevy letters still out of reach, I needed other sources.

Al Alvarez and I were having a pleasant enough conversation that afternoon, mostly about his interest in Sylvia Plath, when his wife, Anne, walked into his office. She barely acknowledged me when he introduced us, but turned to her husband and said, "Did you tell her, Al?" He replied that he was just about to, and then told me the story of Beckett's analysis with W. R. Bion. At last I had the corroboration I needed. We three spent a very long afternoon, with me writing madly as I took detailed notes about people in the analytic professions I should see, books I should read, articles I should consult. They also told me about places where Bion took Beckett, particularly the Tavistock Clinic to hear C. G. Jung. They stressed that this encounter was important for Beckett's development as a writer and that I should study what Jung said on that occasion.

It was good to have the corroboration of Al and Anne Alvarez to support my contention that Beckett had been in analysis. In a later meeting with Dr. Thompson, the moment after we said hello I asked him straight out if what they had told me was true, and he confirmed it, to my great relief. Then he provided further confirmation when he showed me the letters he had earlier dangled. So far, so good: I had three reliable sources. But this was too important to write about without finding others. I was certain that the most important source and the firm foundation for what the others had told me would be Beckett's letters to McGreevy, and I had to do whatever was needed to read them.

19

After my meeting with the Alvarezes, I phoned the elder McGreevy niece to tell her that I would not go to Paris because Beckett was not there, and because no one in London knew his precise whereabouts, the letter could not be delivered. I was almost sobbing as I blurted out my difficulties with both time and money; fearing that I might never be able to return to Europe again, I begged them to let me see the letters if I returned to Dublin. Once I stopped talking, she said very quietly that I should come as soon as I could get there.

It was Thursday and Aer Lingus had one seat on a Friday afternoon flight, and after that none was available until late Sunday. I pulled myself together and arrived at Heathrow for the Friday flight, dripping with perspiration and starving, only to find a huge altercation at check-in and a long wait on the tarmac before takeoff. It was not a propitious beginning. The flight was so late that I arrived at Buswells Hotel only minutes before the elder McGreevy niece's husband came to pick me up and drive me deep into the darkened suburbs to their home.

There, in an unheated hallway closet under the stairs, his wife revealed a breathtaking collection of shoeboxes full of letters and photos. I looked them over swiftly, because the two sisters had decided that I would not read them there but would go to the younger one's house starting the next morning. She lived closer to Dublin, and getting there would require only a short train ride and a fairly long walk. The elder one's strongly disapproving husband drove me back to Buswells, and I barely made it to my room before I began projectile vomiting. Cryptic notes in the *DD* described *"a terrible night. Fever and chills, partly physical I am sure, from exhaustion and head cold caught in London, but psychological, too, mostly mental from seeing the letters and what is in them."* My instincts had been well founded, as a cursory overview of the one or two I had read convinced me that the real truth about so many events in Beckett's life would be found only in these letters.

The next morning I woke up so weak I could barely function: *"I am physically sick and grow mentally sicker at the thought of the falsity I might have published without these letters. It would have been a monstrosity of untrue information."* I was in a panic that I would not get them all read and get myself out of Dublin before Beckett got the nieces' letter, for fear that he would not let me use them. I still had the letter, and the nieces (and I, to a lesser degree now) were still searching for someone to take it to Paris. I feared they could find such a traveler and take it from me at any time.

In my previous drafts of the biography, I had written and discarded two different versions of how and why Beckett left Ireland to live in Paris permanently. The first did not ring true even as I wrote it, and I discarded it soon after. It depended on letters that he wrote to several professors at Trinity College and to members of the Irish literary intelligentsia, trying to ingratiate himself and saying that he hoped to survive on writing assignments they might give him while he tried to write novels. In the second version, I learned from his cousins Ann and John Beckett that Beckett's mother had reluctantly accepted that he would never adjust to living in Ireland, so she had agreed to let him go to Paris and to support him financially until he could find his footing as a writer. They showed me some of Beckett's letters—vague, to be sure, yet hinting that he and his mother had arrived at an understanding and that he would "probably" be leaving sometime soon. The benign portrait of Mae Beckett as kind, caring, and wanting only what was best for her beloved son simply did not ring true, but as I had no other information, that was what I wrote.

As I did further research, the Arland Ussher and George Reavey letters presented a different picture. This correspondence, coupled with my interviews with persons who had known Beckett during his years in Joyce's Paris circle (among them Maria Jolas, Stephen Joyce, his uncle Robert Kastor, Kay Boyle, and the poet/journalist Walter Lowenfels), showed a brilliant, troubled, and conflicted young man still strongly under the influence of his upper-class Anglo-Irish Protestant upbringing. They showed Beckett as incapable of throwing off the constraints of his social class and unable to embrace the bohemian writer's life that, it was obvious to everyone but him, he was destined to lead.

In the Reavey and Ussher letters, he wrote that he was resigned to living in Dublin because he had no money to live anywhere else. He planned to survive on the small allowance his mother doled out as long as he lived in her house, and to keep himself in booze and cigarettes by giving French lessons to Irish schoolgirls who had no interest in learning the language. When he had no pupils, he took some of his personal book collection to the stalls on the River Liffey and sold them for little more than the price of a good drunken evening. Wary of telling the entire truth to his two friends because his situation was so embarrassing, he concluded semi-optimistically by saying that he had set up a work table in a small room at the top of the office building that housed his late father's quantity-surveying business (now run by his brother, Frank). He assured Reavey that he would be able to finish *Murphy* there, and he told Ussher that he intended to write reviews and essays for various Irish periodicals. Frequently he concluded with remarks meant to be reassuring, about how he intended to make a happy go of his circumstances, but more often he ended bitterly, not sure that he could earn a living through either plan and with no idea of what to do if they didn't work out.

The explanation I kept because it was his most truthful (even though I thought it did not ring entirely true) was that Mae Beckett could not stand to see her beloved son suffer, so she chose to do the suffering by granting him the freedom to leave Ireland and the financial support to live while he made his way in Paris. And that

was where I had left things, as it seemed the most truthful explanation of his circumstances considering the available evidence. But
the McGreevy letters confirmed my suspicions about the falsity
of the narrative of a saintly mother's sacrifice. These letters were
truly the most important finding for an honest account of Samuel
Beckett's life.

I was both overwhelmed and relieved to find that my instincts
were correct—that the only person with whom Beckett had been
entirely truthful was Thomas McGreevy, and he had told his truths
in letters that began during his early days in Paris and did not end
until McGreevy's death. When I read them, they showed a dark,
deeply personal dimension to Beckett's decision. I was stunned by
the depth of his violence and vitriol, his bitterness, his anger, and
above all his hatred of his mother. Samuel Beckett not only did
physical damage to himself on his drunken rampages, he was so
emotionally distraught that he made himself physically ill, with
recurrences of the disfiguring boils and cysts he had had as an
undergraduate. His behavior so upset his dutifully patient brother
that Frank exhibited many of the same mental and emotional ail-
ments and feared for his own well-being. Frank knew the mother
and her two sons could not survive living together in the same
house, spacious and gracious though it was, but Mae Beckett would
not listen to any of his proposals for how they could live separately.
Samuel Beckett described in detail to McGreevy how he became
so violent during his drunken debauches that he feared he would
destroy his mother or himself, whichever came first.

As I sat there on that afternoon in the younger McGreevy
niece's study, listening to the sounds of a happy family enjoying
their Sunday lunch in the dining room, I could not decide if I was
shivering and shaking with cold and flu or because of every letter I read. Although I read fast and typed madly, I realized that
there were dozens of letters—each one vital to my understanding

of Beckett's decisions and choices—and I had only six days to go through them all. Even more troubling, they were going to be short days, because I was allowed to read them only between eleven and three that Sunday and from ten until five o'clock on the following weekdays. Faced with a seemingly impossible task, I made the only dishonest decision of my professional life that afternoon.

Even though the sisters examined all the boxes when I quit for the day, no doubt to make sure I was not stealing anything, I did steal some—temporarily. I managed to arrange the boxes so it would not be apparent that I slipped a handful into my purse at the end of every workday to take them back to the hotel, where I spent the night working until my eyes and typing fingers gave out. Even so, by the end of the third day, I knew that I was typing too slowly, so I began to use the tape recorder. That resulted one night in *"a real mess, taped an hour without play button down, then talked over Billie Whitelaw's interview tape until batteries died. Back to typing. Haste makes big piles of you-know-what. Frustrating."* No wonder my health was an equal mess: *"Cold sores, chills, upset tum & runny nose. Everything here so wet and damp. Haven't seen sun for a month."*

My directive to myself was *"must finish by Wednesday!"* But Wednesday came and went and I was still transcribing. I used two sets of batteries in a single day and was nowhere near being finished. I just got sicker and sicker; I had not had a decent meal in days, and I certainly was not sleeping well. All the while, slipping letters out from under the McGreevy nieces' noses was deeply upsetting: *"The McGreevy nieces are the most decent human beings I have met in a very long time. They are going to feel like shit when Beckett writes to tell them not to show me these letters, and so am I."*

I finished copying the letters eight days after I began to read them and lost no time in booking a flight home to New York. Still sick, I took the weekend off to let my family take care of me, and on Monday morning I was on the phone to Carl Brandt to tell him why I had to rewrite the central section of the book, which would make my delivery date of the manuscript even later than it already was. He listened quietly as I told him everything I had learned, both from the letters and from the interviews. He was particularly struck by the news of Beckett's psychoanalysis and said that before I wrote a word he would have to contact my publisher, and no doubt Larry would have to consult the firm's lawyers. The material was so explosive, Carl said, that he was not sure I could use any of it. This floored me.

In December 1974, rules of privacy and propriety were far more strictly followed than under the contemporary "anything goes, nothing is off-limits" attitude in journalism and nonfiction. I had already imposed many restrictions on myself in terms of what I could use in the biography, but I also knew the publisher's lawyers would need to vet the text. Many of the obstacles I had already faced and self-restrictions I had decided to follow generated strong impulses from time to time to say to hell with it and walk away, right back to the news desk or forward into the office of a professor. But this was not one of those moments. I spent the rest of the day trying to think of ways I could incorporate my findings without having to identify where they came from, even though all my other scrupulous sourcing and annotations made the task impossible.

I was not prepared for what Carl told me when he phoned in the late afternoon and told me what the publisher's intellectual-property lawyers had decided: I could not use any information in the letters without either verbal or written corroboration, thanks to common-law copyright. This meant that if letters were on file in a university library and available to scholars, I could paraphrase them. However, I could not quote letters in private collections, although the owner of the physical letters could agree to let me paraphrase the content. My situation was even more perilous because the writer of the letters was still alive and could deny all permissions. Also, the one subject firmly off-limits was Beckett's medical history, which could not be quoted or paraphrased. For all things medical, particularly Beckett's psychoanalysis, I would have to infer, insinuate, or imply. I interrupted Carl's explanation to argue that I was not writing a book of opinion or innuendo, and to omit so much factual truth from the biography would diminish, if not destroy, my credibility as narrator. Carl said this would not happen as long as I had factual evidence that could be called upon after publication to back me up. No, I responded; everything had to be stated clearly in the book so that nothing was open for question.

And then he raised the fear that governed my life for the next month: Beckett could get a temporary or even a permanent restraining injunction if he wanted to, because everyone would be sympathetic to someone whose medical records were being made public. If, however, I could get someone to swear that his psychoanalysis was common knowledge in London psychiatric circles, it would help my case tremendously.

The thought of lawyers, litigation, injunctions—of a huge legal apparatus bearing down on me—rendered me helpless. I was devastated that all my important research had been for naught, that the honest and thorough book I wanted to write was never going to happen: once the lawyers were involved, who knew when or even if it would be published? I had visions of myself languishing in debtor's prison. After a little more than a week of gloom and doom, I decided there was only one thing to do, and that was to write about Beckett's flight from Ireland to France exactly as I wanted to write it and then send it to the publisher and wait to see what would happen. In a blaze of white-hot heat, I did so. Carl and Larry phoned as soon as they read it. Carl said they were both "absolutely wild" about it. Larry said, "Go ahead and write it as if you have permission for everything. We will deal with what happens when or if it does."

All this wonderful support buoyed my spirits and dissolved both negativity and depression. Newly revivified, I remembered what Samuel Beckett had said to me so many different times throughout the several years I had known him: "My word is my bond." And I thought of his promise not to help or hinder me, which I took as his implicit permission to pursue topics in his life that might have embarrassed him or made him ashamed or unhappy. It strengthened my resolve to write the book exactly as I thought it should be written. Now it was time to hold those thoughts firmly in mind and finish.

I used a lot of mixed metaphors back then to describe my situation, but the most coherent ones centered around dropping shoes. Two remained to drop: Beckett's response to the nieces about the letters, and his to me explaining whatever he decided. On December 27, 1974, one of the McGreevy nieces wrote to me. I had left the letter to Beckett with her when I left Dublin, and she found someone going to Paris to leave it in Beckett's mailbox. She received his reply in a roundabout way: the postal strike was still on in France, so he gave his reply to the nieces to someone who was coming to the United States, who forgot to mail it to Ireland for more than a week after he arrived. It had just reached the nieces, and in it Beckett asked them not to show the letters to anyone but to destroy them. *"I expected that"* was my cryptic conclusion to that day's *DD* entry.

They replied to Beckett, as did I, even though I had not heard from him directly. We all explained the constraints I had been under to justify why they had let me read the letters before hearing from him. He made no direct reference when he replied to the three of us, letters we did not receive until almost two months later and which were mailed from London. He thanked the nieces for their letter, and his note to me said nothing about the letters but asked only when I planned to return to Paris; he was leaving shortly for Berlin and the Schiller Theater and wanted to alert me that he would be gone for most of the early months of 1975. I had no idea when I could make another research trip, for the usual reason: I would have to raise the money to pay for it. But I certainly was not going to tell him that. I had never told him of the financial stress writing this book had caused me, and I was not about to start now.

Even more important, I was writing steadily, and my goal of finishing the book—not in early spring, as I had originally intended, but sometime later in 1975—was clearly in sight. At the end of January, my horoscope in the local newspaper said, "You will get money and finish an important project this month." I could not resist thinking, *I hope it knows of what it speaks.*

20

New England winters are always harsh, but January–
March 1975 was particularly bad. Too many snowstorms and too
many personal interruptions, which included dealing with a misbehaving furnace, preparing one child for an exchange in France
and the other for a long stay on the West Coast, and hosting an
exchange student from Sweden. Still, I should have realized how
well I was writing when I took my first electric typewriter to be
repaired by the legendary New Haven specialist, Mr. Whitlock,
and he told me it was so worn that I should abandon it and buy a
new one. I did, and by the time I finished writing, I wore that one
out, too.

As I worked through the early months of 1975, an opportunity
for me to let the world know that my biography was coming presented itself. Grove Press was about to publish Beckett's *Mercier
and Camier* in an English translation, and I contacted the critic
John Leonard, then the editor of *The New York Times Book Review,*
to suggest myself as the perfect reviewer. To the amazement of
my agent and publisher—but not me—Leonard agreed. I simply
assumed that no one knew more about that novel than I did, but I
was still amazed when the review was published exactly as I wrote
it, without cuts, corrections, or other criticisms, for during Leonard's reign, the *TBR* was notorious for making writers submit seemingly interminable revisions.

Publication of the review alerted Tom Bishop, the distinguished
professor of French at New York University, that a biography was
under way. He was editing a special issue of a prestigious French
literary magazine, *Cahiers de L'Herne,* in honor of Beckett's seven-

tieth birthday, and he invited me to contribute an article. That led to circulation on the academic grapevine as well as elsewhere of the announcement that I was soon to publish a biography, and most often it was garbled or incorrect.

My author's identification in the *Book Review* mistakenly said the biography would be published that same year, leading *Book Digest* to announce a forthcoming biography by "Deidre Blair"— the first of many misspellings. If only the wave of criticism that followed could have landed at the feet of a Ms. Blair and not mine!

The first rumble I heard came in a minor newsletter that went out to various grant-giving agencies, in which an unsigned letter suggested that I had "singlehandedly twisted Samuel Beckett's arm to let [me] write his authorized biography." I was horrified, and I prayed the article would never reach Beckett's eyes.

Then various persons who considered themselves authorities on the life and work of Samuel Beckett weighed in. One told me I was not "existential enough" to write the biography, but after reading the *Times* review, he changed his mind and said the book would "probably not be that bad after all." Another told me I needed to "learn how to write" so I could "remove" myself from the book, because the *Times* review was "far too personal" and revealed far too much about me. And still another, a professor at a respected university, wrote a scathing letter saying that I should be "ashamed of the hubris" I had shown by writing the *Times* review, because it should have been his, and I'd better "watch" myself and "know [my] place" if I ever wanted an academic position. Most of these criticisms were more amusing than hurtful, but several, like the professor's not-so-veiled threat, warned of more serious trouble headed my way.

A cadre of Beckett specialists—the "Becketteers," as I called them (all references to Mouseketeers are intentional), white men in secure academic positions of power and authority—formed my primary opposition. They were representative of a larger struggle in academia between the establishment and the perceived threat of women like me and my Danforth GFW colleagues, who were now competing for the same academic positions as the usual male candidates. For the Becketteers in particular, I was a brazen example, the "mere girl" who had "invaded the sacrosanct turf of the Beckett world." One or two younger members who were brave enough to speak to me privately asked if I was completely ignorant of the pecking order, while in public they shunned me so they could "keep on the good side of the powers that be." One of them surreptitiously motioned for me to join him as he sneaked behind a pillar in a hotel lobby at a Modern Language Association conference. "You are a pariah and I can't be seen talking to you," he said with a swagger, clearly feeling brave for engaging in this little clandestine conversation. His childish glee left me (unusually) speechless and unable to think up a quick riposte. When I found my voice, I said I did not understand why I was being ostracized, since my two publications about Beckett had been received positively within the academic world. "Yes," this man said, "in the academic world. But that's not the Beckett world."

Forewarned is forearmed, they say, and so for the first time in the three years since receiving my doctorate, I decided to get serious about finding a permanent academic position. I hoped to find a position at a prestigious university so that I would be less vulnerable to Becketteer attacks. My work was biographical rather than theoretical, which made me think I could escape the internecine battles common in an academic environment. I had seen many of these firsthand in graduate school because biography was still anathema in most literature departments, so I expected potential colleagues to shy away from me and leave me in peace for fear of professional contamination. I thought myself safe on any number of professional fronts simply because of the nature of my research. Theorists would not take biographical work seriously enough to think it deserved critical consideration in the first place. This was just another example of how totally wrong I was about the zero-sum game of academic politics.

The genre of biography relies upon certain conventions, which means that it carries textual constraints. Many topics and multiple subjects pertaining to the principal subject must be identified and explored, but only to the point where they contribute to the under-standing of a particular life. To some critics, this may make the work appear superficial rather than exhaustive. My aim in writing Beckett's biography was to provide a tool that would identify aspects of his life and work for other scholars to explore with rigorous scholarship. Remember, nobody knew much about him before I began, and in my view Beckett criticism had been languishing for some time, full of repetition and dead ends.

It put me in mind of the German round song in *Waiting for Godot*, where the dog goes in the kitchen, the cook gives him a bone, and so on, seemingly forever. I thought Beckettian criticism had been chasing its metaphorical tail and it was time for a fresh infusion. Where others saw Beckett primarily through a lens of existential angst, I found humor and pathos in equal part, much of it stemming directly from what I was learning about his family background and the Irish literary tradition. I wanted to open up new avenues of interpretation, but even more important, of appreciation. I wanted to write not only for an academic audience but also for the intelligent general reader who wanted to understand the creative vision of this writer who had given us so many brilliant novels and theatrical experiences. "In other words," said one of my professor friends, "you want more than three hundred people to read your book."

Above all, I believed my authorial responsibility was to follow the dictum of the critic Desmond MacCarthy that the biographer must be "the artist under oath." In other words, my task was to tell only the "truth" as I could establish it, but at the same time to grip the reader's attention with a page-turner. Wasn't this what scholarship was supposed to be? And weren't other scholars supposed to be appreciative of my efforts? With hindsight all these years later, I was every bit the naive American girl that Vivian Mercier said I was.

Meanwhile, in late spring 1975, I was at the stage of writing where I was in desperate need of a break, a distraction, a way to refresh and renew myself. I had been writing about Beckett since 1971, if I counted the dissertation, or 1972, if I counted just the biography. I was only up to the late 1960s in writing Beckett's life, and at the time I noted, *"Oh lord, let me finish . . . I'm getting anxiety attacks, migraine headaches, backaches. Just awful. Tension all the time."*

I sent birthday greetings to Beckett in early April, and he replied, ostensibly to thank me but mostly to comment on what I had told him about how my writing was progressing. In my letter, I also wrote about a staged reading I had seen, mounted by Lee Breuer and the Mabou Mines company. I only commented, but when Beckett replied, he told me that many others had sent him multiple copies of *Newsweek*'s review. "Sounds a crooked straight reading to me," he concluded, reminding me once again of how well informed he was and how careful I should be with everything I said or wrote about him.

Jean Reavey, true to form, involved me in another mini-conflagration with Beckett when she told me she had found a note from Beckett to George, dating to the early 1960s, explaining that his original intention had been to call his play *Waiting for Levy*, not *Godot*. I dismissed this claim as having no basis in fact when Jean offered no proof, but apparently she wrote to Beckett, saying that I was going to include it in the biography, which ignited another short-lived burst of his indignation.

After I straightened out that contretemps, Beckett told me he was almost finished working with Madeleine Renaud on the French *Not I*, after which he would go to Morocco for a long rest. He said I should let him know when I would next be in Paris so he could be sure to see me, as it had been too long since we had talked about my "project."

But mostly I was just writing, yearning to cross the finish line. One day during that period, I sat for a very long lunch with Alan Schneider and his wife, Jean, while they asked questions about the book's progress. I was nearing the end of the writing, I told them, with only the conclusion left to go. After one more revision,

I expected to give it to the publisher later that summer or in early fall. As we talked, Alan and Jean plied me with questions about its content, which gave me another surprising revelation. That night at home, I wrote: *"Went to see Alan Schneider. Now I really feel ready to publish. I seem to know one helluva lot more about 'Sam' than he does."*

A bit further on I added, *"Jean says I am going to have a best seller. I hope she is right."*

21

The problem of how to pay for another, final (I hoped) research trip was solved by Vivian Mercier, eager to make amends after we settled his attempted use of my research in his book. His wife, the Irish writer Eilís Dillon, told me that the Catholic Church's International Commission on English in the Liturgy (ICEL) was hard pressed to find young Americans, especially women, and she asked me to become a member. Within weeks I was invited to attend the next meeting in London, with a stipend generous enough to pay for side trips to Ireland and France and for my husband to come with me.

Financial needs were pressing, which was another reason I yearned to be free of the Beckett biography. I was to get the last payment of the pitifully small advance once the final manuscript was submitted and accepted, and I needed that money for the upcoming tuition payments for my children. At the same time as I was waiting for a response from Larry Freundlich to my latest draft, I was hearing ominous rumors about the status of Harper's Magazine Press. The parent publisher of the imprint was in the process of severing ties to entities in charge of things like distribution and publicity, which signaled even more drastic separations to come. I also knew from friends whose agents had submitted their manuscripts to HMP that the house was no longer acquiring new books. Every time I asked Carl Brandt, he told me to relax and keep on writing and everything would be just fine for a book as original as mine.

Another worry presaged more to come that very hot summer. One of my neighbors, a respected Freudian psychiatrist, held a gathering to introduce me to some of his Freudian colleagues. Among them was a former analysand of Beckett's analyst, W. R. Bion. There were also two Jungians and a man who claimed to follow "an amalgamation of several important disciplines," those of Freud, Jung, and Laing among them. Several of these men had read most of Beckett's writing, and two had even written "important" (their word) papers about how his fiction revealed so much about his mental state. All of them were united in the opinion that I should "be very careful: Beckett is psychotic and dangerous and a book like yours could tip him over the edge." This was mind-boggling, to say the least, and as I was not writing psychobiography, I did not feel I had to investigate their contention.

But there was worse to come when Larry Freundlich got around to communicating with me at the beginning of August, two days before I was to leave for the ICEL meeting in London. He sent a ten-page letter saying that I was "making the reader work too hard" and that I should tell the reader from the outset what he (Freundlich) believed the book was about: "Beckett's arrested development is the crux of the matter, and his mother is entirely responsible for it. You need to stress the psychotic undertones of this disturbing relationship and Beckett's psychosis in particular." He seemed almost gleeful when he talked about how he would market the book "to destroy Beckett because he will be revealed as so awful a person no one will buy his books." I told him I did not believe this was true, and even if it was, I wanted my book to make readers want to buy and read his work to see for themselves. I was horrified to think that Freundlich intended to present all my years of serious scholarship as something one might read in a muckraking tabloid.

My agent provided no support other than to tell me to relax and keep on writing and everything would be fine.

And so Von and I went to London. I spent long days in working sessions for ICEL and nights and weekends enjoying myself. Jimmy and Tania Stern, Beckett's friends since the 1930s, invited us to stay overnight at their home, Hatch Manor, in Tisbury, Wiltshire, a gorgeous country house with Calders in the bathroom, Picassos in our bedroom, a Djuna Barnes in the hallway, and first editions all over the place. Jimmy had difficulty walking, so we spent the afternoon sitting on Hatch's lovely lawn to talk while enjoying the scenery, the very landscape that Constable had painted.

Jimmy expressed concern about the state of my rapport with Beckett. I had told him of the flare-up after the Molly Howe incident, and he told me he had had what he called "several curious exchanges" with Beckett in recent letters. I described what I had written and how upset I was by the reactions of Larry Freundlich and the psychiatrists. Then he asked a question that was both odd and disturbing: if these psychiatric concerns turned out to be even partially valid, and if Beckett raised objections to the book's publication, would I be willing to withhold it until after his death? I told him I intended to deal with that situation as honestly as I had dealt with the actual writing, and if it became necessary to delay publication, I would do it. I told Jimmy how difficult all this was becoming, and if he had to choose between friendship with Beckett and with me, I would understand why he would choose Beckett. He assured me it would never come to that. I told him we would see. He made me promise that I would contact Beckett in Paris and talk about everything I had written. I promised that I would.

I went to see Tom Maschler at Jonathan Cape because I wanted to tell him what to expect when he received the manuscript and to see if his reaction would be the same as Larry Freundlich's. Tom had none of the same speculations about Beckett's mental health. Instead he was intrigued by how I presented the work within the life and how I incorporated information from the several hundred interviews I had by then conducted. It was energizing to talk about content, structure, and technique in such a positive manner. I took copious notes, many of which enriched the final manuscript.

We could not leave England without a visit to Bridget and Brian Coffey in Southampton. We talked until 3 a.m. as I told them what

I had written and what had been my two publishers' vastly different responses to it. They asked questions about topics they thought needed more explanation and·detail, they volunteered stories of new memories that came to mind, and they offered suggestions about how best to deal with "prickly Sam" when I got to Paris. They were not nearly as concerned about how he would react to the book's content as they were about his friends (and now mine) that I had seen in England. They warned me not to go into too great detail. Bridget said, "You make ever-enlarging circles, while he compartmentalizes. He sees one person at a time and he keeps them all separate from each other. He might not approve of your American openness and might not like having you at the center of all his friendships."

Thus far Von's and my travels had been centered on my work, and as we had not had a real vacation in years, we decided that it was time to do something that would have nothing to do with Samuel Beckett's life and work and everything to do with our marriage. We went to Fornalutx, Mallorca, to stay with our friends the Spanish sculptor Juan Palà, and his American novelist wife, Dolores. They took us to visit their good friends the poet Robert Graves and his wife, Beryl, whom we helped to pick baskets of pods from St. Johnswort plants that she sold for "tonics." One starry night, we watched the Graves grandchildren put on plays based on their grandfather's writings as we sat in a grotto on their property, a natural stone amphitheater carved into a rocky hillside. How we laughed at the mishmash of Greek and Roman mythology, delivered in both English and the local dialect.

We flew to Paris, and thankfully I did not have to deal with any of the concerns I had discussed with the Sterns and the Coffeys during our brief stopover. A letter from Beckett was waiting for me at my agent's office, apologizing for not being in Paris during my time there. He said he had left Berlin in exhaustion and flown directly to Tangier for an extended stay. It came as a great relief, because I was not ready to see him until I had sorted out my differences with Larry Freundlich and was assured that he would be publishing the book I had written and would promote it in the manner I wanted. Even though Beckett insisted that he would not read it before it was published, and he frequently joked that he would most likely not read it afterward, I still feared that he might change his mind and ask to see it. I left a brief note in his mailbox telling him whom I had seen in England and how my few days in Paris would be devoted to fact-checking. To reassure him that all was well, I said the entire trip had been a rewarding one, but I left out the details. I decided that if any disagreements were to come, I would just have to worry about them when the time came.

The European trip ended just as September was fast approaching. I had several weeks to take care of all the things my children would need before their academic year began, but I had only the Labor Day weekend to take care of my own. I was once again filling in for friends on sabbaticals, and for the fall term of 1975, I had an appointment at Central Connecticut State College, where I was to teach three sections of composition, each with thirty-five to forty students, and a fourth course on the short story, with another forty students. These were all required courses, which meant that very few (if any) students wanted to be there, particularly those in the 8 a.m. class. I had to leave my house by 6 a.m. if I wanted to arrive on time, for in those days before interstate highway connectors, New Britain was in such a remote part of the state that the joke was "you can't get there from anywhere."

I scarcely had time to settle into a routine when two life-shattering events happened on two consecutive days. On September 25, I arrived at home late after a long and difficult teaching day to find a letter from Carl Brandt, mailed six days earlier from New York. I didn't even rate a phone call for him to tell me that Harper's Magazine Press was being disbanded, Larry Freundlich was leaving for Crown Publishers, and I had the option of going with him or having my book assimilated within Harper & Row. It was long after business hours when I read the letter, so I could not speak to him until the next day. To say the least, I spent a worried and restless night.

The next day, Friday, September 26, was even more upsetting, because I was able to phone his office only between classes and he was not available to take my calls. After a frustrating day, I was driving home through a heavy downpour on a flooded highway when an out-of-control truck crossed a divider, slammed into my car in the left lane, and shoved it into the right lane and another car. I was trapped inside between them, rain lashing in from shattered windows on both sides. My husband was in Boston attending a museum conference, and all I could think of was my children waiting for me at home to take them to dinner, as the larder was empty and food shopping was scheduled for Saturday morning.

State police extricated me from the car but would not let me go home. Instead an ambulance took me to the nearest hospital, in Waterbury, far from my Woodbridge home and my family doctor in New Haven. I would not let the EMTs move me to the ambulance until the police phoned my friend Allison Stokes, who went to my house, took charge of my children, and contacted my husband, who drove home through the night.

I had hit my head hard and hurt my back, but the doctors said they could not find injuries severe enough to keep me and sent me home the next morning despite a bad headache, a back in spasm, and double vision. There was nothing they could do, they told me; I told the *DD "pills are useless. Put me to sleep. I cry a lot."* Even worse than the pain was my terrible, crushing sense of guilt. Not only had I messed up all our family finances by pursuing this wretched dream of writing a book that was now in publishing limbo, now I was also ruining everything for the people I cared about most. It was a very important conference for my husband, who had to leave his paper to be read by someone else. My good friend Allison, the kindest and most nonjudgmental person I have ever known, had to rescue my children from an unkempt house and feed and shelter them because I was not there to do so. I believed that I was solely responsible for all the trouble I had caused by stepping far beyond the homebody roles women were supposed to accept contentedly. And now I was going to have to pay for it—big-time.

22

We half-jokingly called our house "Ireland West" because it seemed that every *"Irish poet, playwright, or possible prime minister"* knew they could find a comfortable bed and a good meal in Woodbridge, Connecticut. We had a constant stream of visitors, most (but not all) of whom were very welcome. They were people who had helped me in so many ways that I was happy to have the opportunity to return their personal hospitality and professional courtesy. There were many others, however, who took advantage, and the worst offender was John Montague.

The concussion kept me from teaching throughout October and November. To save my job, colleagues at Central took my classes until the burden overwhelmed them. My friend the novelist Kit Reed helped me hold on to the position by taking over, and the department chairman did not complain because he was thrilled to have such a prestigious writer on campus. I still was not well when I returned to teaching and was looking forward to the Thanksgiving break when I received a phone call from (as my children called him sarcastically) "the poet Montague." He was in Seattle and stopping in New York on his way home to Dublin, and asked if he—*he*—could stay a day or two. I told him we were far from New York and suggested that perhaps he had friends there who could put him up. He said he thought it would be nice to be in the country and preferred to stay with us. I told him not to come until after Thanksgiving, as we had family plans that could not be changed and could not include him. (Notice that I said "him.") We ended the conversation with his agreeing to give me advance warning when his schedule was set.

During the first week in December, after a horrendous teaching day that included multiple meetings with students whose dogs had eaten their homework (literally in one case, as a young man showed me a tattered and torn essay with toothmarks on it), I came home with over one hundred term papers to grade before the end of the week. I was not prepared for my husband to be waiting just inside the front door to greet me. The expression on his face was unlike anything I had seen throughout our long marriage. "We have company," he muttered grimly as he took my elbow and guided me into the living room.

There I found not only John Montague but also his wife, Evelyn, and their toddler daughter, Oonagh, who was busy terrifying one of our cats and shrieking and shouting while our two bulldogs terrified her in turn. My husband had found them getting out of a taxi when he drove into our driveway fifteen minutes before me.

The immediate challenge was how to stretch four chops and baked potatoes to feed dinner to seven people, including a small child just getting used to table food. The next challenge was putting linens on the guest bed and towels in the guest bathroom while trying to figure out how and where the child was to sleep. And then there was the next day to think about, when I had to return to the campus at the crack of dawn and leave them on their own. We should have been alerted to trouble when the poet Montague told us we didn't have to worry about him because he expected one of us to drive him to the train station in the mornings, as taxis were "too expensive." We were also to pick him up around midnight after he spent long days in New York kibitzing (drinking) with his Irish friends. Evelyn and Oonagh would be content to spend their days in our house. I did not digest that this meant they planned to stay for some time, because I was too busy worrying about the next day. I knew there was little in the pantry they could fix for their lunch, so instead of grading papers that night, I spent time in the kitchen creating something they could eat until I got home to cook dinner.

Because we were too polite to ask how long they planned to stay, this went on for four days, with me and my family coming home each night to a new form of chaos. Evelyn spent her mornings in bed while little Oonagh rampaged around the house. After several days, Evelyn decided to be helpful in the kitchen, and I returned one night to find that she had used a week's worth of produce to make a huge salad doused so heavily with an inedible dressing that it had to be thrown away uneaten. It was a catastrophe on top of so many others that I asked Evelyn—blurting rudely—how long they intended to be our houseguests.

She said she would talk to John when he came back from New York and let me know. The next morning they announced cheerfully that as they could not afford to go to a hotel or rent an apartment, and as no other friend could host them as comfortably as they were situated with us, they would stay through the holidays, until their flight to Dublin on January 6. This was December 8. We were aghast, but there was no time to discuss it, as we all had to get to work or school.

That night around nine o'clock, Von was working at his desk in our bedroom until it was midnight and time to go to the station to collect John. I was collapsed on the bed trying to grade papers when we heard a timid knocking on our door. Vonn Scott and Katney came in and announced an ultimatum. I will never forget their earnest faces as they said in unison: "Either they go or we'll go. We'll go to Granny's in Pittsburgh before we'll stay with them one day longer." This was an astonishing declaration, for their grandmother's love was too often hidden behind stern discipline, and their visits to her were not always the happy and relaxing occasions we all wanted.

The next morning the four of us confronted John at the breakfast table (Evelyn was still in bed; Oonagh was wandering around the house). We told him they could stay one more day but then they had to leave, as we had to prepare for our holidays. He said nothing and Von drove him to the station as usual. That night when we returned from school and work, the Montagues were gone, leaving behind enormous messes in the guest quarters and living areas and a $400 telephone bill that included transatlantic calls to Ireland. They also helped themselves to a copy of *Horizon* magazine because it had one of John's poems in it, thus destroying a complete set of the original collection. They left no note to tell us where they had gone or to thank us for the eight days we had hosted them.

We found out the next day that they had called a friend from Brooklyn, who had come with a car to collect them. First they went to Guilford, to the home of Susan Howe and her husband, the sculptor David von Schlegell, saying they had had to leave the Bairs because Deirdre was shameless in trying to get John into her bed—and in front of her children and husband, too! David was in bed with the flu and he shouted down from the balcony of their A-frame that this was preposterous and they should leave his house at once.

Susan warned me that this would be the talk of Dublin once the Montagues returned, but I was so exhausted from everything else on top of their disgraceful behavior that I was just happy to be rid of them. I didn't care what they said. Before they left New York, friends telephoned to warn me that Evelyn was telling everyone *"what boors we are and how awful we live and how ignorant we are and how mistreated they were."*

My alleged attempt to seduce the poet Montague really did become the talk of Dublin, as I learned on my last research trip almost a year later. I continued to hear about it throughout the 1980s, after the biography was published and when I was invited annually to lecture and teach at the James Joyce summer school at University College, Dublin. Years later, men (for they were all men) would look at me quizzically as they asked how I could possibly have tried to seduce the poet Montague, *"a nice girl like yerself, and all."* By that time my feminist hackles had been raised seriously high and I knew how to handle them. I neither defended myself nor differed with them. I just gave them my most withering look, and I'm happy to say that most were instantly fearful of my wrath and became totally deflated. It gave me pleasure to see them back down and slink away.

We had one other hilariously awful Irish guest, the actor Patrick (Pat) Magee. Beckett adored Pat, particularly for his voice, which he said was the one he heard in his head when composing male voices for his plays. When he spoke of actors during our "conversations," Beckett's demeanor was neutrally controlled, but when he spoke of Pat, he was animated and his face actually took on a rosy glow.

So there we were, the four Bairs on a calm Sunday afternoon, the newspapers spread all over the living room and the dining table still holding remnants of a lavish brunch, when the phone rang. "Pat Magee here," said the gravelly voice at the other end. He was in New Haven to perform at the Shubert Theater, and Samuel Beckett had told him to call Deirdre Bair, who would keep him company. Pat said I should pick him up immediately and bring him to my home.

It was Sunday, and Connecticut still had blue laws that forbade commerce on the Sabbath. We were not prepared for entertaining, and liquor and grocery stores were closed. I gave an order to the children to clean up the house and told my husband to call some friends and ask them to join us, provided they could contribute food and booze. Twelve good friends came, bringing bounty for dinner and plenty of liquor. When I returned with Pat, he glanced at the people but headed straight for the bottles. He proceeded to fill a large tumbler with scotch, grabbed the bottle by the neck, and headed for the long sofa. "Move!" he commanded the two people sitting there before claiming its entire length for himself.

Everyone tried to engage him in polite conversation, but he either cut them cold in midsentence or said something scathing if someone approached. For the rest of the long afternoon and well into the night he sat in splendid isolation, drinking the rest of the scotch and emoting loudly in his most stentorian voice. "Amazing how time passes when you are having fun," one of my sardonic friends said as she tried to make a quiet exit without Pat's noticing. Even so, he bellowed that she should come back because he "needed a woman."

The theater was putting Pat up at a hotel, and it was quite late when I took him back there. He refused to leave the car until I agreed to spend the night, "just to keep me company." When I convinced him that was not going to happen, he shook his head and said, "Deirdre, you have bluestockings up to your elbows."

"Thank you, Pat," I replied. "That's the nicest thing you have ever said to me." It was exactly the impression I wanted to convey during all the years I worked on Beckett's biography.

The next morning at breakfast, I found my son staring at me. "What's wrong?" I asked. With a deep sigh of resignation, he asked, "Mother, where do you find these people?"

Where, indeed?

23

"*January 12, 1976. My world* came crashing down this afternoon when Carl Brandt called to say that Harper & Row has decided not to publish my book." I had agreed to stay on with the parent company after the press was dissolved, and the legendary editor Simon Michael Bessie had agreed to begin editing it in October 1975, as soon as he returned from the Frankfurt Book Fair. He then claimed that other commitments kept him from it, so he farmed it out to several other editors, none of whom wanted to work on it. One said, "I don't like Beckett enough to endure editing such a long book about him." Another said, "He's not an important enough writer to deserve such detailed study." Harper & Row then hid behind the contractual euphemism publishers used in such situations, saying that I had produced "an unpublishable manuscript." That meant I was free to shop it elsewhere, but if another publisher took it, I would have to pay back the advance Harper's Magazine Press had given me.

It didn't seem right to have to repay the advance if another firm deemed "publishable" a book they called "unpublishable," but as Carl put it, that's just how the system worked. And I, the nicely brought up young woman who had always respected authority and did not yet possess the feminist consciousness to articulate my protest, simply said "Yes, sir" and slunk away. Carl said he would show the manuscript to other publishers one at a time, but he was noticeably curt whenever I asked why he did it this way, why he didn't make multiple submissions, and why it was taking so long. He refused to give me feedback or tell me who was reading it or what they thought of it. I steamed and chafed but got no answers, because he seldom took my phone calls or answered my letters. I thought he was treating me like a misbehaving schoolgirl, but I did not yet know enough published women writers to ask them to share their experiences. I was too ashamed and embarrassed to ask Nancy Milford if this was how he treated her, so I said nothing to anyone. Instead I became more and more depressed.

The double vision after the auto accident had cleared up, but I still had the headaches. My family doctor prescribed a whole roster of different pills, from Valium to who knows what else that was in vogue at the time. At the end of 1975, I wrote: *"I am in deep depression, brought on by terrible finances, dreadful jobs, a book that drags on and on and the feeling that I can't get it all together. I sense deepening crises in my personal life. I have finally discovered that I don't want to do it all anymore. I don't want to be the wonder woman who cooks, bakes, decorates, manages, copes, etc. I'd like to be a good wife and mother, sure. But I want to be a scholar and a writer, too. Everything else is a dead weight dragging me down. I guess what I want is impossible: a satisfying personal AND professional life. Did any woman ever have both? I am so confused. Probably best to do nothing, to make no moves at all until I figure out what to do. I need to put myself into a holding pattern. Hey—that might make a good title for a novel: Holding Pattern!"* I didn't see it at the time, but looking back, I realize that despite my depression, by putting myself into a holding pattern I would eventually know when and where to land. It meant that I was determined to get myself out of all the messes I was in. Now I recognize this as an early feminist awakening.

Freelance writing and part-time teaching were keeping me barely afloat, and I was so confused that when a possible lifeline drifted by just two days after the disastrous phone call with Carl, it barely registered. The English Department at my undergraduate alma mater, the University of Pennsylvania, invited me to be interviewed for an assistant professorship. To say that I was overloaded, overwhelmed, and utterly unfocused would be an understatement. And what was I going to tell Penn when they asked about the status of the biography? The interview went well and the chairman told me that the job teaching contemporary comparative literature (mostly British and French) would be mine if the dean agreed to fund it, but weeks went by without further correspondence. Nor had I heard from my agent, so I still had no job and no publisher. After another month passed, I gathered my courage and phoned him. Carl's secretary told me that there was nothing new, because only the day before, when he was getting ready to go to Arizona for several weeks' vacation, had he sent my manuscript out—for the very first time! I was livid, writing, *"I don't believe the s.o.b. takes me seriously. He's got a real surprise in store for him."* Nor would this be the only time that year when Carl failed to get in touch with highly regarded editors who, I knew from friends, were interested in seeing the manuscript. He was always ready with an excuse for why so-and-so editor or such-and-such publisher was not right for me. And my son was graduating from high school soon and getting ready to start college in the fall. With most of the money we had tried to put toward his education having been spent on my research and travel, I worried ceaselessly about how we could afford it. I knew that Penn offered free tuition to the children of faculty members, but that line remained only a hoped-for possibility.

I must have been in a terrible state, because all my friends started to ask—politely, discreetly, obliquely—if I had ever considered analysis. When I told my husband, he said that he, too, was worried about me because of my headaches, crying jags, and occasional flashes of anger. He thought analysis might be a good idea. We both asked around, and several names were suggested, all men, all quick to dig for hidden childhood trauma or to throw me another prescription (which I refused to take), if they were even decent enough to honor my appointments.

My friend Allison Stokes knew an analyst in Wilton who was highly regarded by her and many of our other friends. "She's a woman, and very sympathetic to women's concerns," Allison told me, adding, "But at the same time I have to warn you." In a hushed tone, almost as if it were something unsavory and a secret that could only be whispered, she confided, "She's a Jungian." That was fine with me, because even though I did not know enough about Freud's canon, I had rejected him in graduate school, like many of my women friends, because of the way he wrote about women. I was more sympathetic to the little I knew about C. G. Jung because of how he wrote about women, particularly his theory of anima and animus. When I met the therapist, Patricia Dunton, for the first time, I noticed the absence of the proverbial couch and joked, "Where is your sofa, and what will we do if I don't want to lie down and talk about my childhood?" She chuckled as she invited me to sit in one of two wicker chairs facing each other and said, "You are obviously here because you have something happening right now that you want to talk about, so why don't we just start with that?" For the first time I knew what the cliché expression of floodgates opening felt like, for as I talked, it was as if years of pent-up dirty water began to drain from behind a dam. The feeling of release and relief I got from talking was extraordinary and unforgettable. That same night I had an experience I couldn't properly categorize until twenty years later, when I began to write about Jung—it was a "big dream." In it, I was in my house when an emaciated female figure covered with slime and sewage was trying to break through the screen door. The trouble was, that woman was me.

I dreamed it during the time I was becoming involved with a number of feminist groups. In Connecticut, I was part of what we called "consciousness-raising get-togethers," small groups of women who gathered to talk about things we could not name until years later, such as why we could have credit cards only in our husbands' names, or why it was so hard to get a job in the first place and then why the man at the next desk was paid more than we were. Most troubling of all, we wondered how we could get almost every guy we met to keep his hands to himself. And I remember the howls of outrage when I described a job interview at a local college, when the department chairman said he probably would hire a man instead of me because I had a husband to "protect me" and didn't need the income. In New York, I attended large marches and meetings where I was a foot soldier in the audience as feminist icons energized us to go home and take political action. I was more concerned with taking personal action and, to use a popular expression of the time, with making the political personal.

There was one curious aspect of my feminist awakening, however, that puzzles me to this day. Several of my new feminist friends were proud to call themselves "Ninnies," devotees of Anaïs Nin. Come with us, they entreated on several occasions as they urged me to go with them to Nin's Greenwich Village apartment, where she often invited small groups to explore her recently published *Diaries*. I still don't know why, but for whatever reason, I always found an excuse not to go. I never met her in person, something I often thought about and regretted several decades later, when I wrote about her. As I pored over the several hundred thousand pages she wrote about herself or read her voluminous correspondence, I saw repeatedly how Anaïs Nin had had to filter every public event throughout the world through her own sensitivities and to put herself at its center even though she had no connection to any of it. All I found about Beckett was her written insistence that she had been the first American to recognize the genius who had written such a play as *Godot* and that she had done so much to enhance his reputation among Americans of influence. I thought about this almost every day when I began to write about her in the 1990s, but as 1976 was lurching steadily toward 1977, my mind was elsewhere.

I had not seen Beckett in quite a long time, but we exchanged regular letters. When I wrote, it was to tell him of my progress; when he replied, it was usually about his recent professional activity. He may have made some remark in reply when I told him of his friends I had seen, but he never asked directly when the biography would be finished, and I certainly was not going to volunteer any information, especially now that the year was passing rapidly and I didn't have a publisher. With the exception of my family and a few trusted friends, I had told no one, because I was so afraid of what Beckett might do if he found out.

In October, Alan Schneider went to Berlin to watch Beckett direct *Footfalls* and *That Time* at the Schiller Theater, and on opening night he flew to London with Beckett to watch him direct a TV production. Alan told me that Beckett quizzed him at length about my book but did not ask anything personal about me. Alan said Beckett never went out of the hotel and saw no one. He said Beckett was very depressed and told him that Suzanne was sick, everyone was dying, and he himself was generally preoccupied with death. The only thing that seemed to please and excite him, according to Alan, was that he knew I expected the book to be published in 1977. I was glad we were talking on the telephone so that Alan could not see my face. I was under too much stress to take pleasure in the news that Beckett seemed pleased, because I still didn't have a publisher. At least by that time I had the Penn appointment and my assistant-professor position on a tenure track was formally secure. However, the work environment was stressful, as my new colleagues asked me repeatedly about the status of the book. I don't know how I managed to smile and say everything was proceeding smoothly, because none of it was true.

And so back to Carl Brandt I went, demanding information about what was going on. He told me that the previous July he had submitted the book to a woman editor who was "everybody's darling" and he was sure she was reading it carefully. She must be, I thought, for it was now going on November. Four months was surely enough time to know if she wanted to acquire it. At the end of October, he phoned my office at Penn to tell me she had invited us to lunch the next day at a very posh restaurant in New York. I rather resented how he instructed me to show up on time and behave presentably, but never mind: we were making progress.

What a fiasco it was! *"She looked me up and down and was more interested in my clothes than my book: My jacket was a most unusual tweed and where did I buy it? Was my scarf Hermès? And then came her voice—from on high down to little me: she wasn't sure I was a good enough writer to pull it off but she had an assistant who was a Yale PhD and he would be delighted to ghost-write."* I was boiling with rage but said nothing, just sat there and glared down at my plate. Before I could erupt, Carl stepped in—thanked her, said we had a lot to think about, and rushed me out of there. I knew he caught my mood because he left his third martini sitting there untouched. He wanted to talk further at his office, but I said no: *"Just get the manuscript back. I never want to see her again."*

To Carl's credit, it was the first time in a very long time that I thought he behaved admirably, telling me something like "It's you and me, kid. We are in this together. You wrote a good book and you are going to have a good publisher." I just turned away and left him standing there. I couldn't bear to talk to him for fear of what I might say about how he had been treating me. Obviously I was still the dutiful girl unwilling to offend the man who knew better.

I didn't know how much longer I could continue to bear these rejections if my fortunes did not turn. Thankfully, two weeks later, on November 10, Carl called in jubilation. He had given the manuscript to Tom Stewart, a young editor at Harcourt, Brace, Jovanovich, who wanted very much to publish it. Carl said, "This book will make your reputation, but it's not going to make your fortune." He told me the offer was much less than the pittance I had received from Harper's Magazine Press, and "we will try to persuade Harper & Row that you have suffered enough and should not have to repay it, but the situation is not hopeful." It wasn't, and I did have to repay Harper & Row. At that point I didn't care. I had an enthusiastic editor, an excellent new publisher, and a likely 1977 publication. What could possibly go wrong now?

24

At 10:45 on the morning of February 28, 1977, I wrote the last words of *Samuel Beckett: A Biography*, the book I had begun to write on November 17, 1971. In fits of hysteria, alternately crying and laughing, I typed out the last words. What an eerie feeling it was to be finished at long last. Now came the nervous part: the waiting.

It had been sheer joy to work with Tom Stewart, and now to have everyone from editorial to secretarial to sales at my publisher giving me nothing but positive feedback was an overwhelming sensation. No expense was spared to produce a beautiful book. The art director, Harris Levine, hired the famed graphic designer Milton Glaser to paint a portrait of Beckett for the jacket, and they decided that the only place to photograph it was *"on a certain wall in Henry Miller's favorite Paris whorehouse."* And off they went to Paris! Jerry Bauer was hired to take my photo, which thrilled me because he had also photographed Beckett. I was not so happy when he told me I was a good subject but I could still stand to lose ten pounds, and I should be happy that he air-brushed out all my wrinkles. Still, it seemed that I could sit back and enjoy my first trade publishing experience: discussing the jacket, sitting for an author photo, letting the book club and review copy requests roll in; everything had been so exciting.

But there was feedback from one corner that was less sanguine: the publisher's lawyers decided that it was time to vet the manuscript, and they said I had to get Beckett's written permission for every single quotation from his letters and unpublished manuscripts. It threw me into a panic.

I remembered how Beckett and I had originally agreed to the project's ground rules, and I marveled at the extraordinary circumstances under which he had freed me to write. I had come to know quite a few biographers and had made good friends with whom I got together for what we called "kvetching and bitching sessions." I listened silently to their horror stories of restrictions and roadblocks set up by their subjects or heirs and executors who determined to impede, if not actually halt, publication, and I told all this to HBJ's lawyers, in person and in letters, as I implored them not to make me ask Beckett to do anything that might make him withdraw his cooperation. I told them he might find my request demeaning, as if I were questioning his integrity, and that he might resent being asked to put his spoken consent into writing. At one point I blurted that "he might tell us all to go to hell, and then what do we do? Do I spend another couple of years rewriting this book and taking all the life out of it?" The lawyers were not swayed and told me to write the letter.

I thought it was the worst possible time to do such a thing, because I had just had a brief reply from Beckett to my letter telling him that I had changed publishers and was now expecting publication by the end of 1977. His reply to this news was noncommittal, along the lines of "That's nice, good luck," but he continued with an unusual burst of personal information. He said he was having a difficult winter. He wanted to spend January and February quietly in Ussy, but his little house had been broken into and burglarized for the third time, and now he was reluctant to go there. The thieves had taken his typewriter, chess set, and kitchen equipment, and, as they had done on the two previous occasions, ignored all his books, papers, and manuscripts, which they left scattered all over the main room. With his distinctive humor, schadenfreude certainly, he congratulated the thieves on their wisdom in choosing what was not worth taking.

He had been more forthcoming to Con Leventhal and Marion Leigh, as I learned when they came to New York again and we met for lunch. They said he had told them he felt violated and bereft, particularly over the loss of the chess set, which was one he particularly loved. And he told Alan Schneider and Barney Rosset that he was so depressed he didn't know if he could ever participate in any activity connected with his work again, let alone try to create anything new.

Armed with all this distressing information, I set out to write a letter that would explain the situation, how it was not my idea but the lawyers' that he should place his initials next to every single typed quotation I wanted to use. I told him I still honored his original word, but the legal situation in the United States was entirely beyond my control. I apologized for creating unnecessary work and set to typing the quotations, twenty-three single-spaced pages.

I sent it off in early February, and a week later I had his reply. It was so warm and courteous that I had to read it several times through, my eyes blurring with unshed tears. He had initialed every single quotation except one, a poem he had written when he was twelve and a student at the Portora Royal School. He said it "shows better your diligence as a researcher than my development as a writer." I have met many honorable persons throughout my long professional life, but there was never one whose integrity equaled Samuel Beckett's. His word was indeed his bond.

Suddenly it was full summer, and even though everything was proceeding smoothly toward publication, the timing for a fall launch was just too tight, so a business decision was made to move the book's publication to spring 1978. To hype it, press releases were prepared, and I was given an enormous pile of them to take to the December meeting of the Modern Language Association (MLA) in New York.

I was looking forward to attending the Beckett session because two British scholar-critics whose work I found useful, John Pilling and John Fletcher, were to give papers, and many American Beckett specialists were also appearing on the program. Most important, James Knowlson, a professor at Reading University in England who had engaged Beckett's cooperation to create an important archive of manuscripts and related materials, and who, along with John Pilling, was the founder of the influential *Journal of Beckett Studies* (*JOBS* in academic shorthand), was the keynote speaker. I was eager to give him a copy of the press release and to discuss having a portion of the biography appear in *JOBS*. Four decades later, as I prepared to write here about what happened, the experience was still so painful and so hard to relive that I chose to do so through the *DD* entry I made then.

"*I met Dougald McMillan, Enoch Brater, Porter Abbott, Calvin Israel, David Hayman, and at least six other sycophantic finks who mostly sniggered or stared at me. [J. D.] Don O'Hara was there preening himself because he asked for and got the Times review and had an advance copy of my galleys. All the others wanted to see it but I guess he wasn't showing it. McMillan told me he 'knew well what a bitch' I am and how I am 'messing up the entire Beckett industry.' Several others jumped in and said no, I wasn't such a bitch after all, and the book was probably not going to be worth much so don't waste time on me. Others were positively salivating as they told me how they were going to review it—negatively. Calvin Israel said he was writing the 'magnum opus' about Beckett and 'Sam' never told him anything personal, so with a big leer he asked what I had to do to get him to open up to me. There was a huge round of laughter when he said this, and lots of eyeball rolling and elbow punching. So naturally he repeated it several more times to even greater giggles and guffaws. Then he told the group how, when they got drunk together on his last visit to Paris, 'Sam' told him he regretted ever meeting me. The trouble is: I knew 'Sam' was not in Paris at that particular time—he was in transit from Berlin to London!*"

As all this was happening, James Knowlson stood firmly planted on the far side of the room, whispering with John Calder. I could see that he was turned sideways just enough to observe everything that was taking place around me. He was obviously not going to talk to me unless I went to him—I knew that I was expected to pay homage—so I broke away from the hostile group to walk over.

I greeted Calder warmly, as he had been generous with his time when I had interviewed him in London, but this time he mumbled what might have been a hello and scampered away as if fearful of contamination.

A complete hush fell upon the room when I was left alone with Knowlson. I could sense that everyone was watching us and straining to hear our conversation. When I introduced myself, he was already moving sideways to get away from me, but I put myself squarely in front of him so that he could not. He said he really could not be seen talking to me, so it was probably best for me to leave. I stood for a very long moment blocking his exodus and stared hard at him. I thought about telling him how childish he and everyone else was being, but instead, without another word, I turned and headed for the exit.

As I left the room, Professor Fred M. Robinson stood hiding in the hallway. He whispered as I passed by, "So you're the little girl who stuck her hand in the cookie jar and ran away with all the goodies." I just shook my head and kept on walking. All I could think of was Canto VII in Dante's *Inferno*, where the sinners are submerged in the marsh of the River Styx, so filled with anger and jealousy that they bite themselves and each other in sheer rage and frustration.

Two of my Penn colleagues were with me, women professors in fields dominated by men and who had suffered similar hostility and insult. They were furious, outraged, in high dudgeon. They demanded to know what I was going to do about it and wanted me to go back into that room and confront all those men. I, however, was just the opposite—cold, detached, distanced. I can remember the sensation of feeling very far removed from what had just happened, stunned by the onslaught. And still, all these years later, I can't explain how—or why—I just let all these insults and insinuations roll off me. Part of me supposes it was because I had such confidence in what I had written that I was sure no right-thinking person would appraise it any way other than objectively. But another reason was surely the consciousness gained from many conversations with my feminist friends, listening to all those talks and attending all the rallies led by feminist leaders. I had always trusted my instincts as a journalist and I was prepared to do so now that I was a scholar. Everything conspired to teach me to have faith in myself and my judgments, and I suppose that was why I was able to ignore the Becketteers.

The first copies came off the press in early May 1978. I kept one for myself and sent one to Beckett. As always, he replied quickly. After thanking me for it, he wrote, "Seems a very handsome *looking* book." He claimed he never read anything written about himself, so I convinced myself that the fact he was not outraged or offended was in and of itself a success. I was relieved when he did not ask my future travel plans, as I had none to return to Paris anytime soon.

The book was published in June, but the major reviews were not timely, and, worse, they paved the way for the unrelenting hostility that followed in every subsequent review written by the Becketteers. J. D. O'Hara had made the mistake of giving a back-of-the-jacket blurb to the book, so Harvey Shapiro, the new editor of *The New York Times Book Review,* took the review away from him and gave it to the British critic John Sturrock. He was so late in submitting it that Shapiro had a London reporter pay a flight attendant to carry it to New York, where another reporter picked it up and delivered it. It appeared at the worst possible time, in the July 4 edition. Sturrock, whom I never met and who never saw me in person, called me "buoyant" and "enviably resilient" as he wrote of the "six hyperactive years" I had spent "in pursuit" of Beckett. Hugh Kenner weighed in with an insulting, unfocused, and silly diatribe in *Saturday Review.* Ruby Cohn wrote a letter praising Richard Ellmann for his attack in *The New York Review of Books* and, by extension, all the other Becketteers who attacked the book. Ellmann in turn attacked her, calling out all the errors she wrong-fully tried to attribute to me. In his review, Ellmann wrote that I had managed a "scoop which in literary history is like that of

Bernstein and Woodward in political history." He said I found "in a shooting gallery . . . a big duck, or drake, named Beckett [and] took aim and brought him down," insisting (falsely) that I "wrote a letter and another letter and another" to persuade Beckett to cooperate. His insinuation was clearly the same as Sturrock's, one that I had been getting from any number of reporters who were interviewing me for features. It was probably voiced best by the late Mary Bull of the weekly *Hamden* (Connecticut) *Chronicle,* when she asked straight out what every reviewer and interviewer from Portland, Maine, to Portland, Oregon, also felt free to ask: "How many times did you have to sleep with Beckett to get this scoop?" It would seem that a woman could not be possessed of a brain, only a vagina.*

Even the headmaster of my daughter's school weighed in when the biography was published, waving a copy of Ellmann's review at her during the lunch hour and in front of all her friends, saying, "Oh boy, but your mother has really done it this time!" You can imagine how upset the sixteen-year-old girl was when she came home that night in tears. Carl Brandt, who was not high on my list of men who treated women as equals, brought my only positive relief when he said he could "not understand where all this male outrage against a woman was coming from. These people are truly crazy."

The surprising, and often saddening, response from many quarters convinced me that my first biography would be my *only* biography. A professor in my department at Penn told me that I had been *"overly aggressive and ambitious to write this book. Didn't I think I had overstepped the boundaries for women?"* Another member of my department wrote a review in the university's alumni magazine—my own alumni publication, which all my classmates saw—that denounced the book: "I don't like Beckett and I don't

---

* I regret to say that in 2017, a friend of the writer Jan Herman asked him to "demand" of me how many times I had to sleep with Beckett to get him to cooperate. I could only sigh as I asked myself, Doesn't anything ever change?

think he deserves a big book like this one." Everyone stared at me in faculty and committee meetings, but few professors spoke to me directly, unlike the student who stopped me in a hallway to ask, "Are you somebody I should know?" "NO!" I thundered and kept on walking. Most disappointing of all were the tenured women in my department, who were heard to say repeatedly, "She's not a scholar; she's only a biographer." Two colleagues in another department who were appalled by how those in my department treated me took me to lunch to celebrate with a bottle of good wine. It was a lively occasion, but they were dead serious when they told me, "If you want to get ahead in academe, your motto has to be 'publish *modestly* or perish.' You cannot write another Beckett."

I had to laugh; how could I take any of this seriously? Unfortunately, I did, and it hurt. And I was truly frightened when I had to call security to remove from my university office a stalker who demanded that I write a denunciation of Beckett because "he is not a Christian and does not believe in God." For an expensive book that sold well but not well enough to make it a bestseller, it was amazing how all sorts of people felt an obligation to offer an opinion.

"Fan mail" (an oxymoron) was heavy. A professor at American University wrote to say that he deplored my invasion of Beckett's privacy but he had already "read it twice and probably could not stop myself from reading it again," after which he would "prepare a list of my intransigencies." I asked the *DD*, *"Intransigencies? Now what the hell does that mean!?!"*

There were, however, many reviewers who understood the book and why it mattered. In England, Anthony Burgess, Matthew Hodgart, and Christopher Ricks praised it—and managed to denounce Ellmann and his like at the same time. The novelist William Kennedy moved me deeply with his *Washington Post* review, and I even respected what Benjamin DeMott wrote in *The Atlantic Monthly*, when he said he liked my book but not my writing style. The distinguished scholar and Stanford professor Albert Guerard told me it was one of the most important biographies of our generation and would be the point of departure for future generations of scholars. Clifton Fadiman echoed Guerard when he wrote in the Book of the Month Club newsletter that my book was a "rescue operation, taking Beckett away from the cultists and the fadists." Well, perhaps, but not entirely.

Praise of another kind came from Orhan Pamuk, the Turkish novelist and Nobel Prize winner. Several years later, when I met him in New York, he told me that he had bought a copy of the book in Paris, and because it was banned in Turkey, he had taken great care to smuggle it into the country. There he passed it around to all his literary friends, who read it so closely that they shattered the binding and actually wore down some of the pages. By the time they had all finished their surreptitious reading, the pages were loose inside the cover. He told me it was the most revered study of Beckett in his country and thanked me for writing it. I was so deeply moved that I had to excuse myself and go into the women's room to compose myself.

But the Becketteers would not relent, and they planned a huge symposium "to rescue Beckett from Bair." The usual suspects, as I called all those who had rushed to (in Calvin Israel's words) "savage Bair," made sure that I knew all about it, and also that I knew I was not invited. Beyond that tight little group, very few genuine scholars attended. I don't think it was over for ten minutes when the phone rang for the first time with "friends" who wanted to tell me about it: *"The whole damn thing revolved around 'THE biography' (it was the only book not written by SB that was on sale there). Seems everyone in the audience wanted to know what the 'in crowd' thought about it. Barney [Rosset] defended it while the rest of them sneered. I told myself I should consider the sources."*

Yes, I should have shrugged it all off as I had done before, and I should have moved on. Instead I suppose I had a minor breakdown. I dropped everything—opportunities for publicity, offers of articles to write (and I needed the money), invitations to interesting parties, and most of all family, friends, house, and home. I went to my brother's house in San Diego, where I paced up and down the Del Mar beach, communing with the seals and crying.

One bleak morning, after two weeks of Jungian "creative depression," in which I let every changing emotion I felt play itself out, I confronted a mama seal guarding her two pups and surprised myself when I shouted in an amazingly strong voice that I needed to go home and get on with my life. Mama seal gave me a snort in reply and waddled off with her babies while I kept talking, telling her that the kids would be coming home from summer camp and my family needed and wanted me at home, which my husband told me daily in our phone conversations. Even more, I needed them.

I was suffused with shame for what I saw as having selfishly run off, and I felt that I needed to make amends. But . . . didn't I also have an obligation to myself? If my head was not in the right place, could I really be useful to anyone else? Raw emotion triumphed over reason—I loved my husband and children, and quite simply, I wanted to see them. I had dedicated the book to Von, "who shared it," and to Katney and Vonn Scott, "who grew up with it." I should have added, "To the three I love most who were strong enough to survive it."

That morning, as the sun broke through the fog and haze earlier than usual and my seal friends headed back into the surf, I sat on their rock talking to myself. I told myself that I had written the best book I could and I had nothing to be ashamed of or to apologize for. I would hold my head up high and not let a bunch of spiteful mediocrities tell me otherwise. I went back to my brother's house, changed my reservation, got on the last flight that day, and went home to face the music, sour and off-key as it mostly turned out to be.

25

When classes began in September 1978, for the third year in a row I was commuting each Tuesday morning on Amtrak from New Haven to Philadelphia and then back again on Thursday evening. When I look at the *DD* for those first few months, I see only unfocused ramblings, mostly about all the professional responsibilities I should but could not bring myself to fulfill. I told the editors of book reviews and journals a flat-out lie, that my schedule was so full I could not accept new work. My siblings and I joked that as the oldest child of three, I was the one blessed (or cursed) with an overdeveloped sense of responsibility, but in this hazy period I was so indifferent that I didn't even care that I was blowing off one obligation after another. My contract with HBJ specified that they had the right of refusal for my next book, and my agent urged me to "strike" while I was "still hot." I demurred, insisting that I would never write another biography.

A year went by, and I drifted along. I could not think of anything I wanted to write, and as for biography, I insisted that I would never put myself or my family through that ever again! In fact, I found it impossible to write anything beyond a grocery list. I often taught classes without having read the texts thoroughly or preparing good lectures. I went through the motions of getting through the days at Penn, letting all the continuing sarcasm, backbiting, and general bitchiness wash right over me. I went home to Connecticut for the long weekends and relished being there, playing with the bulldogs and the Persian cats, cooking, eating, and generally doing nothing much.

We moved to Philadelphia in September 1980, when my husband took a position at Penn's University Museum. It was an unhappy move for me, having to give up my beloved house in Woodbridge, and my unhappiness was accompanied by back spasms that kept me confined to bed and on medical leave that semester. Doctors told me that half the paralyzing spasms were due to scoliosis but the other half were emotional and most likely exacerbated by the hostile responses to the Beckett biography.

Meanwhile Carl Brandt phoned periodically to suggest meetings with editors to discuss subjects for another book. Conrad Aiken and Anne Sexton emerged as possibilities, but neither grabbed me strongly enough to snap me out of my funk. I thought I was truly finished with the genre of biography until one day in June 1980, when I found myself in Boston with my husband, who was participating in a museum conference. I was in desperate need of a vacation and eager to avoid schmoozing, which I thought I could achieve by spending several days alone on Cape Ann, in Rockport and Marblehead, before the conference began.

Carl had other plans for my free time. I did not know that he had been receiving inquiries from Dick McDonough, an editor at Little, Brown & Company, who wanted to offer me a contract to write a biography about anyone at all who interested me. Carl said I would like Dick, and even if I never wrote a book for him, I would at least have a glorious lunch.

Dick was an admirer of the Beckett book, and he turned on his considerable charm at the elegant Maison Robert, one of Boston's finest restaurants at the time. It was a stunning June afternoon and we had a table on the terrace. Excellent food and wine coupled with witty conversation did their magic, and for the first time in ages I was relaxed and happy, laughing at jokes, trading quips, and enjoying all the publishing gossip. The afternoon drifted by in a haze of pleasure until, inevitably, Dick broached the subject of my next book. He said all the wonderfully flattering things an editor intent on wooing a reluctant writer might say about her abilities. He said he would offer me a contract to write about anyone I wanted, but his first candidate was Eudora Welty, and after her, he was convinced I could "tackle anyone Irish or even Virginia Woolf." I thought he was joking until I realized he was deadly serious, and the afternoon became slightly tense as I told him repeatedly that I would never write another biography. Finally, and I think in exasperation, he gave up and accepted my decision. Or so I thought, until the moment that changed everything.

"All right," he agreed, and I remember him saying something along the lines of "But let us ponder, just for the fun of it, if you were to write one, whose life would you choose? You can pick any person in the world, living or dead, but you have to explain your selection."

So each of us tossed out names, most of them highly inappropriate, mostly supermarket tabloid mainstays of the time. After fifteen or twenty minutes of this, I stopped, saying I didn't have a name but I did have an idea. "If I were ever to write another biography, it would have to be of a woman who made a success of every aspect of her life. She would have to have had a solid professional life, one that garnered respect and admiration, but even more, she would have to have had a happy and satisfying personal life. And since I cannot think of a single woman who had both, I guess I will never write another biography."

In my astonishment over what I had said, I gulped down a big slurp of the wine I had hitherto been sipping discreetly. I wondered where that remark came from, and thinking about it later in my hotel, I had no doubt it was a manifestation of the cultural moment.

McCall's magazine's 1957 campaign for "togetherness" was a glorified paean to domesticity, using an image of the larger family unit to conceal a message that women should suck it up and be content as happy housewives. That message fell on a lot of deaf ears, and it gave way in 1963 to Betty Friedan's *Feminist Mystique,* in which domesticated women, particularly those with good educations, were asking, "Is this all there is?" Like most of the feminist friends in my small groups, I had read Simone de Beauvoir's *Second Sex* in college, but I did not pay much attention to it until after

I read Friedan's book. Then I read Beauvoir again, this time more carefully and with considerably more life experience. I remember being astonished by her wide-ranging examination of the lives of women, but like most of my feminist friends, I was moved more by Friedan's American version of female dissatisfaction. Hers was the book that gave rise to the life changes made by the women I knew best.

By the 1980s, the contemporary feminist movement was fully ramped up, and everything about women's lives—their goals, aims, ambitions, sexual identities and preferences—was in flux. In my case, it was a struggle to stay married, raise two teenage children, get an academic career solidly under way, and oh yes, figure out how to write that all-important second book I needed to secure tenure. I told my feminist friends that the choices we were all making had made "Holding Pattern" obsolete as a possible novel title. Two others captured the moment far better: "Splitting," and "Sticking," because they described much better what we all seemed to be doing.

I must have gone on at great length as I told Dick I was less interested in a specific biography than I was in an examination of the lives of contemporary women, a collection of examples of the many and varied choices contemporary women were making, quite possibly managing to construct and offer a model for how they should conduct their lives.

That was all fine and good, he said, and of course I had a proven track record as a journalist, so there was no doubt that I could write such a book. But after Beckett, "Wouldn't you rather examine the problem through the example of a woman who did indeed do it and have it all? Wouldn't you rather express your concerns through the life of an exemplary woman?" Dick insisted that such a woman must exist—"We just have to identify the perfect example." He began to toss out names of various women, from Joan of Arc to Margaret Mead and Ayn Rand, all of whom I rejected.

To this day we joke about who said Simone de Beauvoir's name first, but all I remember of that magic moment was the "Eureka!"

burst of recognition that hit me when I heard her name. *"Of course! She is probably the only modern woman who made a success of everything."* At that time, and like every other woman who had read her four volumes of autobiography, I believed that her relationship with Jean-Paul Sartre was the perfection she claimed it was. Like so many other women who counted *The Second Sex* as an important coming-of-age book, I regarded her as both paragon and icon. It made so much sense—all those concepts that I had been thinking about, all the possibilities for the perfect life and relationship that I knew I could never use in a bio of, say, Anne Sexton. Everything fit Simone de Beauvoir so naturally that I couldn't believe I hadn't thought of it on my own, long before.

I was wildly enthusiastic about the project, but my agent was not. Nor was Mary Kling, who represented me in France. When I asked why, Carl said, "Nobody is interested in an over-the-hill French feminist." Mary said succinctly, "She is not popular in France just now." I mustered every argument I could think of as I asked them both to begin contract negotiations, after which I would decide if it was doable. My entreaties grew heated and passionate, and they were all met with reasons why I should not "waste my time." Reluctantly, and I think only to put an end to my phone calls, both grudgingly agreed to try to sell the idea. Carl's bottom line was, "She is passé. Nobody cares about her anymore." Even more shocking was Mary's attitude: "What is she without Jean-Paul Sartre? Now that he is gone [he died on April 15, 1980], she is nothing." I was stunned, but having come this far toward another biography, I was not yet ready to give up.

A month passed with no further contact. At the end of June, I wrote: *"No word from Brandt yet so they must still be talking. If that's the case, I guess the project might live."* It was alive and limping along, but months passed before there was resolution, and the outcome was nothing I could possibly have envisioned.

26

I was on fire when I returned to Philadelphia. For almost a year we had been camping out in a rented house, because interest rates on mortgages had risen to a shocking 15 to 18 percent and we could not afford to buy anything and get settled. Every room looked like a hoarder's paradise, filled with boxes that we hoped to unpack as soon we could move to something permanent. Despite the dreary surroundings, the energy that had eluded me for almost two years kicked in as I thought about Simone de Beauvoir. I set to work clearing my desk of everything that had piled up on it: articles for academic journals, reviews for newspapers, long-overdue correspondence, and invitations to give lectures and talks at theater openings of Beckett's plays. All this cleaning up was accomplished in several short weeks, by the end of June 1980, and still there was no word from my agent. I had expected a quick offer of a contract but none was forthcoming.

Summer settled over us, hot and heavy, and with it came all sorts of family crises. First Katney came down with a serious bout of mononucleosis, which left her bedridden for a month and which she then gave to her father. He was ill with so many unsettling symptoms that we spent most of July in the offices of various medical specialists, who were convinced it was not mono but a strange and perhaps life-threatening virus. When not chauffeuring the two patients to doctor appointments, I was tending to them at home, shuttling between their bedrooms and the kitchen, trying to entice them to eat. As August's stifling humidity overwhelmed our non-air-conditioned house, I told myself that my agent's silence was perhaps for the best, as I would not have been able to do any research anyway.

Carl Brandt finally replied in mid-August, after his refusal to take my phone calls drove me to fire off several impassioned letters demanding to know what, if anything, was happening. He cited layoffs at Little, Brown (although Dick McDonough still had a job) and warned that now was not the time to request funding for "an over the hill French woman." If Little, Brown did not offer a contract, he would probably not contact other publishers, as none would likely want the biography. I didn't care, I told him. I was going to write it no matter what, and I'd find another way. And then he erupted, berating me for wanting to write it at all: *"It's going to take four to six years of your life. It might—but probably won't—get you tenure, and if it has any success at all, it will only be 'critical,' meaning maybe 300 people will read it. You won't get any European sales, not even in France. You are still paying off your first advance and you'll go broke writing this one."* He brought up Anne Sexton's name again, claiming that that biography would have been the bestseller and how foolish I had been not to pursue it when her daughter, Linda Gray Sexton, had asked to meet me.*

I chastise myself now for letting this man scold me and belittle my project. It took me a few weeks to recover from this lambasting, but recover I did, and I wrote at the time: *"I've decided to write the SdB bio no matter what. I'm doing this one for me. I need to write this book. I really want to do it, so I'll just apply for grants and fellow-ships and get started."* It was late in the year and most deadlines had passed, but I planned to start work on two fronts at once: while I was reading or rereading everything Beauvoir had written, I would fill out an application for every grant for which I thought I might qualify. However, real life had a way of messing up my best-laid plans.

---

* Wisely, she chose my friend Diane Middlebrook, who wrote a splendid biography.

Interest rates fell back to percentages we could afford, and we were finally able to buy a house and get settled. Simultaneously I was enduring a tenure review that required nonstop concentration for weeks, collecting or preparing all the supporting documentation that was required. On top of these distractions, I was teaching three overenrolled courses and being trotted out by the university as a prize trophy, cordially directed to perform for trustees, rich donors, and anyone else the administrators wanted to impress or recruit. And all the while the department's powers that be chuckled as they told me how I had published "too well" to get tenure. One did tell me that Walter Kerr had called the biography the best book ever written about Beckett, chuckling gleefully that he was only telling me because Kerr misspelled both my names.

It was not the happiest of times for me. I learned to get by on four to five hours of sleep each night because there was so much work to be done to care for the recovering invalids and move into the house that I could not do my own work until they were settled for the night. I found myself doing something I had not done since working on the Beckett book, when I so despaired of ever finishing it that I sought Jungian therapy. Once again my dreams were so unsettling that I began to keep a record of them. They were mostly what I called "can't get it together" dreams, and the one that recurred most frequently was of me riding the New York City subway in my Columbia graduate student years. As I jumped up from my seat to exit and change trains from the express to the local at Ninety-Sixth Street, my briefcase burst open and all my papers spilled onto the floor. I could not gather them up in time before the doors closed, and the train sped on to Harlem with me trapped inside. This was when I usually woke up in the sweat of panic. As I replayed the daily stresses during the 4 a.m. galloping anxieties that usually followed the dream, I wrote, *"This really can't go on. Too much stress."* I asked myself how I was going to get out of all these messes, especially since *"you created them all by yourself!"* My feminist awakening had not yet taken strong enough hold for me not to think that I was to blame for everything.

By September the move was over, all the boxes were unpacked, and the invalids had recovered and resumed their usual activities. I decided to get on with my next book, contract or no contract. It was probably time to let Simone de Beauvoir know that I wanted to write her biography.

Just as I had done with Beckett, I wrote a letter. With it, I sent a copy of the French translation of the Beckett biography, saying I thought it was important for Beauvoir to know what I had written about my last subject before she agreed to become the next one. Her reply was as swift as Beckett's had been. She said she had already read my book and was impressed with the way "an American"—then a disdainful appellation in French literary and cultural circles—had so captured "the French writer"—for indeed the French were happy to claim Beckett as their own. Most of all, she said she welcomed me because I wanted to write "about everything and not just my feminism or Sartre." She closed by inviting me to come to Paris as soon as possible "so that we can begin."

• When I conveyed this news to Carl Brandt, via a message left with his secretary, he told me that a contract was being prepared. It would offer an advance that would scarcely pay for one round-trip plane ticket and a week or two in a cheap hotel. I was insulted and asked if I should take my own peanut butter and jelly to make sure that I would have something to eat. And then he revealed what I called "the kick-in-the-face clause": at any time during the writing of the book, even before anyone had read a word, the publisher could decide not to publish it, and I would have to pay back the advance. I couldn't believe he expected me to sign it. So I didn't.

Meanwhile my family and I celebrated the happy news that Simone de Beauvoir was waiting to welcome me. As children often do, mine lovingly teased me, about my French in particular. "I guess you'll be enrolling in Berlitz any day now," they joked. Actually, it was not all that funny, and it was something I thought about but didn't do for lack of time. I had studied French since high school and had taken advanced literature courses all through college, and in graduate school I had easily passed the language proficiency exam. I could read novels and poetry without having to translate in my head. However, in all those years I had never really learned to speak the language properly. I could chatter away in French to everyone from waiters and desk clerks to scholars and writers, but I always had to rely on the simplest forms of nouns, verbs, and sentence structure. French people often corrected my appalling grammar, and I was grateful for it.

With Beckett my spoken French was never a problem, because everyone in his circle, no matter their nationality or native language, had enough English and I had enough French for us to understand each other. I wasn't worried about communicating with Beauvoir's circle because I assumed my "franglais" would suffice, but I should have been concerned, because so few persons close to her spoke any language but their own.

I assumed that everything I had learned about the genre of biography while writing about Beckett would simply carry over and apply to the writing of a biography of Simone de Beauvoir. That was only the first of many—no, the first of *all*—my assumptions about biography that I would have to discard when I returned to Paris.

27

As 1981 began, I had ten free days between the holidays and the start of the new semester, when I would begin yet another grueling term of overenrolled courses. I needed those ten days to prepare for the onslaught to come, but it was the only time I could go to Paris. Instead of preparing syllabi, I spent the last days of the old year making increasingly frantic phone calls to hotels along the rue Jacob where I had stayed previously. None would give me a room confirmation, but all told me to come anyway, as something would surely be available. It was an inauspicious start, but I decided to do just that.

The flight was a nightmare, delayed by bad weather and then turbulence, after which the airline lost my luggage. Bleary-eyed and frazzled, I had the taxi drop me at one end of rue Jacob, intending to work my way to the other until I found a hotel that had a free room. Fortunately, the second one I reached took me in, disheveled, dirty, and without a change of clothing. I was such a sorry sight that even though breakfast was long over, the desk clerk took pity and sent coffee and croissants to my room, "with compliments." At least something started nicely.

I showered and hastened over to the nearest Monoprix to buy some inexpensive clothing before I tried to telephone Beauvoir. At that point I learned that the telephone system throughout France had recently been changed, adding extra digits to every number and making the one she had given me invalid. My first thought was to call her publisher, but then I realized that Gallimard would never release her number to a stranger. I phoned Mary Kling instead and asked her to intercede, because Beauvoir knew I was arriving on

January 3 and she expected me to phone on that day to set up our first meeting. That day was almost over and I had not found a way to reach her.

Mary was sick at home with the flu and her staff had no luck in tracking down the new number. Once again, as I had with Beckett, I resorted to the little blue pneu. I sent one that gave Beauvoir the name of my hotel and my direct line, and once again I waited. By midmorning the next day I had not heard from her, so I wrote a letter in my grammatically imperfect French, ran to the Métro, and rushed over to her apartment building.

I had no idea what I would do when I got there because the doors required a code to open, and I could not even see mailboxes in the entryway. If I did manage to get inside, I did not know where I might be able to leave a letter for her to find. Fortunately, an old man came to the building as I was standing in front of the door wondering what to do. He asked what I was doing, so I spilled out my entire sad story, clutching and waving my letter the entire time. He listened until I ran out of breath and had exhausted my limited French vocabulary, unsure if anything I had said made enough sense for him to understand me. Without a word, this old gentleman reached out and took the letter, assuring me that "Madame" would receive it. Now, he said, I was to remove myself from the entrance so that he could enter his building, making it clear that I was not to enter after him. I had little recourse but to step aside, hold the door, and bow him in.

Two days passed, during which I wandered aimlessly around Paris in miserably cold weather. There was not much snow, but constant sleet made the streets slippery and me wet, so I popped in and out of bookstores and coffee shops, trying to kill time and keep warm. Even though Beauvoir had assured me before I made the trip that she was remaining in Paris throughout the holidays and would be at my disposal, I worried that something might have happened to change her plans. Drawing on my experience with Beckett, all sorts of scenarios went through my mind: perhaps she had become ill and had had to go somewhere warm to recuperate, or she was having second thoughts about the book. Naturally the latter was the one that played over and over in my mind.

My anxiety increased exponentially until January 8, when I found a letter in my mailbox from Simone de Beauvoir. She apologized for having given me the old number—she didn't realize she had done so—and asked me please to phone her new one to make an appointment. I collapsed in a heap of relief before I could compose myself long enough to dial it.

I spoke in French and so did she. I don't know what I expected, but hearing her voice for the first time took me by surprise. She spoke clearly, but her tone was loud and brusque, one that indicated she did not suffer foolish conversation and was in a hurry to make the appointment and get off the phone: "Six o'clock tomorrow at my apartment." I was trying to stammer my way toward ending the call with some pleasantries when she surprised me again by continuing the conversation in an unexpected direction. She told me how happy she was to have a scholar of my reputation writing about her, one who "so understands the French character." And then she began to lavish praise on the Beckett biography. I could not get over how closely she must have read it to be bringing up so many specific points. She told me she had already asked Claude Gallimard to buy "her" book—the one for which I had not yet written a word. I was happy about all this, but it also scared me to death.

Then she said something like "Good! Until tomorrow!" (*Bon! À demain!*) and hung up as abruptly as she had spoken. I sat on the edge of my bed for what must have been a very long time trying to digest what had just happened. When I reached for my date book to enter the time and place of our first appointment, I realized that it would be on January 9, her birthday. I was already a fairly nervous wreck, but here was another level of stress. Perhaps she had made a mistake giving me the rendezvous for that important day. Surely the world would be beating a path to her door, especially at the hour when her friends would be gathering to take her to cocktails and dinner. I wondered whether I should call back and ask if I had misheard the date or do nothing and just show up. If she tossed me out for my ineptitude, I could offer jet lag as an excuse for not hearing correctly and make another appointment. Needless to say, I did not sleep well that night.

Early the next morning I created another dilemma for myself as I wondered if I should take her a gift, and if so, what kind. And how was I going to kill the hours between 6 a.m., when I woke up, and 6 p.m.? I had been introduced to quite a few French feminists who were friends of my American colleagues and who taught in French universities or worked in the publishing community, and I could have called any one of them to keep me company. But I was so nervous that I decided to keep myself to myself, doubting that I could carry on a coherent conversation. I was one of the first people in line when the Louvre opened that day, and I stayed there until late afternoon, wandering through every gallery and stopping now and then to drink coffee, for eating would have been impossible. I stared vacantly at items in the gift shop, in the end deciding that nothing was appropriate, not even a card.

I was empty-handed when I arrived at the Denfert-Rochereau Métro station at 5 p.m. Beckett had once chastised me for being three or four minutes late to one of our earliest meetings, so every time I went to meet Beauvoir, I imitated his character in *Murphy*, carrying the virtue of promptness to an extreme. There was a café on the corner, but I was afraid to get too close to it for fear I would see Beckett, whom I had sometimes met there. It was a preferred haunt of his after his walks, a place to drink coffee and play chess with several local men who were always happy for a game.

Beckett had been much on my mind during the few days while I waited for Beauvoir to phone. As soon as I received her first letter telling me she wanted me to write her biography, I wrote to tell Beckett that I had decided to do it and that I would be coming to Paris from time to time. He did not reply to that letter, or to the one I wrote once I had fixed definite dates, saying that I would be available should he wish to meet. Still reeling from the negative onslaughts of the Becketteers, I was initially relieved that I would not see him and perhaps have to defend or explain anything about my book.

When I saw Con Leventhal and Marion Leigh later, they explained Beckett's silence, losing no time to tell me that I had made a big mistake in "deserting Beckett, for he expected any scholar who wrote about him to remain faithful." So now, on top of every insult others leveled at me, Beckett considered me a deserter because I was not planning to spend the rest of my professional life writing about him.

But on that cold January day, as I stood staring at the enormous statue of the Lion of Belfort that dominated the Place Denfert-Rochereau, I realized that if one began at the statue, and with only a slight stretch of the imagination, one could say that Samuel Beckett and Simone de Beauvoir lived at opposite ends of the same street—she just up the rue Froidevaux where it met the rue Schoelcher, and he a straight shot in the opposite direction down the boulevard Saint-Jacques. Because he and I had met several times in that café on the corner, I gave it a hasty and guilty glance as I rushed past, hardly daring to look in the window for fear I might see him. I was relieved to find only empty tables near the window where he usually sat.

Just beyond the café I saw a flower stall where the clerk was closing for the day. All she had left were several bunches of wilting yellow tulips and a large, cheerful bunch of yellow acacia blossoms. I bought them all, and thus equipped, I headed—exactly on time—for 11 bis, rue Schoelcher.

Simone de Beauvoir buzzed me in and I walked down the long ground-floor hallway until I could turn a corner to the right and take the shorter hallway that led to her door, also on the right. Years later, when I was writing about Anaïs Nin and had befriended her brother, the composer Joaquín Nin-Culmell, we were having a casual conversation about the Nin family's early years in Paris. "We lived on rue Schoelcher," he began, as he described their first apartment in the city. How interesting, I said, because Simone de Beauvoir also lived on that street. Yes, he said, he and his mother lived "in 11 bis on the ground floor, down the long corridor, then the short one on the right, with our flat on the left in the rear, and Anaïs and Hugo's to the right and in the front." I still remember the chills that shook me as I learned that Beauvoir's beautiful studio apartment had been Anaïs Nin's first home in Paris.

When the door opened, tall woman that I am, I looked straight ahead and saw only air. It felt like a cartoon moment as a beat passed before I lowered my gaze to look down and see a very tiny woman looking up at me. I remember thinking how small Sartre must have been, for in all the photos I had seen of the two of them together, she was always the taller. I thrust the flowers toward her and mumbled something about birthday greetings while she gestured dismissively and told me to come in. She walked in front of me and dumped the flowers in a sculpture of a pair of human hands on a small round table; I later learned this was a cast of Sartre's hands. Abruptly, as if she decided that this was not an appropriate place, she excused herself to go into her kitchen and find a vase. I noticed the difficulty she had walking as she shuffled slowly back and forth.

I also noticed how she was dressed in what looked like a shabby red bathrobe over a nightdress. How strange, I thought, that she would be dressed this way on the evening of her birthday. This robe became familiar, as she wore it for many of our conversations during the next five years. She also wore a turban, which I unkindly came to call "the ubiquitous rag," because I never saw her without it. Her eyes were a brilliant blue, although the color was muted by the pale yellow tinge of the whites around them. Her flawless skin was marred only by a similar color and not by wrinkles, even though she turned seventy-three on that day. The yellow deepened over the years I knew her, a worrisome symptom of the cirrhosis of the liver that would contribute to her death.

She left the flowers in the kitchen and shuffled back into the living area, where I was still standing. I was too overwhelmed on that first meeting to observe closely the furniture and decorations, except to take in the two daybeds she used for sofas, arranged perpendicularly along the walls and faced by three tiny slipper chairs with a coffee table in between. As she returned, she indicated with a sweep of her arm that I was to take the nearest slipper chair while she positioned herself on a significant dip in one of the sofas, where her body had made an impression. It was clearly the place where she spent most of her time, and it was where she always sat whenever we were together.

I began to make stuttering conversation, starting with my thanks that she would give me time on her birthday. Her quizzical look as she replied let me know I was not making a very positive first impression. "Why not?" she said. "What is a birthday anyway but just another day?" I didn't know what to say to that, but she didn't pause long enough to let me answer as she asked, "Shall we get to work?"

I had assumed that this was to be a brief getting-acquainted session and I had not brought anything with me; I had no notebook or tape recorder, and I had not prepared any questions. My only preparation had been to practice how to tell her, in my best French, that I had to go home on the twelfth to teach during the spring semester and would not be able to begin serious interviews until at least the summer, and then only if my schedule allowed enough time for me to prepare myself with serious reading and research during the term. I stammered something about how I did not wish to impose upon what I was sure would be a festive evening, so I had not brought any work materials with me. She snorted in derision. There was to be no celebration, she told me; her friend Sylvie would be coming later with something for dinner, but until then we should probably get started.

I fished in my bag for something to write on and could find only my date book, so I pretended it was a notebook. I got a reprieve of sorts from asking questions because she launched right in to tell me how we were going to work: "I will talk, and I will tell you what has been important in my life—all the things you need to know. You can write them down, but you must also bring a tape recorder, and I will have one, too. We can discuss what I tell you if you need me to explain it, and that will be the book you need to write. That will be the one you publish."

I remember clearly how I lowered my head into my hands and said out loud, "Oh dear." I had the sinking sensation that the book was dead and done before I even got started. "What is the matter?" she demanded. "What is wrong?" I was so flustered that I could not think in French and asked her if I could reply in English. She said of course, because she read and understood the language far better than she spoke it.

"That is not how I worked with Samuel Beckett," I told her, and then I proceeded to explain how he had given me the freedom to do my research, conduct my interviews, and to write the book that I thought needed to be written. I told her how we had agreed that he would not read it before it was published, and I even told her how he had said he would neither help nor hinder me, which his family and friends interpreted as his agreement to cooperate fully. I told her that, having worked in such extraordinary circumstances, I didn't see how I could work any other way. I hoped that she would be generous and gracious enough to give me whatever help I asked for, but that she would also allow me the independence to construct a full and objective account of her life and work.

She sat there quietly for what seemed an eternity with her eyes cast down. Finally she met my eyes and said, "Well, if you worked that way with him, then I suppose you will have to work that way with me as well. After all, my book must be equal to the one you wrote for him."

I was sure the enormous breath I had been holding would break her windows as I expelled it. I cannot describe the relief I felt, relief that was later confirmed by both Beckett and Beauvoir when I asked them each to confirm a story about their relationship. When he was a struggling writer, Beckett submitted the first part of a story to Sartre's magazine, Les Temps modernes. Everyone knew it was Beauvoir who did the hard work of putting the magazine together, and also that it was she who made most of the editorial decisions. She accepted the submission and it was published to critical acclaim among the small readership of the magazine. Some weeks later Beckett submitted the second half of the story, only to have Beauvoir refuse it and tell him that the magazine could not waste any more space on such trivia when there were so many important political issues that needed to be addressed. Beckett never forgave her, and he made his resentment public. He wrote her a scathing letter, a copy of which was published after his death in his collected letters. She threw the original away and dismissed him as unworthy of further consideration.

From that day on, they cordially detested each other. I had placed myself squarely in the middle of their contretemps, but in this case it worked in my favor. I would have the same freedom to write about her that I had had while writing about him. I considered myself the most fortunate of writers as we said goodbye that day.

28

I returned to Philadelphia the day before classes began, to a schedule that had me running from one end of campus to the other. My mailbox was overflowing with notices of committees to which I had been appointed, graduate dissertations I was asked to advise, and proposals from undergraduates interested in pursuing independent studies. Requests for Beckett-related reviews or articles alone could have occupied me full-time. Because I was expecting any day to have the all-important second book contract that would be required for tenure, I also asked to be brought up a year early for consideration, which created a major stir and elicited howls of outrage over my presumption and effrontery. Or, as one of my more sympathetic senior colleagues put it while clucking in mock derision, "What chutzpah!"

To my surprise, the English Department did recommend me for tenure by a mostly positive vote, even though I was not exactly the kind of woman they wanted because I was an untraditional "scholar" and, even worse, far too public a figure. My few allies among the full professors told me that the official letter recommending me put "scholar" in quotes because my colleagues were not sure what to make of me. I should have been concerned when they also told me that two senior members of the department had put "damaging and destructive letters in my dossier." They would not tell me who wrote them, but it was easy enough to guess their identities based on who exerted the most effort smarming and sucking up after their knives proved ineffective.

As for my being "too public," the many accolades that were coming my way probably generated that impression, foremost among them being the National Book Award, the most significant honor of my professional life, which I received that April. Such high-profile recognition did make it seem that I was not following a traditional academic path—whatever that was supposed to be— but I had no doubt that my being a woman was also a problem for some of these established gentlemen. They resented that women were successfully climbing the barricades for admission into other boys' clubs, but it was inspirational for me to know that I was not alone in forging an untraditional path toward tenure. A woman before me had fought and won at Penn, and there were other very public ongoing battles by women at Harvard, Princeton, Rutgers, and probably many other universities I didn't know about.

Everything seemed fine for several weeks, "fine" being my shorthand for quiet days passing without incident, when I was able to sit at my desk and work on my book. All that ended one morning when the dean of the university called as I was drinking my morning coffee. Even though the department had put forward a robust recommendation, his committee (the next step in the tenure process) had rejected it. The full professor in the English Department who had written the more damaging letter of the two in my file, a man who enjoyed a reputation in the world of literature, had gone before the dean's committee in person to argue that "she is not a scholar; she is *only* a biographer." He had enough influence with several members that they succeeded in convincing the rest to reject me. If that vote stood, it would mean that after the spring of 1982, I would not have a job. And I still did not have a book contract.

In the aftermath of this bombshell, I learned who my true friends were. Professors I did not know came from other departments to commiserate and offer advice. Some urged me to fight the decision; others (the majority) told me to start looking for another job and offered to help me find one. The dean, a quiet and dignified man and a genuine scholar, told me to keep quiet and let him work on my behalf. The current committee would be replaced by new members for the fall term and he would present my dossier to the new group. He told me to "keep to your plans, go about your business, and let your dean work for you." So that was what I did.

Things were equally chaotic at home, even though both children were in college and my only daily responsibility was to my husband. From the beginning of our marriage, we had shared household and family responsibilities as equally as possible. This surprised me, growing up as I did in a household where my father never fetched a glass of water if my mother was within hailing distance. Von grew up on an Idaho farm with four siblings, and there was never "man's work" or "woman's work." There was simply work to be done, and everyone pitched in and did it. So it was with us most of the time, but there were periods when one of us felt overburdened, and the years we lived in Philadelphia saw a number of them. In the winter of 1981 our weekly house cleaner retired and we were without one for several months, a period when we were so busy professionally that we had little time to find a replacement or take care of things ourselves. As dust bunnies accumulated, newspapers piled up, and laundry went undone, things grew tense.

Von's job as a museum administrator required extensive socializing, and I, who had hitherto been willing to attend events, was now so involved with my own career that I often could not, nor could I entertain at home with casual suppers or formal dinners as I had always done before. With the success of the Beckett biography in the wider world beyond the Becketteers' sphere of influence, I was receiving offers from other institutions to give lectures or be a guest lecturer on a longer-term basis. There were even hints from other universities that teaching positions might be available in my field, with invitations to visit other campuses and let myself be looked over as a possible prospect. Ever mindful of the precarious tenure situation, I tried to accept as many as I could. Several times each month I packed up and Von had to drive me to or from various airports or train stations, which meant leaving him in charge of a large house and four pets on top of his day job and evening obligations. He felt neglected and abandoned, and rightly so. Yet while I felt tremendous guilt for not being available, I also felt a certain degree of resentment.

I was no longer the "housewife who dabbles," as I had been dubbed by former friends in the Junior League and the PTA, even as I supported the family with a full-time job as a newspaper reporter while my husband was in graduate school. I remember a lot of *tsk-tsk*ing and head shaking when I gave up volunteerism to forge a career as a scholar-writer. Despite the broader social changes under way, it was still a man's world. I had a full-time job that most men in my immediate circle envied, but I had very little of the professional support they enjoyed. I had 215 students in a British novel survey course and 24 in a British novel seminar, and no teaching assistant to help me with the grading. Nor did I have a work-study student, that all important gofer who would perform the many adjunct services to my teaching that I did not have time to do. I could not help but think the double standard in most households applied in the office as well: we women were being told that we could have it all, but only after we agreed to do it all.

It was not an easy time for either Von or me, and after far too many heated exchanges, we eventually agreed on the old saying that what we both needed was a good wife. And because we were not going to get one, we would have to respect each other's commitment to our professional lives and work something out.

Meanwhile, my work on the Beauvoir biography was at a standstill. My plan was to have myself ready to go to Paris as soon as the semester ended, by the first of June at the very latest, and I would rent an apartment big enough to house Von, the children, and several other family members who would come for visits when they had free time. However, the semester was so frenetic that I did not have nearly enough time to prepare for the intense interviews I envisioned, both with Beauvoir and with her family and friends.

At the end of the semester, just when I was in the deepest confusion over my disorganized life, I was asked to host a panel at a Beckett conference at Ohio State University. I accepted, in the hope that this meant the unrelenting hostile attacks were finally over. (Sadly, they were not.) While there, an Australian professor at Griffith University asked if I would be interested in becoming the visiting scholar in their Institute for Modern Biography. I laughed off his query, because it seemed that the only reason I had been invited to the conference was so I could hear in person criticism that ranged from the snide to the overt. I could not wait to get home to start paying attention to Simone de Beauvoir. I had put that work on hold for far too long.

My one promising stateside interview was scheduled for May 10, when I was to go to Sag Harbor to interview Nelson Algren, one of the most important men in Simone de Beauvoir's life. Algren and I had exchanged several phone calls to settle on a date, and in each one he had gone on at great and angry length about how eager he was to tell his side of the story about their romance. I thought that meeting him would be crucial to my work and would do much to help me organize questions about the men in her life besides Sartre. I woke up on May 9 to several phone messages telling me that Nelson Algren had been found dead after an apparent heart attack. I was stunned by the news but also angry with myself. I had put off seeing him for the previous five months because of the unrelenting pressures of academic responsibilities, and now it was too late forever.

I had been in touch with Algren's agent, the legendary Candida Donadio, throughout the many months I had been unable to find time to meet him, and we spoke again two days after he died. She told me to give her two weeks to sort things out on her end, and she also suggested that I call Algren's lawyers immediately so that when I phoned her later, she might have their permission to show me the "goldmine" he had left behind, especially the 350 letters he had exchanged during his love affair with Beauvoir. However, she warned that he had died without leaving a will, which meant that the lawyers had to find his nearest heirs, and they might present an insurmountable stumbling block.

Dick McDonough at Little, Brown, and Robert Ginna, Algren's editor and friend, painted a similar, if more colorful, picture. They told me everything was probably still in the Sag Harbor house. No relatives had claimed Algren's body, so Candida did, and took care of all the arrangements. The day before he died, Algren had given an angry interview in which he made all sorts of ugly remarks about Beauvoir, ending with how he was going to sell the letters and make a lot of money.

I wrote in the *DD* that *"this could well be the goldmine I will never see. And to think I let all this tenure shit keep me from getting it!"* I was so furious with myself for allowing academic politics to keep me from seeing Algren that I could hardly think straight, let alone write to his lawyers. It didn't help when colleagues and friends joked that "some people will do anything to avoid having to talk to Deirdre Bair." I have always regretted not having Algren's personal testimony for Beauvoir's biography, but it became a catalyzing moment: from then on, I never let anything stand in the way of seeing an important source.

I still did not have a book contract as May became June, but I did get a fellowship that would give me the academic year 1981–1982 free from teaching. The Mary Ingraham Bunting Fellowship at Radcliffe College was a mixed blessing; indeed it was a significant honor, for which I have been eternally grateful, but it was also one that required residence on the Harvard campus. If Von and I found it almost impossible to coordinate our professional and personal lives while living in the same house, how were we to manage with me commuting such a distance?

And speaking of distance, another shock came with a phone call in mid-June from Australia. It came at our dinner hour, and it happened that we had both children, some of their friends, and two of my colleagues dining with us that evening, all of whom were eager to weigh in on the news. The professor I had met at the Beckett conference had been serious about the offer to visit Griffith University in Brisbane. A formal invitation was extended for me to accept a residency at the (alas, now defunct) Institute of Modern Biography from mid-July through September, which would coincide nicely with the beginning of my Bunting Fellowship in October. It was a rollicking evening as everyone around our table was insistent that I must accept. Everyone, that is, but Von and me. We were unsettled by the possibility of how much more upheaval this second separation would cause, but somehow we managed to be good hosts even as we avoided looking at each other, letting the questions about how we would manage swirl around us, unanswered.

After several days of nonstop debate, we decided that I would accept the Australian invitation instead of going to Paris to conduct research. The children's annual college expenses were about to hit, Australia paid handsomely, and I still did not have an official book contract. Also, the family would visit me "down under," a welcome change from the old haunts that made going to Paris almost as routine as going to New York. And I would also accept the Bunting Fellowship, but try to come home every weekend.

With everything I had to do before I went anywhere, I was actually happy to fall back into the happy-housewife mode for a brief time, even if it meant putting the Beauvoir research aside. I lined up a dependable weekly house cleaner, spent days and nights filling the freezer, and created a master calendar of all the chores that had to be done, the dates for paying bills, and the family birthdays and anniversaries that I had always acknowledged but would now have to leave to Von. Frustration over not being able to do my own necessary work bubbled on low heat in the background, but I felt that all these things were my responsibility and I had to keep them under control. I still thought that way, even though I knew it was not my job "to make the world safe for democracy," as the analyst I had consulted during the Beckett book once told me. But somehow I could not get it out of my head that I should still be trying.

29

There was one pressing Beauvoir-related task, to tell her that because of the Australia invitation and the Bunting Fellowship, I could not go to Paris until the start of 1982, when I could dedicate the two months between Bunting semesters to being there. I composed a very careful letter outlining my reasons for accepting these honors and postponing our meetings. I included a slightly embellished version of the preparatory background research I was doing and a long list of people I had identified to interview during my time in Paris. From the beginning I recognized that Beauvoir liked schedules and plans, so I adopted the habit of keeping her informed. I saw no problem with telling her whom I wished to interview and what archives I would need to consult, but the one thing I never told her in advance was what documents or correspondence in her personal possession I would need. Working with Beckett had taught me not to risk creating a possible difficulty until I absolutely had to.

I sent this letter in June, after several weeks of worry. I had called immediately after Algren died to ask if there was anything I could do for her and had been unable to reach her by phone, a silence that persisted. I phoned several people in Paris who were normally in contact with her, but she had told no one where she was going, and none could explain why she was unavailable. Later Beauvoir told me that the press was hounding her, so she went to hide at her friend Sylvie Le Bon's apartment.*

One of those close to Beauvoir to whom I reached out was Ellen

---

* Le Bon became known as Le Bon de Beauvoir after Beauvoir adopted her.

Wright, the widow of the novelist Richard Wright, who sometimes acted as Beauvoir's agent and liaison with English-language publishers. She told me the alarming news of rumors that Beauvoir was ill with a possible cancer. Ellen, who often expressed unorthodox opinions, said she herself was worried because she believed people could wish cancer on themselves, and in her view Beauvoir had that kind of mind-set: "Who knows what losing Sartre and now Algren might have done to her." I learned fairly soon after this conversation that Ellen, like Maria Jolas before her, could be an unreliable source.

As Maria had done with Beckett, Ellen Wright maintained her own version of Simone de Beauvoir's reality, which was not rooted firmly in fact. Beauvoir did not have such a mind-set: in all the years I knew her, and despite obvious signs of failing health, she considered herself wholly healthy—invincible, really. She did pay attention to matters of her physical well-being, but only to those that could be addressed with holistic methods of healing, particularly kinesthesia. She ignored anything that would have required medication or other conventional medical treatments.

At the end of May, I finally connected with Beauvoir on the telephone. She told me that it was *"probably Sartre's daughter who is spreading the rumors"* that she was ill. In fact, she told me, she was so healthy that she was planning a trip to New York, *"probably around July tenth with her girlfriend Sylvie."** She hoped to spend time with me then. However, it took two years to finalize her on-again, off-again travel plans before she went to New York, and throughout that time I learned something else about her, best expressed by her American friend John Gerassi: *"She could turn on a dime."*

When I asked him to explain, he told me of the curious contrast between the woman who could form instant opinions but then

---

* Beauvoir was referring to Arlette Elkaïm-Sartre, whom Sartre adopted in the last years of his life. And "girlfriend" was her word for Sylvie.

become utterly inflexible in her judgments, stubbornly holding to views that she knew were inaccurate or incorrect, and the woman who could be instantly spontaneous when she decided to do something or go somewhere; she was famous for going away without telling anyone, which created enormous worry for her close friends. And, Gerassi added, *"She is also a terrible procrastinator, and you have to be careful when she makes delay after delay, or tells you why she can or can't do something. It isn't that she's lying, but she does make an awful lot of excuses, and when she finally gets around to going somewhere or doing something, she hates to be called out for the lies and excuses. You better be careful with how you approach her when you ask about these things."*

This was hardly what I wanted to hear as I set off on my worldwide travels. On top of no tenure (and the possibility of no future job), no book contract, and a household in disarray, this insight into Simone de Beauvoir was not the most encouraging information. Nevertheless, I could not dwell on it, so I fell back on one of my favorite expressions: I would worry about it when the time came.

I flew to Brisbane and spent three highly rewarding months meeting Australian scholars and writers who became lifelong friends. There was a strong feminist presence throughout the country and a burgeoning interest in studies relating to women's issues, so I talked as much about Beauvoir as I did about Beckett and his biography. When I left Australia and arrived in Boston at the end of September, I was still reeling from the exhilaration of the engagement, only to find the same sort of excitement among the women who were my colleagues for the upcoming academic year. Early on, several of us who gathered for brown-bag lunches at the big table in the conference room discovered that even though we were in very different disciplines—historians, literary scholars, political scientists, economists, and folklorists—we approached our research topics with a surprisingly similar technique and methodology. Our research centered on issues pertaining to women, and the only thing that differed among us was the professional vocabulary unique to each of our disciplines.

By the time the semester ended in December, after three months of intensive reading and conversations, I had gained many insights into Simone de Beauvoir's writings, her place in French cultural life, her intellectual contributions to her society, her friendships, her travels, even her love affairs. I had accumulated a huge pile of file cards with questions I wanted to ask her, and all I needed now was to go to Paris and get her answers. I could hardly contain my enthusiasm as I set off for two months of her company.

30

I arrived in Paris in January 1982 to find the exact same circumstances as the previous year. Once again Simone de Beauvoir was all business, her brusque voice telling me to come again on her birthday, January 9, but this time at 4 p.m. (which became our usual time for every meeting thereafter). She said she looked forward to seeing me and ended the call. Even though her blunt directness was always slightly unsettling, I actually found it comforting after the mind games I had played with Samuel Beckett every time I tried to arrange meetings.

I had flown over with my daughter and her classmates, who were returning to finish their junior year at the University of Bologna in Italy. Katney and I were to spend a week together in Paris, but we arrived with such severe colds that neither of us could venture further out of bed than to the nearest shop that sold chicken soup and orange juice. I was renting a new apartment on this trip, which the owner had not told me was at the bottom of an air shaft in an interior courtyard where no daylight penetrated. The heat seldom worked, and the weather refused to cooperate. I desperately needed to replace my elegant dress boots with a sturdy outdoor pair that would let me navigate the frozen ice and snow on dangerous Paris streets that were neither cleared nor sanded.

Such topics did not come up in my conversations with Simone de Beauvoir, because small talk was not her strong suit. Several years would pass before I told her anything about myself, simply because she did not ask me until then. All she was interested in during the initial interviewing sessions was the book I was about to write, and despite our earlier agreement that she would not impose herself on it, I retained the distinct impression that she expected me to write it under her direction.

I could not help but flash back to my earliest meetings with Samuel Beckett and contrast them with what I faced in early meetings with Simone de Beauvoir. He did not take me seriously at the beginning, but once he realized what kind of book he had agreed to cooperate with, having given his word, he let it happen. Perhaps it is too strong to say that Beauvoir tried to control what I wrote, but I do think she tried to influence me. Considering the kaleidoscopic range of topics she would discuss in a single session and the intensity with which she discussed them, it took me awhile to sort out her strategy.

On her birthday, snow fell steadily, and it was bitterly cold. The weather system that was making my trip miserable had been battering the entire country—there were floods all over France, and the Seine was about to overflow onto the quays. Part of the extensive preparation I had done beforehand was to confide everything from thoughts to fears in the *DD*. This time I wrote: "*I am very nervous and filled with anxiety. She is 74 today and I am not sure what I will find when I get there.*" What I found was "*an absolutely charming woman, warm and friendly, telling me if it would be easier to speak English with my terrible head cold and laryngitis, I should go ahead and she would reply in French.*"

Beauvoir plunked herself down in her usual spot in the corner of one of the daybed-sofas while I stood there, still in my coat, uncertain of what I should do. I took off the coat and decided to sit in one of the three slipper chairs facing her while putting it on the one next to me, as she had not offered to take it or hang it up. In every subsequent meeting I would perform the same little routine of making myself comfortable. Her only concern was for the work ahead.

I noticed that on the coffee table between us she had already set up her own tape recorder next to three or four carefully arranged fountain pens and a small writing pad. I chattered away nervously as I dug into my bag for similar equipment, which I then placed opposite hers. I made a spontaneous gesture of pulling out the pile of notecards with questions I intended to ask, my "intellectual solitaire" cards, probably to show her that I, too, had the materials of "work." Beckett had never seen the cards I made during the time we worked together, and he had no idea how I slaved before each meeting to memorize and mentally arrange the order in which I wanted to ask them. But Beauvoir was different, and her eyes actually lit up when she saw the first pile I presented. It proved to her that I took the forthcoming book seriously and that I had indeed spent the previous year doing research, reading intensively, coming up with various theories. This initial pile, a good two to three inches thick, contained only the easy questions I thought we might cover at the first meeting. I had several more such piles back in the apartment, ready and waiting for future sessions.

And so we began. I thought I would ease into my questioning by asking about her earliest childhood memories, but she went first because she wanted to thank me. "Women come from all over the world to write about me, but all they want to write about is *The Second Sex*." Here she pounded one fist into the other open hand as she said, "I wrote so much else. I wrote philosophy, politics, fiction, autobiography . . ." She seemed to be pausing to catch her breath after every genre, and then she said, "You are the only one who wants to write about everything. Everyone else only wants to write about feminism." It threw me off-balance, but I did not have the luxury of reflecting on her generous appraisal until after I left, when I grasped the truth in it. During the 1970s and 1980s she had been slotted into the niche of feminist icon—all well and good, but she did not want to be there in perpetuity. Aware of her many different contributions to culture and society and extremely proud of them, she wanted posterity to acknowledge all her accomplishments.

After I thanked her for her comment, I launched into my first questions about her childhood. Her answers to the first one or two were perfunctory, and I could tell she had something else on her mind. She interrupted me as I began to ask another and said, "Look here, I understand you have made arrangements to talk to many people here in Paris. Who will you see?" I stopped the questioning and pulled out the date book with the list of all my appointments. She seemed impressed, nodding her head repeatedly and making a little noise that sounded like clucking. I was to be in Paris for two solid months, until the end of February, and I had booked interviews and appointments for every day that I did not see her. She and I were to meet at least twice each week, reserving the possibility of a third or even a fourth session if need be.

I told her I would begin my interviews with the persons to whom she was closest, those she and Sartre had chosen to call their "family." Among them were Jacques-Laurent Bost and his wife, Olga; her ex-lover and good friend Claude Lanzmann; her Sartrean friends Jean Pouillon and Jean-Bertrand Pontalis; her childhood friend Geraldine "GéGé" Pardo; and her friend who had just become her newly adopted daughter, Sylvie Le Bon de Beauvoir. Equally important was her sister, Hélène de Beauvoir de Roulet.

She was inordinately pleased that I had arranged interviews with Nathalie Sarraute and Marguerite Duras, for she was extremely proud of being ranked in their company. She had the same reaction when I told her I had talked to Mary McCarthy, for she was always eager to hear what American writers thought of her work. I showed her the list I had made of writers, publishers, professors, and feminist activists and asked her to contribute the names of anyone I might have omitted. She was quite excited about all those names but was thrilled most of all that I would meet Yvette Roudy, the minister for the rights of women, a cabinet position in the French government.

I also showed her the list of people I had interviewed during the previous year, mostly Americans but also French scholars and writers who had attended conferences in the United States or Canada. She liked it that the list contained the names of scholars whose specialty was Sartre, for she felt that many of them did not take her seriously: "They ignore me; they don't want to admit how important Sartre and I were to each other."

Once Beauvoir saw how intensely I had studied her life and work and how much preparation I had done to write about both, she relaxed and said that because we had done enough for one day, we should stop now and have a relaxing drink before I left. This first encounter set down a pattern that would repeat, with little variation, for the next five years. "Do you drink scotch?" she asked, and before I could answer she was up and shuffling toward her refrigerator, which was not hidden in her kitchen but in clear sight on the back wall of the living area. When she opened it, I could see that it was spotless, pristine, and empty save for a large bottle of Johnnie Walker Red—and sometimes in subsequent meetings a bottle of vodka as well. At one point there was also a plastic-covered arrangement of petits fours on a shelf, but it remained untouched and unmoved for the better part of a year. I thought perhaps it was not real food but an art object of some kind. Occasionally there would be a dried-out slice of something she had forgotten to eat or some fruit long past its prime, but most of the time all the refrigerator contained was the liquor. She told me she did not keep food because either Sylvie brought her dinner or she went out with friends. In her later years, when she did not go out to lunch routinely, Sylvie also brought her something for the next day.

While she was fussing to collect the bottle and glasses, I had the opportunity to look around the seating area. I saw the thick gold satin spreads on the daybed-sofas and the pillows that topped them in gemlike colors of amethyst, emerald, and sapphire, the same colors that graced each of the little chairs that faced them. The sofas were clear on that first occasion, but by the time she grew used to my visits, she did not bother to hide the clutter that accumulated where she usually sat and which gave the setting a slightly comical aspect. Beauvoir, like her mother before her, exhibited the practical behavior of a frugal bourgeois housewife: to protect the gold coverlet of the sofa where she liked best to curl up and read, she covered it with a flamboyant American Indian blanket. It was especially jarring in the midst of her one attempt at decorative elegance, since the blanket was where she kept her telephone and piled books, manuscripts, stacks of unanswered mail, wadded paper handkerchiefs, a comfortable old sweater, and the other detritus of a writer's workplace.

It was dark outside when we finished the work session, and she had reached up from her perch on the sofa to turn on the floor lamp made for her by Diego Giacometti. It was next to the shelf where she had a collection of his brother Alberto's tiny metal figures, and it threw enough light to make them cast magical shadows. She shuffled back to the coffee table, carrying the bottle, two glasses, and a battered pewter jigger. There was a large Mexican glass tumbler for her and a small plain glass for me. Into mine she carefully poured one jiggerful of scotch, putting it aside before filling her own glass to the brim. She told me that "Sylvie waters the scotch because she thinks I drink too much. She thinks I don't notice, but I do." It had not been diluted too much on that first visit, but in later years I had trouble swallowing what was little more than faintly colored water. Beauvoir, on the other hand, hastily downed several glasses to my one, as if that would be the only way she could get enough.

She was an old woman when I met her, and as she was comfortable in my presence, she was often dressed in the dowdy red robe she had worn on our very first meeting. There were times when I took someone to meet her, or when I was escorting her to an event or a dinner, and on those occasions she made an effort to impress. Her usual outfit then consisted of neat brown trousers, a beige shirt, a patterned sweater-vest, and of course the ubiquitous turban. When she was in the red robe, I tried not to dwell on how I described her in the *DD*, as "*lumpy, grumpy, frumpy, and dumpy,*" but instead to envision the beautiful, vital, and dynamic young woman she had been. That was the woman I wanted to write about and the one I wanted to describe most strongly, an accomplished woman in the fullness of her life.

The whiskey at the end of each session—usually running two hours, if not longer—became our ritual. Those post-interview conversations were never tape-recorded, nor did I take notes, for this was our social hour, when we were to enjoy random conversation as we decompressed after what were sometimes fractious and argumentative sessions. That did not stop me from taking extensive notes immediately after they ended, when I rushed down to my favorite café, the Dôme on the boulevard du Montparnasse, to sit at a little table overlooking the street where I could people-watch, drink a glass of white wine, and write or record my impressions.

Very often Beauvoir volunteered information in these post-interview conversations that surprised me, as she did on the first meeting. I had the feeling she was trying to woo me when she launched into a diatribe about how my book would differ from some of the recent ones about her. It was clear that she read everything, and unlike Samuel Beckett, who professed ignorance but revealed significant familiarity with those about him, Beauvoir did not hesitate to express her opinions. She liked Carol Ascher's 1981 book but was disappointed because Ascher wrote "too much about herself and forgot to write about me." Of Axel Madsen, "I thought I should sue him for all the lies he wrote, but Sylvie told me not to bother. It would give him too much attention." Benny Lévy (also known as Pierre Victor), who wrote about Sartre in the last distressing years of his life, drew her most furious ire: "I hate him! I hate him!"

She often switched topics rapidly, sometimes more quickly than I could follow. After dissecting all the books about her, she asked what she should call me. Should I be "Madame Bair," or could she call me—and here she tried to pronounce my first name, which came out sounding something like "Dared" but with an extremely long and highly emphasized r, that French glottal roll I could never manage. I told her she must call me whatever was easiest for her, and she decided on "Darrred" (or so it sounded to me). I never asked what I should call her, for to me she was always "Madame" or "Madame de Beauvoir."

It was she who, from the first meeting, moved naturally to a kind of personal closeness that I had never had with Samuel Beckett. All during the years I wrote about him, I regretted the formality and sometimes resented how he would engage more personally with relative strangers who contacted him about some aspect of their work which couldn't have been nearly as important or innately personal as mine. However, once Beauvoir began to invite "Darrred" to join her at meetings such as book publication parties and gallery openings, and to go to dinner with her and some of her friends, I always pulled back. If the event was something I thought useful to observe for the book, such as a feminist meeting to plot some sort of activity or action, I accompanied her. If, however, it was purely social, I tried to invent a prior engagement or some other excuse.

Once the Beckett book was published, I realized that Samuel Beckett had done me a favor by keeping me at a distance. It ensured that our relationship was entirely professional and it freed me to be totally objective when I wrote about him. From the beginning I realized that I really liked Simone de Beauvoir, and I recognized that it could be a dangerous emotion. It would be far better for me to keep to a professional distance, but she made it very difficult for me to do so.

"Ah, Darrred," she would begin, and I would mentally cringe: *Uh-oh, here it comes . . .* And indeed it would, for she always had "a nice young friend" who wanted to come to America and needed a job, and she was perfectly sure that my university was always in need of a native French-speaker on the faculty. Of the half-dozen or so candidates she proposed, none had any sort of qualifications, but that didn't matter to her, and she refused to accept that I had no authority to hire them and no clout to persuade anyone else to do me this favor.

One whom she was determined to send to Philadelphia was someone who had no desire to go there, the novelist Claude Courchay. He had just won the prestigious Prix RTL for his novel *Retour à Malaveil* and bought a typical turn-of-the-century house on the last remaining street of them in Montparnasse. Beauvoir was extremely close to Claude, and he was her one friend to whom I became close also, as he did much to help me gain an accurate understanding of Beauvoir's place in French culture and society.

Of all her protégés, there was only one for whom I was successful in finding a teaching job, and in the process I also found him a wife. Serge Julienne-Caffié, who had written an eloquent and perceptive book about Beauvoir, was living in New York when Penn's Wharton School needed a French professor for its international business program, and he agreed to teach the course. I introduced him to my colleague the anthropologist Peggy Sanday and was delighted when they married.

The miserable January days were passing in a blur because I was too busy to notice how often it snowed and how cold it was. I was up and out of the dark and gloomy apartment early every day for interviews, and when I was not interviewing someone, I was in the Bibliothèque nationale or one of the other archives where there were documents I needed to see. I worked with Beauvoir two or three times each week, and because the questions were still dealing mostly with her childhood, girlhood, and youth, none raised any red flags and the sessions unfolded pleasantly. I told her I would be seeing her sister in early February, and I had contacted her two cousins and girlhood companions, Magdeleine Mantis de Bisschop and Jeanne de Beauvoir Dauriac, who still lived at Meyrignac and La Grillère, the family estates in southwest France where Beauvoir had spent her summers. She was delighted and said she was "content with 'our' progress." I was not sure how I felt about her use of *our* progress.

I was not quite so content, because aspects of my "real life" kept intruding. Carl Brandt contacted me to say there had been another round of mass firings at Little, Brown and this time Dick McDonough had been among them. Carl was still after me to sign Little, Brown's insulting contract, but I had no idea if that would remain an option now that Dick was gone. I received some better news from Penn, where the dean had indeed done his work and his new committee had awarded my tenure that fall. It was bittersweet news for me: I was relieved to know I would have a job to return to in the fall of 1982, if only because it seemed unlikely that I was going to have a book contract to support me and my research.

I was very grateful to be away from academic politics, and I was also relishing every day in Paris, as each one brought something new and exciting for my book. I was energized by the way things were coming together on so many different levels. For example, articles about conservative right-wing newspapers in the early years of the twentieth century explained so much about Beauvoir's father's attitude toward his daughters' upbringing. Coupled with the memories of her girlhood friend GéGé Pardo, passages in Beauvoir's memoir helped to explain some of the rebellious decisions she had made during her teen years. Things were going very well that winter, and I especially enjoyed having the luxury of time to sift through ideas, sort through information, and posit conclusions. My mantra had become "this is what I think today, no doubt subject to change tomorrow," and most often it was.

I made some lifelong friends on that research trip who provided the necessary socializing over lunches and dinners, where convivial conversations often led to ways of thinking or research modes I would not otherwise have learned about. Here, too, I was helped by journalists working for American and British publications and longtime residents of France, who became important sources for deep background and were often instrumental in helping me navigate bureaucracies that would otherwise have remained securely closed. Among the prominent and outspoken French feminists who became good friends, I counted the professor of American literature Marie-Claire Pasquier and the feminist publisher (and no relation) Françoise Pasquier. Mary Lou Decossaux, an American graduate student of French descent, became the research assistant I truly needed. Karen Offen, an American scholar of French women's history who was working in archives, became an excellent sounding board for my ever-changing thoughts. It was such a pleasure to meet them for drinks and dinners after my tranquil daily routine, and I was thoroughly enjoying it—until the bombshell of a phone call.

I had just returned from a long day of reading microfilm in an archive and was damp and disheveled after trudging through a sleet storm, eager to take off my wet shoes before any more blisters could form. I could hear the phone ringing as I unlocked the door. The call was from a professor in another department at Penn who was on sabbatical in Paris and who said he had been appointed by the university's honorary degree committee to offer one to Simone de Beauvoir. Officiously, he told me he was "authorized" to order me to provide her contact information. Then I was to step aside, as he would take over all meetings with her to conduct this business.

My mind was a sieve after my long day in the archive, and his arrogance left me befuddled. It was fortunate that I had only the evening and a restless night to stew, for early the next morning the concierge delivered a formal and polite letter sent by the university's president saying that the professor would be contacting me and asking if I would be so kind as to use my influence in helping him persuade Beauvoir to accept the degree. No one had informed me that this honorary degree was on offer, and no one had included me in planning how to approach her. It seemed that although my scholarship was that of "only a biographer," my subject was of sufficient merit to be honored, even though I—the creator of the project—was to be marginalized. The irony rankled. However, it was a tribute to a remarkable and deserving woman, so of course I would help the university, even though I resented the gall of, as I wrote at the time, *"the big boys who just take over and push the little girl aside."*

The day I received the president's letter was also the day I received another blow, this one not quite so upsetting but still a disruption. Simone de Beauvoir phoned to tell me that she had decided suddenly to go away from Paris for two weeks, from February 1 to 15. She thought she might be coming down with a mild case of the flu, and Sylvie had persuaded her to go to Biarritz to take the waters at a spa she liked. I spent the next several hours fuming until I told myself no matter, never mind that we had set meetings for three days during each of those weeks; I had plenty of archival work I could attend to. But before she left, I had to talk to her about this degree.

She moved to end the telephone conversation as abruptly as usual, but I managed to jump in to say I had something I needed to discuss with her and asked to see her that day even though we had not scheduled an appointment. She told me to come at two and not stay long because she needed a post-luncheon rest before seeing some of her feminist friends at four.

I got right to the point when I saw her, telling her that a professor from my university wanted to be introduced to her so that he could present the offer of an honorary degree. I wanted her permission to give him her telephone number and her address, in case he wanted to write and not call. She said, dismissively, that she would give him the courtesy of a meeting the next afternoon at four. She asked if I wanted to be there, and I would have been, except that she had already arranged for me to meet Sylvie at 4:30 in her apartment on the avenue du Maine, and I preferred to keep that appointment. She said I should warn the professor that she had been offered many such honors before this one and had refused them all because they required her to be there in person: "I am an old lady now, and no longer capable of making such extravagant journeys." I thought it ironic that she was still talking about flying to New York and then traveling up and down the East Coast by car and train. I kept the thought to myself and said I would tell him about the appointment but I would leave everything else to her.

When the professor told her that she would be required to accept the honor in person, just as she had suspected, she declined the invitation (as he later told me) "most graciously," saying that she could no longer travel. I could tell that he was upset by her refusal, especially after he blurted out in a rage, "How, then, could she tell me about making a trip to New York one year from now, when she will be even older?" My jaw dropped to think that she had told him this, but he explained that after she asked about his accent and he said he was a native New Yorker, she told him quite casually that she was planning a visit. That was how I learned that the trip she had been planning off and on for the past several years was back on again. But because she had changed her mind two or three times previously, I knew not to take it seriously and I said nothing to the professor.

The end of my two months in Paris was fast approaching, and the pleasant days of setting my own schedule would soon be over. I dreaded having to return to all the intrusions upon my book. I would be going back to Cambridge and the sabbatical would last until May, but I doubted I would find the tranquility for reflection and writing that I was counting on. That night, while plotting how many interviews I could fit into the time when Beauvoir would be in Biarritz, I made a list of all the things other people expected me to do in my professional life. It was a long one, and at the end I felt close to hopeless about how I was ever going to write this book and where the money, never mind the time, would come from.

But counting the current one, I still had three weeks in Paris, and I decided to make the most of them.

31

During the two weeks Beauvoir was away, I conducted interviews every day. As I met her relatives, friends, and acquaintances, I noted a clear distinction between her French friends and Beckett's French friends. To start, hers did not like to hold meetings in the mornings, and the idea of an early-morning breakfast meeting, popular in America, was horrifying. Some of her writer friends who had spent time in the United States actually shuddered at the suggestion, reliving how they had been subjected to such meetings in New York or Los Angeles. Occasionally someone would meet me for morning coffee, but never before eleven. That suited me just fine, as it gave me time to prepare my questions for that day's work.

I found another difference with Beckett's friends, who tended to speak good English because they had participated in the wider cultural world. Many had lived, worked, or studied in England or the United States, and they brought a broader perspective to France's place—and by extension theirs—in the intellectual and cultural firmament. Despite Beauvoir's extensive travels and her work analyzing other cultures, her circle at home in Paris was curiously restricted. Her milieu was the philosophy, politics, and literature of her native country, and the people with whom she associated most closely reflected that. Few spoke any language but their own, and if they traveled, it was mostly for holidays and vacations to places where others just like them congregated. Few saw much need to move away from Paris even for their work; professors who held positions in universities far from the city commuted to their jobs and kept their primary residence in the capital. Everyone

I spoke to was highly sophisticated, but compared to the French people I had met working on the Beckett biography, this group was relatively less diverse in their outlooks and ways of thinking. This was their conscious choice, to be sure, a simple preference to concentrate their interests and endeavors on their society of origin. By spending time with them, I gained insights into French history and culture that helped me to understand why Simone de Beauvoir had made so many of the controversial decisions her non-French readers questioned.

I thought that understanding Beauvoir's relationships with men was a good place to start my interviews, and with Sartre and Algren both dead, Claude Lanzmann, renowned as the creator of the film *Shoah*, was one of the first men I contacted. He was a journalist and her junior by seventeen years when they met after he wrote an article about Sartre, and they were together as lovers from 1952 to 1959. They remained devoted friends until the end of her life.

Unlike most of her other close friends, Lanzmann said he preferred to come to my apartment rather than meet in a restaurant or hotel lobby, and on a Saturday morning, when he would be free for the day and could talk at length. I agreed, even though I was not happy to have even my most understanding friends come into that dark and dreary place at the bottom of an air shaft. And on that freezing day when it was sleeting, the heat was so minimal that I worried I would have to greet Lanzmann in my coat and hat. When he all but burst in, though, I soon forgot about the cold. He was a large man and a formidable presence, flushed with the success of *Shoah*, and he quickly got down to his own agenda.

He illustrated another difference between Beckett's French friends and what I called in the *DD* Beauvoir's *"French" French friends*. The Beckett interviews usually began with an exchange of pleasantries before I eased into my questions, beginning with general ones, such as when did you first meet, what was he like in the early days of your friendship—always something that would lead to pleasant memories and positive responses. Conversation would flow rather leisurely, during which time I would be on the alert for nuggets of new information so that I could casually shift toward a topic for which I wanted more detail, more depth. I was seldom able to do this with Beauvoir's *"French"* French.

With Lanzmann I tried to begin the conversation by asking about the weather—a safe topic in any country or culture, I thought—and offering coffee to warm him. He brushed off my attempt at small talk by saying he had come on the Métro and was well caffeinated, and before he even removed his coat, he launched into a discussion of the woman he had known for so many years, first as her lover and now as a devoted and protective friend. Over the next several hours, he talked and I listened. He knew what he wanted to tell me, so I let him hold forth, because everything he said was both relevant and important. Occasionally I broke in to ask a question that related to his topic; sometimes he stopped to answer it directly, but mostly he kept on with what he was saying until he came to a natural conclusion. Only then would he answer my question. He was always this way whenever I saw him throughout the rest of Beauvoir's life, and even after her death, when I consulted him to fact-check the manuscript. He was abrasive, seemingly irritated by my probing (and often repeated) questions. He was a difficult and opinionated man, but also extremely insightful and honest. I could argue with and dispute some of his views, but his ultimate defenses of them usually checked out, so I trusted him.

Lanzmann's agenda illustrated another difference between the Beckett and Beauvoir biographies. In the Beckett world, there were not that many people with whom I needed follow-up appointments. With the exception of those who were closest to him, one interview was usually enough to help me ascertain the role an individual had played in his life. In the Beauvoir world, almost every single person I spoke to, no matter how close or how peripheral, required multiple meetings. Each had a specific agenda, which perhaps in proper French intellectual terms I should call a theory or a thesis, and only when they were satisfied that they had expressed it would they allow me to proceed with my questions.

To give some other examples, in my first meeting with Olga

and Jacques-Laurent Bost, they wanted to talk only about Beauvoir's life since Sartre's death. But they had been her close friends throughout her entire adult life, so there was much more I needed to learn from them. I had the feeling that seeing them together was inhibiting what each wanted to tell me, and I was right. It worked out naturally to see them separately when Olga came down with the flu and Bost asked me to meet him in the bar at the Pont Royal. Sitting where he had sat with Sartre and Beauvoir for so many nights was a great tongue-loosener, as he recalled story after story, person after person. Those sessions with Bost alone, usually over many drinks in the early evenings, were immensely rewarding. Olga, perhaps because of her personal past as Sartre's lover and the subject of one of Beauvoir's novels, was far more guarded. I always saw her in their apartment, and after the third meeting I realized that I was upsetting her too much by asking her to relive her intimate relationship with Sartre as well as with Beauvoir. I ended my one-on-one encounters and saw her only one other time, in her husband's company and over a hasty drink.

Pouillon and Pontalis had both read the French translation of my biography of Beckett and written critiques of it, as well as separate articles detailing their respective interpretations of his psychology. They would not talk about Beauvoir until I let them talk first about Beckett, and when they talked about her, they did so in terms of how her life and work differed from his. So many of Beauvoir's friends had read the Beckett biography, and I think many assumed that I would write about Beauvoir through a comparison of her life and work with his. Those who held that view would not discuss Beauvoir until they had exhausted their list of differences between the two writers, from their writing styles to their personalities. Each was determined to see my second book as a continuation of what they deemed the "thesis" of my first, a thesis to which they did not hesitate to offer their "corrections." I could only listen with a polite smile until the first opportunity to break in and get them back on track to talk about Simone de Beauvoir.

Because I was so well aware of the animosity between Beckett and Beauvoir, I was scrupulous about never mentioning one to the other in conversations with her or in correspondence with him. I let them be the ones to bring up each other's name or to ask questions (usually about something connected to my work with them), and I trod carefully when I answered. I found it curious that after so many years, the animosity he held against her and the indifference she showed toward his resentment had never changed.

I was lucky that winter because all the primary players in Simone de Beauvoir's life were in Paris and available for interviews. At the top of the list were her sister, Hélène, and Sylvie, now her officially adopted daughter.

I think Sylvie was leery of me before we met, and she remained cautious and distanced for the remainder of my time working with Beauvoir. Early in January, after our second meeting, Beauvoir and I were having our post-interview *verre* of watered-down scotch when we heard someone inserting a key into the apartment door. Beauvoir's face brightened; she blushed, sat up straight, and leaned forward eagerly. "That will be Sylvie," she said. "She wants to meet you." She sprang this on me as a total surprise.

A slim dark-haired woman of medium height looking to be in her fifties came in and crossed over immediately to Beauvoir without glancing at me. They exchanged multiple kisses in greeting and a few words about the bad weather and heavy traffic before Beauvoir turned to introduce "Darrred" to her friend Sylvie. At such first-name familiarity, I thought I saw a dark shadow cross Sylvie's face, so I, who had risen as a sign of respect, held out my hand and called her "Madame."

She eyed me intently but said nothing in reply and addressed her conversation entirely to Beauvoir. I sat quietly smiling but not attempting to join in. Soon after, Sylvie included me by explaining that she had stopped in only briefly to see what Beauvoir wanted for dinner and now she was on her way to shop for it. As she was leaving, I told her I was very pleased to meet her and asked if she would be willing to grant me a separate interview. She seemed surprised and was clearly flustered until Beauvoir jumped in to say, "Of course Sylvie will see you. We will set a date tonight when we have dinner."

Several days later I went to Sylvie's apartment on the avenue du Maine. Again she was guarded, wary, and, I felt certain, seeing me only under duress. Beauvoir had cautioned me to "be gentle" with Sylvie and to let her know as much as I could about the book I intended to write. I had the feeling that she wanted me to reassure Sylvie that I had no desire to replace her in Beauvoir's affections and no intention of trying to do so, so that was what I set out to do. I spent the first part of our meeting telling her about myself, about my husband and college-age children, my career as a professor. That struck a collegial chord, as she, too, was a teacher. We commiserated about the indifferent attitudes our students had toward learning, and that provided a good segue into some of the topics I hoped to address in the biography, particularly Beauvoir's years as a lycée teacher.

The next several hours passed smoothly—but neither of us let down her guard. I did not want to ask any question that she might consider controversial or negative, because I felt that she did not fully trust me. In fact, throughout our subsequent meetings I always had the feeling that she simply did not like me. I did not dwell on this, nor did I try to change her attitude, because I was not looking for a new best friend or any sort of personal connection. All I wanted was a successful project, a book that would do us both proud.

I was reveling in the work for the new book, but the old one continued to intrude. Aside from the constant questions about Beckett from Beauvoir's friends, I received requests from journalists who heard I was in Paris to interview me about him or to appear on radio shows to talk about him. I declined most of these offers, as the publications involved would be of little benefit to sales of the French translation, and trying to schedule appearances on these very-early-morning programs or after-midnight talk shows was impossible. I did speak on the phone with quite a few of the friends I had made in the Beckett world, but I managed to persuade most of them that I had so little time and so much to do for the new book that I could not see them. In retrospect, I think I did this because I was so fearful of contamination. This was a new and completely separate project, and I needed to make a clean break.

As for Beckett himself, I paid him my usual courtesy of letting him know that I was in Paris and gave him the address and phone number of my apartment. He sent one of his usual replies midway through my stay, one of his calling cards inserted into a letter-sized envelope. He wrote that he was overburdened with translations of several of his new plays and planned to stay in Ussy as long as possible to complete the work. Once again he was my phantom, never in my presence but always flitting in my background. It was always unsettling to find out how much he knew about my doings, as this time he knew that I was going to Kassel at the conclusion of my time in Paris to speak at a Beckett symposium—for which he wished me luck.

I was not looking forward to it, but I had accepted the invitation from the German university because I persuaded myself that I had to stand tall in the face of opprobrium and should therefore accept all such invitations. Just after the Beckett book was published, I read a remark made by the sculptor Louise Bourgeois, who told an interviewer that "a woman has no place as an artist until she proves over and over that she won't be eliminated." It became one of the mantras with which I fortified myself for possible combat.

Besides, I could put the conference in Kassel mostly out of mind because on my way I was going to stop at a tiny Alsatian commune called Goxwiller, where I would meet Hélène de Beauvoir. And that I could hardly wait to do.

32

I took an evening train to Strasbourg and spent the night in a properly heated hotel that was so hot after my freezing apartment I had to open the windows before I could sleep. The next morning at ten, Simone de Beauvoir's sister came to take me to her home, where we were to spend the day in conversation. I recognized her the moment she entered the hotel lobby, for Hélène de Beauvoir de Roulet had the same fine bone structure, fair coloring, and exquisite complexion as her sister. The only physical difference between them was their hair; Simone's was a rich brown while Hélène was a natural blonde.

Hélène must have recognized me, too, as I stood at the concierge's desk trying to get his help in changing my incorrect reservations to Kassel on the late-night train. Without a moment's hesitation she took over, and after a single phone call she had corrected the huge mess. She verified something I had learned from talking to Simone's closest friends, those whom she called her "family," and also the feminist women she met with either in groups or singularly: the sisters may have looked alike, but their behavior was entirely different. Simone was completely unable to handle any sort of detail and would become bored or impatient when asked to deal with it. She who had managed every aspect of Sartre's life for years had since his death ceded everything connected with hers to Sylvie. The feminists were often in despair over her unwillingness to contribute to any sort of logistical discussion or to make a decision. Hélène was the exact opposite; to her, problems were meant for solving.

As we drove to Goxwiller, the village on the Route des Vins

where she lived in a renovated seventeenth-century farmhouse, she pointed out every site of historical interest while engaging me in a conversation in which I did most of the talking, mostly about myself. Unlike her sister, she was interested in people, particularly (as she called me) "young ones." She, too, had read the Beckett biography, as had her husband, Lionel de Roulet, a retired diplomat, and she told me they both were eager to talk about it over lunch. But before then she would show me around her house and we would have coffee and talk about her sister.

I was surprised when she turned down tiny village lanes to enter the courtyard to her compound, for I had imagined something on the order of a rural farm. Inside the courtyard was a sort of barn overflowing with what looked like several centuries of farm detritus. Next to it was her summer studio, an enclosed but unheated space where she painted large canvases in warm weather. The main house was a warren of rooms on different levels, evidence of a structure that had been added onto haphazardly over several centuries. It was, however, a cozy and comfortable place where life was obviously lived in contentment. Lionel had a bedroom and study at one end of the structure and Hélène had her bedroom at the other. The bedroom also served as her winter studio, where she worked on smaller projects, and in pride of place on a sturdy table next to her bed was a large flat stone that she used for the work she had recently begun to enjoy, the painstaking etching of copper plates.

We sat there throughout the morning, talking so intensely that Lionel had to call from the other part of the house to remind us that it was getting late for lunch and he was hungry. Hélène was an excellent cook, and the lunch she served, at a beautiful table set with antique china and old family silver, was bountiful. Later, when she served afternoon tea, it was lapsang souchong presented ceremonially in porcelain cups so thin they were translucent. Everything this woman touched was graceful and beautiful, a stark contrast to life on the rue Schoelcher. We joked about how Simone was hopeless with all things domestic, and Hélène imitated her sister's disdain with a dismissive wave of her hand and her sputtering insistence that she had more important things to do.

We talked for long hours as the afternoon became evening, of her days as an art student in Paris and as a diplomat's wife in Portugal and Italy. When we talked of her girlhood, I told her how her colorful memories differed in so many ways from Simone's gloomy ones. I told Hélène how Simone described the family apartment as always dark because it got little outdoor light and her mother would not permit artificial illumination. She burst into laughter as she described the light-filled apartment on the third floor of the building that houses the famous Café de la Rotonde, with large windows that open onto balconies just above the trees that line the boulevard du Montparnasse.

Simone remembered formal occasions during which ladies in hideous black bombazine dresses gathered around a dining table in dour disapproval of the fidgeting children, who were expected to sit in silent respect of their elders. Hélène remembered Sunday afternoons as the happy time after a huge luncheon when their grandfather would request music and someone would play the piano while others sang and the family darling, little doted-on Hélène, would dance, often to a tune from Offenbach's *La belle Hélène*, which was highly popular in Paris at the time. "What did Simone do while you danced?" I asked. "Oh, she probably sulked because she wanted to be off somewhere reading a book instead." Hélène's laughter trilled at the memory. From their girlhood summers on the family estate, Meyrignac, to the relationship between Simone and Jean-Paul Sartre, the discrepancies between what I had heard from Simone and what Hélène was telling me mounted.

These discrepancies created a quandary for me as a biographer, for how could I determine which sister's memory was the more valid? How was I to present "the real truth," and how, in my writing, was I to persuade my reader that it was the objective truth and not my reliance on one witness over another because that was how I wanted it to be and not how it actually was? I wondered why I was so willing to take Hélène for the reliably objective witness and to cast Simone in the role of the unreliable narrator who wanted to shape her personal truth into the story she wanted the world to believe. It was early days in my interviews with Simone de Beauvoir, so this question of objective narrative truth became something I kept in mind always, something I worried over and wrote and rewrote until the manuscript went to the printer and no more changes could be made.

Here is where one of the methods I adopted to write about Beckett carried over into my writing about Beauvoir. Whenever I had multiple sources and whenever they could provide accounts of the same event, incident, situation, I factored them all into an informal compendium. Sometimes it resembled a list, other times a chart, and other times an example of my "three p's," the passionate purple prose where I wrote everything into a kind of narrative that I needed to see in order to pick out what seemed important, accurate, honest, objective—so many qualities were involved here—to arrive at the "real" reality. And even as I was doing all this, I was aware that I might be indulging in the biographical fallacy of giving privilege to one set of facts over another. I liked to think that I showed scrupulous objectivity when I wrote about Beckett and factored into his life story the testimonies of so many of his close relatives, but after this first meeting with Hélène and my early meetings with Simone, I had to wonder if I might be skirting perilously close to giving pride of place, if not actual preference, to one sister's account over the other's. Was I tending toward accepting the version that I wanted to write rather than the one that had actually happened?

I talked about this with Hélène as she drove me to the Strasbourg train station on that cold, rainy night. She urged me to give her sister's memories validation above all others because, as she said repeatedly, "my sister is the most honest person I know. She will never shade the truth to make anything she tells you favor her." And then she qualified her statement: "She will tell you the truth as she knows it, or as she believes it to be. *Not*," she insisted with some vehemence, "not as she *wants* it to be." And as I found, in almost everything I asked Simone directly, Hélène was right.

The conference in Kassel added to my concern about what constituted "the real truth." I knew all the old jokes about how history is written by the last person still living, and one event proved how that last person can perpetuate a lie that future generations should examine carefully. Knowing that Beckett had spent long periods of time in the German state of Hesse, where his Sinclair cousins lived and where the conference was being held, the conveners had searched for anyone who might have remembered Beckett or his cousins. They were especially interested in any information about Peggy, the cousin who died tragically young of tuberculosis and who many scholars believe was the inspiration for the woman in *Krapp's Last Tape*.

When Peggy died, she had a younger sibling who was eight years old and whose very good friend was a little German girl, also eight. The conveners were thrilled to find her, now an elderly woman, and they invited her to share her recollections of being in the Sinclair house during Beckett's visits. She had often boasted throughout the town that she retained many memories of him. Her appearance was billed as a special presentation, and all the attendees were on the edges of their seats as she began to speak.

She was a woman of modest background and little education, and as her memories of the Sinclair household unfolded, it became clear that a small child could not have observed such adult behavior as she described. When the audience pressed her with questions that only a much older observer could have answered, she became red-faced, flustered, and loud. And then she began to invent. She was trying to impress her audience, to give them whatever version of reality they wanted that she could create on the spot, for clearly she had little, if any, recollection of the young Samuel Beckett. It was sad to see how determined she was to please.

Eventually one of the conveners interrupted what had become

a shrill monologue, thanked her for coming, and led her off the stage. As she passed through the audience, she tried to make eye contact, but most people refused to look at her. She was clearly embarrassed and humiliated, and I felt sorry for her. However, it proved once again how a biographer had to weigh and measure every memory before committing anything to posterity. If you can't trust the teller, you cannot trust the tale.

33

The minute the conference ended, I took the train to nearby Frankfurt and then flew back to Paris, not wanting to waste a moment of my last weeks to work. I already had a good fourteen hours of Simone de Beauvoir on tape, six of Hélène, and I had not yet counted how many hours I had of others. I would have several more sessions with Beauvoir and another round with Olga and Bost, which would give me more than enough to listen to on the flight home.

Over coffee on my first morning back in Paris, Ellen Wright surprised me by saying that publishers were suddenly eager to meet me to talk about book contracts. She thought the interest in a book about Beauvoir stemmed from Benny Lévy's new book about Sartre: *"Papers and magazines are filled with stories about Lévy breaking his '2-year silence.' They are all on his side and against the 'vielle clan' [Beauvoir's self-appointed 'family'], but particularly against SdB. I don't know why I am so surprised by this. I should know by now that people just don't like her."* However, if this made French publishers want my book, I would not complain. And when I saw Beauvoir for our interviews, I thought it would be time to start asking the hard questions I had put off until now. It was going to be an interesting week, no doubt about it.

Simone was eager to hear about my visit with Hélène, so we began with my recounting Hélène's recollections. Simone was animated and laughing as she remembered girlhood escapades, particularly the one about how Sartre made his way to Meyrignac one summer during their student years and how she hid him in the pigeon cote at the neighboring estate of La Grillère because of her father's disapproval. Beauvoir became animated while she imitated her cousin Magdeleine smuggling him food hidden in her apron. She was in such a cheerful mood as she told how she sneaked out at night to be with him that I thought this would be an opportune moment to bring up some touchy subjects she had hitherto been reluctant to talk about.

To shift the conversation in that direction, I told her the good news that the publisher of the Beckett biography, Claude Durand at Éditions Fayard, had offered a contract. She was pleased that her biography would also appear under the imprint of this respected publisher. That provided the segue for me to tell her that I had just read the book then dominating the literary news, Benny Lévy's book about Sartre. Could we discuss it? Her mood changed in an instant. Her face flushed and her voice thickened as she began to talk about Sartre's last years. Whenever I had asked about Lévy before this, she had denounced him as a manipulative liar but had been reluctant to go into detail beyond saying that Sartre's "Jewish conversion was all Benny's invention." Now she elaborated: "Yes, Sartre was part Jew, and of course that was one aspect of his being. But he was also French, and his French identity was paramount to him. He was a writer, a political figure, a good son to his mother, and a lover to many women. He was all of these, and they were all part of him. There was no Jewish conversion: Jewish identity did not become the defining part of him, it was only one of the many parts of him. It was a terrible lie to make Sartre renounce everything he stood for all his life."

She was reluctant to go into the details of how Lévy became one of the two dominant figures in Sartre's final years, someone who had managed to marginalize or exclude everyone else, particularly Beauvoir. Whenever I had pressed for more detail in previous interviews, I had sensed that her hesitation was linked to what she considered a personal failure: her shame that she had abandoned the man she loved when he was helpless. Now I asked if she had willingly given his care over to others because of that love, because she could not bear to witness his decrepitude. She verified this when she blurted out that much of Sartre's daily life had become sordid and sad, and it was just easier to let the two young people who didn't mind being around him perform the onerous duties that were needed to keep him going. Years of smoking and drinking had hardened Sartre's arteries and enfeebled his brain. He was often incontinent and frequently soiled himself; he paid no attention to his personal hygiene; often his clothes were dirty, his breath foul, and he smelled bad. But he was still demanding that young and nubile bed partners be brought to him, and many, wanting to brag about being with the great philosopher, came. According to Beauvoir, one in particular, a foreigner with visa problems, was happy to comply repeatedly.

Once Arlette Elkaïm entered Sartre's life, Beauvoir let her take center stage in it, only continuing to keep the task of placating his two longstanding mistresses, Michelle Vian (widow of Boris Vian) and Wanda Kosakiewicz (Olga Bost's sister). Beauvoir had never been a nurturer, but when Arlette prohibited the two women from seeing Sartre (their main financial supporter) and they became unmoored, she felt she had little choice. Michelle was in the early stages of dementia, and Wanda's lifelong mental instability worsened, alarming her friends, who feared she would cause serious harm to herself. It was Beauvoir who saw that the money Sartre paid every month for their upkeep continued to flow, and it was she who rushed to calm them when they acted out irrationally.

As her sister said, and as was evident in Beauvoir's book about Sartre's last years, *La Cérémonie des adieux,* Beauvoir did not hide from unpleasant truths, nor did she try to soften or prettify any of the ugliness that characterized Sartre's final years. Neither did she try to sugarcoat how her abdication of responsibility for him contributed to it. By the time she spoke to me, she had nothing good to say about Arlette Elkaïm-Sartre, the young Algerian Jewish woman who was first his lover and then his adopted daughter. She lashed out repeatedly about how Arlette had managed to dupe all Sartre's "family" into accepting her presence as his "girlfriend." Once they allowed her to take over the daily management of his meals and personal hygiene, it was just as easy to let her take care of his apartment and see to his literary affairs. Not until Sartre announced that he was adopting Arlette and making her his sole heir did they realize that they had all been "duped."

But by then it was too late. Beauvoir saved face by presenting herself to the public as Arlette's staunchest advocate, pretending to show such approval of Sartre's decision that she consented to be Arlette's sponsor during the legal process required by French law, for only a family member was entitled to inherit an estate (and Sartre's was significant), and a non–blood relative could inherit only if legally adopted. Beauvoir was aghast in private but to the world at large said she had been in favor of the adoption from the beginning "of their [Sartre and Arlette's] 'friendship.'" Only to me and a small group of others, which included Sylvie, Hélène, and Lanzmann, did she rage at the betrayal that transpired behind her back.

Having succeeded in getting Beauvoir to tell me why she so despised Benny and Arlette, I thought the time had come to press on the major topic that had long been a source of disagreement between us, her sexuality. I wanted to move beyond her affairs with men to those she had with women, but I knew I had to tread carefully.

Whenever I approached this subject in my mind, I thought of it in tennis metaphors. I always began with an easy lob, saving the hard slams down the line for later, and there was always the hope that I could sneak in a drop shot when she least expected it. The easiest practice volley was to ask her to talk about "the contract" she made with Sartre when they were students setting out on their life together. The agreement stipulated that they would always be primary, "essential," in each other's affections, but they would also be free to indulge in "contingent" relationships. As far as she was concerned (at least in the beginning of our talks), everything connected to Sartre throughout their relationship had been exactly as she wanted it, sheer perfection. And yet everyone else in their "family" told me of how they thought Beauvoir coped with Sartre's rapacious sexual appetite, and their stories hardly depicted one partner who willingly accepted another's ongoing infidelities. Instead they were of a woman so devastated and racked with emotional pain that she would often drink herself into a stupor as she sobbed to exhaustion.

We talked of all this as we sat in our usual places, Beauvoir on her daybed-sofa, I in the closest little jewel of a chair, the coffee table between us. She had stopped using her tape recorder soon after our earliest sessions and no longer set out her "work" apparatus. Her fountain pens remained capped in the little dish, and she never used the small notepad set next to them. I, however, still prepared my questions on the little file cards and put them out next to my own recorder. I held my steno notebook and jotted all sorts of things as we talked, including the occasional French word or phrase that I needed to look up later. Her vocabulary was so rich and varied that there were times I was not sure I was understanding her correctly and I needed to verify her words. Sometimes I asked her friends to listen to parts of the tapes and provide me with accurate interpretations as well as translations.

I took her more relaxed attitude as a sign of growing trust, but she still needed to see me as a working professional, and my little file cards sometimes created touchy situations. At most sessions my single pile quickly split into two as we talked, one of questions asked and answered and the other of those still to be asked. Sometimes, when I could see that one question was leading into sensitive territory where she might not want to go, I'd try to push that card to the bottom of the unasked pile as something to come back to later, when the time was more propitious. She was incredibly sharp and observant. "What's that?" she would ask. "Not important," I would try to say with as much nonchalance as I could muster. "We can always come back to it later." She was undeterred. "Ask it now," she would insist as I tried all sorts of feints that would not incur her anger. Often whatever I dreamed up was something so insipid that I knew that she knew I was inventing as I went along!

But there was the occasional flash of real anger, as happened, for example, when I pressed her to talk about what she and Sartre did (or did not do) during the war. In one session she literally jumped up from her usual perch and stood straighter than I had ever seen her and shouted, "This interview is over! You must leave at once!" I was shocked by her outburst and didn't know what to do, but as she was standing, I stood up, too. I must have been hesitating too long, as she was yelling "Leave! Leave!" I gathered up all my things as quickly as I could, and with coat half on and scarf dangling and tripping me up, I headed for the door. Apparently I was not moving fast enough, for she literally gave me a shove in the small of my back and slammed the door behind me.

"Now what do I do!?!" was what I thought constantly during the next few days, even as I did nothing to reach out to her, mainly because I could not think of anything that seemed appropriate. Instead I simply showed up at the appointed time for our next interview three days later. We resumed the conversation as if nothing had ever happened. That was when I learned I could press her only so far before what I called "the Lucite curtain" would come crashing down.

I could ask Question A, and she would answer it, knowing that most likely I would then go on to Question B. That was all right, too, even though she could sense that Question C was next on my list. She was not going to answer Question C, because that was the one that would get me to where I wanted to go, which was to Question D, and she was definitely not going to answer that one. Down would come the Lucite curtain. I could see through it clearly and so could she, but we could not hear each other, nor could we make any other sort of contact, and that was exactly how she wanted it.

Still, I was not to be deterred: sometimes I knew that if I wanted the answer to Question D, I would have to lead with it. There would be a smile on my face but dead seriousness in my voice as I told her that the time had come when I really needed the answer to Question D before I could write anything further on that particular subject. And that was when she sat there in her lumpy, dumpy, frumpy, and grumpy mode for a fairly long time before finally letting out a great sigh and telling me what I needed to know to ensure that what I wrote was an accurate account of the subject at hand. Beauvoir's relationship with women was exactly one such subject, but in the case of Sylvie Le Bon, I didn't even need to get to Question D. Beauvoir did it for me.

When I first met Sylvie, I asked Beauvoir a few general questions about why she had adopted her. Beauvoir insisted that it was "the only sensible thing to do because Poupette [Hélène's childhood nickname] and I are old and Lionel is sick." She said she "had faith" that Sylvie would carry out her wishes toward the two of them should she die first. I was perfectly willing to accept her explanation, even though I knew from Hélène how deeply hurt she had been by her sister's action. Sadly, she was right to be fearful of Sylvie's behavior, for after Beauvoir's death, Sylvie committed despicable actions. But all that happened after my biography was published.

The adoption gave me the answer I always gave when people asked me just what was going on between Simone and Sylvie: *"Madame de Beauvoir's trusted friend will ensure that her family and friends are protected and her estate is administered properly."* But the suggestion that they were lovers cropped up again and again.

Paris is a very small town, and the little fiefdom of the literary world was often particularly nasty. The usual rumors about me that were sometimes carried to Beauvoir usually concerned something connected to what I would write about her, and even though they were very different from those about Beckett and me (that I had used sex to get his permission to write the book), I found the Beauvoir rumors far more upsetting. Often what they told her was more than a simple misinterpretation; it was an outright falsehood. A number of times I had to explain that the stories she heard about me were lies, and in every instance she believed me and her trust deepened. I trod so carefully in all those years, but even so, it was often not good enough to keep the gossip at bay, and that gossip created temporary upsets between us.

I thought I was succeeding in keeping things on an even keel until two Frenchwomen who lived and worked in the United States decided that they, too, were writing Beauvoir's biography and set out to sabotage mine. Professors Claude Francis and Fernande Gontier came to Paris on sabbatical to meet Beauvoir and interview her. She asked me what she should do, and I said the decision to cooperate or not was hers to make, as was how much she wanted to confide in them. At our next meeting she told me she had seen them and said dismissively that they were not going to be competition because all they had asked about was her feminism. She said she would see them a few times more but that I was not to worry. However, they did want to meet me and she had given them my telephone number.

They phoned and invited me to dinner, so as a courtesy I went. From the moment I met them, I didn't trust them. The only thing they talked about over a dismal meal in a grim café was "Beauvoir's new-found lesbianism with Sylvie." I beat as hasty an exit as I could and decided that from then on I would not have any further contact with these two women.

When I arrived for our next session, I could see that Beauvoir was in a nasty mood. I found a festering, smoldering woman sitting in her little hollow on the sofa, her face a molten red and her conversation curt, abrupt, even rude. There had been times when she was short-tempered as I began my questioning, but usually she would recognize that whatever was bothering her had nothing to do with me—her feminist friends were making too many demands, she did not want to see an old bourgeois school friend who had suddenly materialized after many years, Sylvie wanted her to do something she did not want to do—and she would resume cooperative behavior. This time the mood not only persisted, it deepened. Beauvoir seldom blushed the pink of pleasure, but her face always darkened when she was angry or upset. I was thinking I had never seen it so mottled when she suddenly burst out, "You are going to write that Sylvie and I are lesbians! You are going to tell the world!" When she said the word "lesbian," she all but screamed it.

I had not yet gotten around to asking about the exact nature of their relationship, because I thought it was a subject best left until the end of my research and interviews. Why stir up trouble before need be, was how I reasoned; why not lob until the perfect moment to slam one down the line? This barrage of anger was obviously instigated by someone else, and my logical conclusion was that it came from Francis and Gontier. When I asked, Beauvoir confirmed it, saying that the two women had "warned" her that all I talked about was her "lesbian sex," and that was how I intended to write the book. I told her I thought she knew me well enough by now to know that it was not true, and I do believe she blushed pink when she said yes, of course, she had never believed it for a minute. I think she expected me to drop the subject, but instead I continued. I spoke quietly as I told her I was glad the topic had come up, and now was the time for her to talk about the relationship so that I would know how to write about it.

"We are not *lesbian!*" Again she practically spat out the word. "We do not do—" and here she did not use words but rather held out her hand, palm up, and flicked it downward toward her vagina with a hard, sure movement.

"I'm sorry," I said, "but you have to tell me what"—and here I flicked my own hand downward—"means."

"Oh sure, we kiss on the lips, we hug, we touch each other's breasts, but we don't do anything"—and here another downward flick—"*down there!* So you can't call us *lesbians!*"

Well then, I thought, *what am I to call them?* She was flat-out determined to deny her encounters with women despite so much evidence to the contrary, and as her biographer, I could not ignore this part of her life. I solved the problem some months later when I was back in New York by convening a group of feminist scholars in various fields and of various sexual persuasions to help me find the best way to write about her sexual identity. I adopted the consensus view that Blanche Wiesen Cook, then writing about Eleanor Roosevelt, expressed best: "If she does not identify as a lesbian, you cannot call her one." And so I wrote a carefully worded endnote, scholarly in the extreme, that came as close as I could make it to a definition of what I concluded was a complex sexual identity, and I left it at that.

There were other times, often after the official end of an interview, when a throwaway question would result in an astonishing discovery. The time I will always remember most vividly came at the end of a long and intense session during which I had succeeded in persuading Beauvoir to lift up the Lucite curtain and let me through. We were both exhausted from the effort as we were having our ritual scotch. As we sat there, she gulping hers down and refilling her glass while I tried to sip mine as slowly as possible, I spotted the clunky silver band she wore on the middle finger of her left hand. I had seen it many times before but had never thought to ask about it, and now I was only making polite conversation until I thought I could make a graceful exit. "That's such an interesting ring," I said, and I told her that I had often admired it.

"Algren gave it to me. I wear it on this finger because it was supposed to be my wedding ring and I am going to be buried with it."

I had no time to digest this stunning admission because she launched into the entire story of their relationship, of how much she had loved him and how romantically he had proposed to her on their Mexican holiday, and how she had thought seriously for the first time ever of leaving her life in France—or, more accurately, of leaving Sartre—to move to Chicago and become an American housewife. As she talked, I was in a quandary. This was vital information for her biography, but the work session, when everything was on the record, had ended, and I didn't dare pull out my recorder or steno pad for fear that I would interrupt her reminiscing and cause her to stop talking. I certainly could not break in and ask if what she was telling me was on the record and I could use it in the biography, so I let her talk. I don't remember any other topic that moved her so deeply and gave her such a high as telling me about Algren. I thought I saw a young woman deeply, romantically, ecstatically in love. She had never once talked about Sartre, or Lanzmann, or any of what she called her "passing fancies" (men with whom she had one-night stands or casual, fleeting affairs), with any of these emotions. Instead she talked about them with such detachment that I often envisioned her in a white lab coat, examining them as specimens under a microscope throughout the sexual act. It was only when she talked about Algren that she became girlish, flirtatious, gloriously happy, and deeply sad— all in the single telling.

She was euphoric after this session, and I, too, was emotionally moved, but even more, highly alarmed over how to write the story that she had just confided. We were off the record when she talked about this important moment in her life. Would I be breaking ethical boundaries if I used it? I decided to think about it and ask her later. I had to get it all down while it was sharp in my mind, so I hurried down her street and up to the boulevard du Montparnasse and the Dôme, where I took my favorite front-row seat before the window. I ordered my usual white wine, whipped out my notebook, and started to write down everything she had said.

At some point I paused to breathe and raised my head to look out the window. There I saw Samuel Beckett, swaying slowly as he crossed the street, probably about to look in the window and see me sitting there. Now what was I going to do? Indeed, it had been quite a day, and it wasn't over yet.

34

The evening when Beauvoir told me about Algren's ring was the first time I had seen Samuel Beckett since finishing his biography. In order to process the sighting, I had to record it in the *DD*: *"The most amazing thing happened today. I was sitting in the Dôme after SdB told me about Algren, trying to digest it, and I don't know why, but I started thinking, what if SB should walk by just now? What would I do? And just then—he did!!! I almost fainted is what I did. And then I just sat there, unable to move and sure I was about to black out and cause a big scene. My heart was pounding as I watched him pause at the door and I held my breath but he didn't come in and he didn't see me. He walked on down the street. I was turned into stone. I couldn't move."*

I suppose that on some deep level I knew that I was too emotionally overwrought to converse with him. Fearing that he might turn around and come back, I managed to get myself up and out of the Dôme, and as I looked in the direction he had gone to see if the coast was clear for me to leave, I saw his tall figure sway into La Coupole. I toyed briefly with the idea of following him in and pretending it was a serendipitous coincidence. But no, it would be a waste of money, as I would be too nervous to eat the expensive food, either with him or alone at a separate table.

Still revved up from Beauvoir's revelation and then the close encounter with Beckett, I walked all the way to Saint-Sulpice before taking the Métro to my usual stop. I collapsed into my apartment but spent most of the night sleeping fitfully, waking repeatedly to hunch over a notebook and scribble something I had just remembered or some new thought that I would want to explore about why

I had behaved as I did. In retrospect, hiding from Beckett seems rather silly, and I am embarrassed by it. So many years later, I still blush when I think about it.

I had no appointments until the evening of the next day, and I needed that time alone to decompress and decipher why I did not want to talk to Samuel Beckett. Was it because I was so deeply immersed in writing and thinking about Beauvoir, which was very different from how I had written about Beckett? That may have been part of it, for once I began to write about Beauvoir, I chose not to read any biographies while I was actually writing. I had developed the possibly irrational fear that I might inadvertently adopt stylistic tics or even plagiarize the work of someone else. It's a habit I keep to this day. Perhaps the reason I did not want to talk to Beckett came out of a related concern, that a conversation with him might influence how I talked to her, which in turn would allow the book I had written about him to influence the one I was writing about her. That was a genuine possibility, but I think the most probable reason why I avoided him was my "anxiety of influence," one based upon the general uproar the Beckett biography had caused in France, where Becketteering had become a favorite pastime of the intellectual elite.

As I tried to fill every available moment when not with Beauvoir with interviews, I depended on letters to set up as many as possible beforehand. Word of my arrival would spread among the chattering classes, which led all sorts of people to seek my time. Either they wanted me to interview them for the Beauvoir book, or, as in the case of the journalist and writer Pierre Assouline, they wanted to interview me. And not about Beauvoir, but about Beckett and the book that had been published four years earlier.

Assouline invited me to lunch, and I arrived late and out of breath because I had misheard the name of the street and had had to race across the sixth arrondissement when I realized my mistake. I had hardly sat down when he launched into *"a third degree about SB. Suddenly he tells me all the American Becketteers hate me and have convinced the French to do the same. He says they hate with a violence he has never seen. And now the French believe them and spew the same hate. [Avigdor] Arikha says if Assouline even speaks to me, Arikha will never speak to him again. The same with [Jérôme] Lindon who denies ever having met me and says everything I wrote is a lie. I break in here and tell him to see Mary Kling, who introduced us, and to ask Lindon how I could have gotten access to all those files and photos if he had not permitted it. And with glee in his voice Assouline prattled on, describing more of this irrational insane gossip, all to my complete disgust."*

I should have been well prepared for this. Just that morning I had received a phone call from Mary Kling telling me that the Swiss publisher Diogenes Verlag was canceling their contract to publish *Beckett* in German translation because *"'the publisher fears the negative French reaction will influence German sales, especially all the sexual innuendo about you and him.' Mary warned that it seemed I had powerful enemies who were out to sabotage the book."*

Assouline continued to tell me about all those who hated me while I tried to explain the Becketteers' jealousy with an onslaught of my own: *"I wrote the book none of them dared to write and now they cannot stand their continuing powerlessness to derail its success and my career. I launch into a diatribe about the position of women in the workforce in general, and specifically in academe. He says it's all too typically American—feminists out of control and men furious—and of course things are far more sophisticated in France. I guess we end up being friends when we leave, as he gives me one of his books, lavishly signed, and invites me to contribute an article on Beckett to Lire."*

I did write an article for the magazine he edited, and it was published along with Assouline's interview of me. I suppose he had to cater to his base, for sure enough, he could not resist taking gratuitous swipes at the biography and at me personally. I said nothing to him but channeled my rage into the *DD: "Pierre sent his article with the usual 'homage to Saint Sam' in it. I sent a gracious thank you despite the barb against me and my work. What no one seems to ask, perhaps because they are too stupid, too enamored of*

SB, or perhaps too frightened of offending him, is why this pathologi-cal veil of secrecy surrounds him, and what this says not only about his personality but about the personalities of the people who are part of his world. Why all this two-faced, behind-the-back stabbing and biting? Why not come right out in the open? I am everybody's favor-ite object of hysteria because I wrote the bio and afterward refused to tiptoe around him and be one of that crowd. One should ask why these so-called mature and successful men need to create the role of whipping-girl for me. And one should ask why—of all the books written about SB—mine is the one they always mention and always quote (sure, mostly negatively), which is even more telling, I think. What is important to me is that I did a good and honest piece of work and that it will last a long time after all these Becketteers disappear into their own assholes."

The real problem was that if Assouline, a perfect stranger before this meeting, knew all this gossip about me, Beckett had probably heard even more of it. I was so happy to be in the straight-forward world of Simone de Beauvoir that I had no desire to return to his, where people walked on eggshells for fear of being ostra-cized by him. As I put it, *"How much healthier—and fustier, and gustier—is the world of SdB. What a pleasure to be with people who are not terrified of their 'monstre sacré.' People who respect her and love her but don't hesitate to stand up to her. People who tell her (and me) everything straight out, come what may."*

During the years I worked with Simone de Beauvoir, I could not avoid Beckett's world. The invitations to write articles and attend conferences and seminars never stopped (especially from Germany, the one place where the focus was always on an honest assessment of his canon and what I had written about it). I hated how these diversions kept me from steady and sustained writing about Beauvoir, but I felt that not to accept them would be tan-tamount to cowardice. Like Louise Bourgeois, I gritted my teeth and girded my loins and went charging on. Simone de Beauvoir's example was influencing me, as were my ever-expanding friend-ships with French feminists. Even if I wasn't ready to see Beckett yet, I was ready to make some major changes. And the first one was firing my agent.

Carl Brandt had always treated me like the neophyte to publishing that I certainly was when he asked to represent me, but I had learned a lot in the years since I had signed the contract to write about Samuel Beckett. Every so often I would propose ideas for things I wanted to write, from magazine articles to future books, and every time he would tell me why none of them had any merit. I often met people in the publishing world at book launch parties or other receptions, and more than a few editors expressed regret that I had not accepted their invitations to write something I would have liked, had I been told about them. When I asked Carl why he had not given me the opportunity to accept or refuse, he said they were not my concern because he made the decisions for me.

What he said rankled, as I was constantly trying to raise money to pay for research and travel. I was still spending far too much time applying for grants and fellowships when one of his so-called decisions cost me a sizable advance, and that was the final straw. A British publisher had invited me to write a short book about T. S. Eliot, someone I had long wanted to write about, as part of a series suitable for a general audience. The money offered was (to poor me) a staggering sum, most of it payable up front, and best of all, I would not have to start until after I finished the Beauvoir biography. But Carl never told me about this offer, and I didn't find out until the contract had been accepted by someone else. "What a shame you refused," said the series editor when I met him at a party. "You were our first choice."

I told this to two of my good friends, the writers Judith Rossner and Barbara Seaman, who were as appalled as I was. Judy, always forthright and outspoken, had the answer: "What you need is a good woman who will work for you! Fire that man! Get yourself out of that insulting [Beauvoir] contract!" And so I did. I telephoned Carl, and for a change he accepted my call. As I was telling him why I wished to leave his representation, he said "Fine" and hung up. We never spoke again.

Judy gave me the names of four women agents and told me to interview them and choose the one I liked best. Even after all I'd been through, I was unnerved by the idea of interviewing these women who held such amazingly prestigious reputations in the literary world. However, there was no need to meet the others after the first one, Elaine Markson. Our connection was immediate, and her friendship and wise counsel sustained me for the next twenty-eight years.

Being in Paris and away from Penn had relieved me of that other thorn in my side—snide colleagues, tenure battles, etc. The phone in my apartment did ring often with calls from the university, but these were not only positive but highly intriguing. It seemed that the extraordinary woman who had recently become director of communications, Mary Perot Nichols, was envisioning a groundbreaking international feminist conference. It was to be paid for mostly by the French government, which would also pay expenses for twelve to fifteen important women scholars, writers, politicians, and artists to attend. The centerpiece would be, as I wrote, *"live and in person: Simone de Beauvoir!!! Yeah, sure—in their dreams."* The project seemed so ambitious that from the beginning I had reservations. However, if it happened, it would be truly amazing. Knowing that I was working on the Beauvoir biography, Mary hoped I would be a valuable ally in securing Beauvoir's participation.

Since Sartre's death, Frenchwomen had sought Beauvoir as their spokesperson on many different fronts. In 1982 a women's center was created and named in her honor: the Centre audiovisuel Simone de Beauvoir. Founded by (in their words) "three militant feminists"—the film director Carole Roussopoulos, the actress Delphine Seyrig, and the director Ioana Wieder—the center was dedicated to collecting and preserving all things connected with the history of women. Beauvoir was exceedingly proud that it bore her name.

These were the years when much of her activity was devoted to supporting women. She had signed the Manifesto of the 121, joining other women who admitted to having had abortions; she agreed to participate in every program Yvette Roudy sponsored through the Ministry for the Rights of Women. When younger groups of feminist women asked her to attend their meetings, she did not hesitate. She worked closely with Roudy's private adviser, Michelle Coquillat, whose brilliant insights into the condition of women enriched my own feminist education. Beauvoir agreed to let small groups meet in her apartment to plot strategy for protests by the MLF (Mouvement de libération des femmes), and she gave them advice on how to write manifestos and proclamations. When some of their names came up in our conversations, she spoke warmly, and among those she mentioned in passing were Anne Zelensky, who represented the MLF, and Claudine Monteil. She liked it that the journalist Josyane Savigneau wrote about her and that Professor Geneviève Fraisse gave lectures based on her writings. Beauvoir thought nothing of phoning the feminist publisher Françoise Pasquier to suggest she publish someone's new book. She kept in touch with her contemporary Colette Audry, who told me proudly that now that she was so old, she liked to call herself "France's first feminist and Beauvoir's inspiration." And although Claire Etcherelli was seldom an active participant, Beauvoir had come to depend on the writer she had become fond of through her work on *Les Temps modernes*.

I never asked to be included in the small planning sessions and meetings she held in her apartment and she never invited me, but I always attended the public occasions—not with Beauvoir, as her escort, but close enough to observe her behavior. I could see that she gloried in being part of this activity and was particularly proud to be singled out so often by Yvette Roudy.

All these activities marked a dramatic change from her daily

schedule when Sartre was alive. Until Arlette shut her out so completely, almost everything she did revolved around catering to his
daily demands. Without him, it was as if she had reinvented herself and could spend her days as she liked. She continued to be an
early riser, even though she was seldom eager to confront the day.
By drinking tea and reading newspapers and correspondence, she
was able to get herself going by midmorning. Usually she answered
letters, made phone calls, and wrote a little if there was time. She
no longer had to go to Sartre's apartment for a one o'clock lunch,
so she usually ate something at home, brought by Sylvie, unless she
had a date. She tried to schedule social engagements for the early
afternoon because she liked to get back to work by four or five, but
she could not often work until nine or later, as she had when Sartre
was alive, because her life was no longer as private as it had been.
Such freedom was not without a price, as her feminist activity put
her smack in the middle of the public eye. She was indeed France's
monstre sacré, their beloved and respected "sacred monster."

Mary Nichols was bursting with so many amazing ideas for
bringing feminist recognition to Penn that in our numerous
follow-up calls she had my head spinning. After one of her creative
bursts, I asked what she hoped to gain by tossing all those idea balloons up in the air, and she had a ready answer: "It's good to send
up three hundred because if you can get ten to stay up, you are
way ahead of the game." But when it came to "the Beauvoir conference," as it quickly became in our shorthand parlance, at least a
good hundred or so stayed there.

By the time I was home at the end of February 1982, Mary
had secured the cooperation of everyone who mattered in New
York's French Consulate, and with their help she received the same
enthusiastic support from French Embassy officials in Washington. They helped her plan a trip to France during which she and I
would be the guests of the government and officials would make
sure that we had access to everything and everyone whose par-

ticipation we wanted. But first Mary asked me to go back to Paris alone and persuade Beauvoir that, even though she had refused to come to Philadelphia for the honorary degree, she really had to come to the conference.

Thanks to Mary's budget, I was back in Paris several weeks later for a quick ten days in March, busy ones both for me and for Beauvoir. Hélène was having a *vernissage*, an opening to show her newest work at her gallery, and Simone was planning to attend. Publicity was under way, too, as journalists and interviewers wanted to feature both sisters in articles and broadcasts. She groused a little about how much of her time it was taking, but she didn't really mean it. She told me something that had to be "off the record, just between the two of us": that she feared the most recent attention Hélène was receiving for her painting came only because of the newfound attention Simone was getting because of her outspoken cooperation with French feminists. However, the sad truth was that Hélène had been involved in feminist activities for many years before her sister. As early as 1975, Hélène had been instrumental in establishing a home for battered women in Alsace, and since then she had participated in marches, contributed to manifestos, done whatever she could to help women. But her name did not command the attention of her sister's, and when the women in Paris mobilized in so many ways, it was Simone they chose to lead them. Hélène, always wanting only what was best for women, graciously stepped aside and left the leadership to Simone.

Simone loved her sister, although she sometimes complained that she could not understand Hélène's paintings and wondered why she kept at it when she sold so few and gallery exhibitions were so far between. Unfortunately, she made the mistake of confiding these thoughts in fairly ugly language to several letters that Sylvie collected and published years later, after Simone's death, when Hélène was still alive. I was with Hélène on several occasions when I saw how deeply hurt she was by her sister's thoughtless, offhand remarks. No one in "the family" could understand how Sylvie could have been so cruel in publishing them, and to this day I know of no suitable explanation.

Simone de Beauvoir said a lot of things that she really didn't mean, and some of her general comments about the feminists fall into this category. Just as she was so dismissive of her sister's painting, she told me she was upset that we would have to curtail our meetings during these ten days because of the "demands those feminists" were making on her. She still managed to meet me every time I said I wanted to talk, and each time she had something good to say about how well the "strategy meetings" were going. It was obvious how much they energized her, and how, despite griping about how much time they took, she relished these contacts.

"Ah, Darrred," she would say as she mock-complained about having to go off to yet another meeting and suggested that I should escort her. I was probably overreacting when I searched quickly to come up with an excuse for why I could not do so but said I would go along later on my own. I think this attitude went back to the days when I had been involved in Beckett's world and was determined to practice scrupulous objectivity by not becoming a part of it. Many of these feminists had become my good friends; indeed, some of them were my houseguests when they came to the United States. When I was in France, I often cooked "American dinners" for them. American "daube" (beef stew) and meatloaf and baked potatoes were two specialties they requested often. I suppose I always found a reason not to be Beauvoir's escort because I did not want anyone to think that the book I wrote about her would be the book she dictated.

And now here I was, having to impress upon her the importance of her presence at the conference in Philadelphia, and no doubt to have her as my houseguest if she chose not to stay in a hotel. I talked as persuasively as I knew how, telling her how everything depended on her presence. She listened attentively, and after a long silence that gave me hope she was seriously considering it, she said, *"I just can't come. I'm too old and I get too tired."*

When I wrote this in the *DD*, I also wrote how upsetting it was to hear her say that, after all her earlier talk about the *"private vacation"* she wanted to make to New York in July 1982. And I was irritated further by the fact that as soon as she told me she was too old and too tired, she brightened up and said that the minute she concluded our business, she was leaving for a vacation. She had told me on many earlier occasions that she was on her way to visit London one last time (a trip she never made), so I asked if she was going there: "I am not going to London, but I'm not telling you where, either." (Later she told me she was going to take the waters at Biarritz.)

What had I said or done to bring this on? She was often feisty and secretive with me, but this was something new. Before I could digest it, she added offhandedly that she would give me the list of Frenchwomen whom she wanted the government to sponsor for the conference, but "there is really only one American I want you to invite, Kate Millett." And in conclusion, "I will do everything you want me to do, but I will not come in person." I tried for the last time to impress upon her how important her presence was and how the French government was not going to sponsor so many women without her. "Of course they will send the women, because I will tell them they must."

Obviously she was letting her recent popularity among feminists go to her head, but how could I tell her that the French government would not trip over itself to allocate many thousands of dollars just to glorify her reputation? And how was I to convey her decision to the conference organizers, who had spent so much time, energy, and money to get this far? She had an answer for that, too. "I will write you a formal letter tomorrow. They will accept my decision." I think my chin dropped down to my ankles after she said this. I wrote that night: *"She never ceases to amaze me. Just AMAZING!!!"*

It was good I had no evening engagement after I left her, because I needed to figure out how I would present it to Mary Nichols. It was the evening before my last full day in Paris, one that was booked from early morning to late night, so I took myself down to La Coupole and ordered a good half-bottle of wine and an expensive dinner. I had had little time for socializing on this trip, so I decided to indulge myself (on my own credit card) and enjoy my oysters and Dover sole. I would not let myself think about how to present Beauvoir's astonishingly unrealistic attitude until I had to. Once again, no sense worrying until the time came.

35

I worried throughout the flight home about how to tell Mary Nichols that Simone de Beauvoir would not be coming to the conference. I can't say I was angry with her, but I was certainly miffed. And I feared that the French government would withdraw its commitment and that Mary would not have enough balloons left to keep the conference afloat.

I should not have worried, because the always-innovative Mary knew exactly how to overcome Beauvoir's refusal. She got in touch with her contacts at PBS in Washington, and within a week or so we had their solution: a satellite hookup that would enable Beauvoir to address the conference, live and from the comfort of her apartment. We in Philadelphia would be able to interact with her, and audience members would be able to greet her and ask questions. A live satellite hookup was something fairly novel in the early 1980s, and Mary sent out a press release explicitly announcing it, generating an avalanche of interest from people the world over who volunteered to participate. We could have created a program that would have run for a month if we had accepted everyone.

All this was happening as my Bunting Fellowship ended and my teaching at Penn resumed. Mary and her staff took care of everything connected to planning and promotion, but I was expected to construct the program. I asked for a reduced teaching schedule and didn't get it. And then there was the committee work, especially my membership on the advisory board of the university's press, which took an enormous amount of time. I did get a work-study student to assist with the conference for four hours three times a week. He had a decent command of the French language and was a splendid help just answering the phones. I remember him at the end of each workday, sitting dazed in his chair, his eyes glazed and voice raw from dealing with people who were determined that they deserved a place—if not a starring role—in the program. Imagine, then, if he was reduced to this, how I was at the end of what was usually a sixteen- to twenty-hour day. For the better part of a year I wrote next to nothing on Beauvoir's biography.

After nine solid months of nonstop planning, Mary and I thought we had the program essentials together and were ready to go to France to talk to the fifteen women the government wanted to sponsor. In April 1983, I joined Mary and a woman she had hired to help with public relations on an Air France flight to Paris, courtesy of the French government. We were met by a driver with an official car and were whisked into the city in more posh comfort than I, always the poor writer on a tight budget, had ever enjoyed. The driver took us to the hotel the French government was paying for, the PLM Saint Jacques, on the boulevard directly across the street from Samuel Beckett's apartment building.

I did not know our destination when I wrote to him before my departure. I had his reply before I left, telling me he would be between Paris and Ussy but was overburdened with new writing and dealing with nervous actors and directors in Germany and was not sure he could see me. Period. I was relieved to think that I would not have to worry about upsetting him if he ran into me unexpectedly in the hotel's coffee shop, where I knew he often held meetings and where I had asked several friends to meet me during the few brief breaks in my official schedule.

Once I arrived, I sent another letter to explain why we were staying just across the street from his house, because I didn't want any surprises if our paths happened to cross. I think he was curious about what I was doing there, for he left a telephone message asking me to meet him at two o'clock several days later. I had to see Beauvoir at four, so the timing was perfect. I did most of the talking, telling him about the preliminary plans for the conference. He talked very little, saying again that he was overwhelmed with writing and going back and forth to Ussy in search of the privacy he needed to finish several works in progress. We said a cordial good-bye, and I could not help but think that he was slightly annoyed. My university was going to all this trouble for Simone de Beauvoir, but nothing had ever been proposed—by me or by others—to honor him.

We were in Paris for two weeks, and I knew from the start that I would have a problem with Mary and her PR woman whenever we had to interact with the French. Mary was ebullient and outgoing, and she never hesitated to express opinions that were often tactless and could shock people who did not know her well. Her associate must have patterned her professional conduct on a single public relations primer she had read who knows how long before, for she was never able to discern what a person or a situation required and stuck unwaveringly to her preordained script. She knew nothing about French history, culture, or language, but she did not hesitate to present our initial ministerial contacts with a list of outrageous and completely inappropriate actions she expected them to take. I had tolerated her in Philadelphia because Mary insisted that she was useful, but in Paris she was an officious woman whom I muzzled after our first official meeting, a lunch with Minister Yvette Roudy. After that, unless we were attending a large reception or lecture, I usually did not allow her to accompany us. I told them both repeatedly that we were never to discuss our real thoughts about any of our meetings until we were alone. I warned Mary and her associate that they must never—ever, with three exclamation points—say anything negative or derogatory in the car, where the driver could overhear us. My cautions went, as one of my dear friends often said, in one ear and out the same one.

And when I arranged for them to meet Simone de Beauvoir, I

thought they would give me a heart attack. After a brief exchange of pleasantries in Beauvoir's apartment, she in her usual place and the three of us lined up on the little chairs like students in a classroom, Mary launched into comments about Beauvoir's refusal to travel that I could see were making her angry. The obtuse associate, who probably thought she was defusing the situation, interrupted Mary, only to make the situation worse. Beauvoir's expression showed me that she was smoldering, and I knew I had to get them out of there. I jumped up and nudged Mary up and out of her chair and motioned to the associate that we were going. I told Beauvoir we were late for our next appointment and had to leave at once, thanked her for her kindness, and hustled them out before they could do any more damage. I saved my scolding for the sidewalk as we waited for the driver to bring the car.

I always sat in the front passenger seat, because I spoke French to the friendly young driver, who claimed she neither spoke nor understood English. It was good that I did so, for it allowed me to turn around and glare at my two companions whenever they misbehaved. They called it my "straighten up and fly right" look. On the last day of our stay, our driver said goodbye to us in perfect English and told us that she was the kid sister of the high-level cultural attaché who had arranged our itinerary. She cheerfully explained that she had gotten the job because she spoke English and could make daily reports to her sister. And because we were so highly positive about everyone we had met and everything we had seen or done, she told her sister that our conference was well worth supporting. My two companions had the grace to look sheepish and avoid my eye contact when they heard this.

On my own, I managed to see Beauvoir almost every weekday during our two-week stay. She listened attentively as I told her of all the ministers who were cooperating and of the feminist women who were going to participate. I also told her how the cultural atta-ché at the American Embassy had invited us to tea in order to offer whatever cooperation could come to us directly from France.

I think she liked that best of all. And then she asked me about my book's progress, and I had to tell her the dispiriting news that I had not written very much since she and I had finished our last working sessions.

I did write a lot in that nine-month interim, but mostly pieces I accepted for the brownie points I needed to secure promotion to full professor: reviews and op-ed pieces, an introduction to a book about Beckett's canon, and even the entry for Simone de Beauvoir in the *Encyclopedia Brittanica*, complete with a photo of the two of us taken by my husband, who was the only photographer she would trust with the assignment. After he hastily snapped a few photos and left the apartment, she said, "He's very nice but he's very quiet." I didn't tell her that I had instructed him not to speak unless spoken to, and then only in pleasantries, and to beat as hasty a retreat as he could make!

Everything about the French visit was more positive than I could have hoped for. I slept all the way home to Philadelphia, confident that once the program was officially set, all we had to do (besides deal with the many colossal egos involved) was wait for it to happen. I was able to find enough free time on the weekends to return to the book, even though it was hard to pick up where I had left off. The semester was ending soon, and I looked forward to a summer at home in my office. I was certainly not prepared one fine spring day to see Mary, who seldom left her department office, appear in the doorway to mine. She was uncharacteristically sub- dued as she came straight to the point: she had been fired. I had to ask her to repeat what she said several times. When the university president had summoned her to come to his office that morning, she had thought all he wanted was an update on the progress of the conference. Instead he told her to leave as soon as possible.

We were both flummoxed, going around and around until we had exhausted ourselves without arriving at an explanation for such devastating news. Eventually we moved on to talk about what would become of the conference. Mary said that all her programs and promotions then under way would continue to their conclusion, but that she was to make her exit a swift one. "But who is going to be in charge of the conference?" I wailed.

"You," she said.

Several weeks later, at a reception for the university trustees, I thought I found out why Mary had been summarily dismissed. One trustee I particularly disliked said how lovely it was, now that Mary Nichols was gone, to wake up in the morning and not have to worry about seeing a story on the front page of *The New York Times* highlighting some achievement connected to Penn. Philadelphia was such people's little backwater fiefdom, and they wanted to keep it that way.

There was no way I could run the conference Mary had envisioned. I had none of her contacts and none of her administrative abilities. Almost immediately her friends at PBS withdrew their cooperation for the satellite hookup. Their allegiance was to Mary and certainly not to the university that had harmed her. When the French government heard that Mary was gone and PBS had pulled out, the various ministries said that perhaps they could scrounge funding for four or five women but no more. At Penn, faculty women did not come to aid their beleaguered colleague (me) but formed several partisan factions and battled for control of the conference. I was too tired to fight for something I no longer believed in. I gave it to them willingly and resigned from all participation.

The conference happened, but no French feminists came, and neither did those from other countries who had volunteered to pay their own way just to honor Simone de Beauvoir. The program became decidedly American and focused on women's issues that had little or nothing to do with her. With attendance dropping off, the conveners moved the event to coincide with the spring semester break, and hardly anyone came. I left, not only the city but also the country. I went to Oaxaca and spent the spring vacation visiting artisans in Mexican villages and scouting for the ceramic Trees of Life (*Árboles de la vida*) that I collected.

As soon as I resigned from the conference, I hauled out my credit card and flew to Paris to tell Beauvoir in person what had happened. On that rainy afternoon, as darkness fell in her apartment, she expressed a range of emotions—at first dismay, then sadness, and then I think resignation. When she twisted her body to turn on the Giacometti lamp beside her, I saw that in the end she had settled on compassion. It was one of the very few times that I saw her express genuine concern for me as a woman and a person, not just as the writer with whom she maintained a professional relationship and with whom she was collaborating on a book she very much wanted to see published in her lifetime.

I had always found her awkward whenever I saw her try to comfort her friends, and some of that awkwardness inflected her speech as she tried to be kind to me. She volunteered stories of disappointments she had suffered in her professional life and insisted that none was equal in magnitude to mine, even though they seemed far more significant to me.

She insisted that I stay resolute, and while she spoke, I thought of phrases I often used in such situations: "what's done is done," and "things beyond repair should be beyond reproach." I told her I would have to express my personal way of coping with adversity in English because I could not think of the French slang equivalent: I told her I dealt with rejection, failure, or disappointment by saying, "Cut your losses and run." By that I meant that since nothing can change the past and we cannot be sure of the future, we have only the present and should make the most of it. She said yes, that was always how she lived her life, too. I flew home feeling much better.

My peace of mind lasted for a good long while, because at last I could devote myself to finishing the book. It was 1984, and I had been awarded two fellowships, the Rockefeller and the Guggenheim. At first the English Department's chairman said that I could be released from teaching for only one year and would have to decide which I wanted to accept, but when I said I would not allow the university to take credit for these prestigious awards unless I could accept them both, the decision came down from the powers that be to let me have them. I could not believe my good fortune: two years to sit in my office and finish my book, or so I thought. My new agent, Elaine Markson, had placed the book with the visionary publisher Jim Silberman at Summit Books, and he was starting to press for a manuscript that was long overdue. It was high time I knuckled down, because Elaine was running out of excuses to persuade Jim to be patient a while longer.

I worked steadily through the winter of 1984–1985, until I arrived at a point where I needed more conversations with Beauvoir and a break from the daily grind. An American friend offered to let me use her apartment in Paris for three weeks starting at the end of January, a stroke of good fortune that would let me dig into two important topics in Beauvoir's life that she had hitherto kept firmly behind the Lucite curtain. I could proceed no further on the book: in order to write about them, I had to make her explain them.

When I wrote to tell Beauvoir that I was coming to Paris, I said that I had specific topics we would need to cover in greater detail than we had before, but I did not mention what they were. Sometimes I found that if I gave just enough information to pique her curiosity, I would get fuller responses, because she would not have had the time to prepare her answers in advance. The first topic was her doctoral dissertation on the German philosopher Leibniz, which I thought might offer an important glimpse into her development as a philosopher. Beauvoir claimed the document had been lost years before; she insisted she did not have a copy, nor could I find one in any library or archive even loosely connected to the École normale supérieure. I had searched every possible academic archive and so had most of the French friends who had volunteered to help me. I could not understand why Beauvoir refused to talk about something so seemingly straightforward. Usually when I wanted to see something specific—a manuscript, photo, or letter—it was best to be upfront with her beforehand, but in this case I knew she would make the same excuses as before, so a more oblique approach was best.

When we met for our first conversation, I told her I had been reading Leibniz's philosophy in preparation for meetings and I was struck by the notion then current among philosophers and Leibniz scholars (before being disavowed and then accepted again) that he had been influenced by the Kabbalah. At the time Beauvoir was writing the dissertation, some scholars proposed that mystical and occult writings contributed to the development of general scientific theory, and they argued that Leibniz enfolded some of these studies into his theory of monadology, or monads. I asked Beauvoir if she had included any of this thinking in her dissertation or if she had been influenced by what was then called the kabbalistic philosophy of optimistic perfectionism and universal salvation, and if she had perhaps accepted it as her own. One of the arguments prevalent when she was writing was that Leibniz took these various theories and incorporated them into his notion of reality. He melded this collection of separate and individual entities into the idea of a unified infinity.

I remembered that she had been writing this dissertation before she began her involvement with Sartre and his student-philosopher friends. It coincided with the last years of her infatuation with her cousin Jacques, before she came under the influence of their existential theorizing and when she was fascinated by the romantic character of Alain in *Le Grand Meaulnes*. Both schoolgirl anguish over unrequited passion for her cousin and the heavily romantic fictional character she so admired were the exact opposite of Sartre's theory and fully aligned with certain interpretations of Leibniz that she might have embraced.

Non-philosopher that I am, no doubt everything I said as I tried to explain why I was asking about the dissertation was confused and unscholarly, but when I got around to what I really wanted to know, my language was perfectly clear: Was the reason she never wanted anyone to read her dissertation that she was embarrassed or ashamed of it, as it had no basis in or correspondence with Sartre's existentialism? Had she perhaps put forth a totally opposite view from his, one that she had wholeheartedly embraced at the time?

She seemed astounded that I could even ask such a question, or so I thought when I saw the expression on her face. Rather than let her anger build, I kept up a rapid-fire commentary of possible differences between what I thought she had probably written and Sartre's burgeoning theory. When I ran out of nervous chatter, I concluded by saying that perhaps she did not want anyone to write about her thesis because, for whatever reason, she wanted to disown it.

Meanwhile she just sat there and stared without speaking. In my mind I saw the Lucite curtain hurtling down, and I could only sit there silently until it crashed. Silence is a well-known journalistic technique with less-than-forthcoming sources, but on that occasion I was using it only because it was my last resort, and this was probably my last chance to get her to talk about Leibniz. If I was kicked out of her apartment again, so be it, but I was determined that she would be the one to break the silence, and eventually she did.

She did not tell me to leave, but I could tell there would be no ritual scotch that afternoon. When she spoke, all she said was, "No." When I still said nothing, she elaborated, claiming to have no memory of "schoolgirl thoughts," which was interesting, because she could remember in full detail so many other things she had written during that period, or books she had read and films she had seen. All she could say was that the dissertation was lost and she was tired of talking about it, and she warned me never to bring it up again. I knew when I was defeated, and on this topic I had to accept what she told me. My speculation could not go into the biography with no one's testimony to back it up. Thus I wrote another of my very careful endnotes to explain the true beginning of her philosophical writing and quite possibly her earliest credo.

Beauvoir's reluctance to discuss the second major topic of my trip—how she had colluded with Sartre in the seduction of one of her pupils, Bianca Bienenfeld Lamblin—was much easier to understand.

When I had asked about Sartre's liaisons in previous sessions, Beauvoir had usually been blunt and candid, no matter how seamy her participation in helping him to seduce women had been. She insisted that their own sexual relationship had continued for many years and that they had each found it (among the many expressions she used over time) "loving" or "tender" or, most often, "satisfying" and "necessary." Yes, he liked beautiful women, and because she knew how much she meant to him, first above all others, it did not matter how many other women he took to bed, for they meant little beyond physical release. And if she had to help persuade reluctant women to be with such an ugly man who had bad breath and body odor, she did what had to be done.

Her sister, Hélène, explained Simone's complicity in much the same way, as she implored me to understand the role that Sartre's physical ugliness played in his need for a constant stream of sexual partners. Although Hélène never assisted in these tawdry acquisitions, she urged me to accept that her sister's unconditional love for Sartre was the reason she helped make them happen. I accepted this explanation for most of the other cases, but it did not explain Beauvoir's attitude toward Bianca. Whenever I asked about the affair they both had had with her lycée student, she always said we were not going to talk about it and tried to change the subject. After a while I stopped persisting so that she would not send me away without the ritual scotch, which was her way of letting me know that I had gone too far.

I saved the topic of Sartre's women for our next session, two

days later. It began on a somewhat strained footing, as I could see
that she was still wary after the intense exchanges about Leibniz.
Since I could not think of any other casual conversation after we
compared notes about the dreadful winter weather, her head cold,
and my sniffles, I went directly to the point. I asked her the one
question that I knew angered her more than any other: was her
"essential" relationship with Sartre a construct of her own determined creation? This time I couched it in the context of why she
had chosen to publish Sartre's letters but not hers: by suppress-
ing her half of the correspondence, did she not give credence to
Arlette and everyone else who claimed that their "essential" relationship was her fiction? Once again her face was black with rage.

Beauvoir had gone against almost everyone's wishes after Sartre's death when, in 1983, she had published his letters to her. She
told me she had done this to preempt Arlette's claim that she held
copyright, for she feared that not only would Arlette never publish
them but, worse, she would destroy them (she did destroy the origi-
nals). Beauvoir believed that Arlette was determined to undermine
her, if not to remove her entirely from the supreme place she had
held in Sartre's life, and by publishing his letters she could guar-
antee that it was indeed her rightful position. She took this action
despite the fact that everyone in "the family" advised against it.
The general attitude was best expressed by Bost, who told me that
she should not "air such dirty—no, no, such filthy—family linen."

Some of the dirtiest of this linen described how she colluded
in his seductions, and how, as in the case of the eighteen-year-old
Bianca (called Louise Védrine in the letters), she had seduced the
girl first so she and Sartre could compare notes that would be useful for when he seduced her. These letters do not make for pleasant reading. I could sense Beauvoir's reluctance to take the girl
to bed, and there was no question in my mind that Beauvoir was
ashamed of her intimacy with Bianca. Why, then, did she publish
her role in this sordid episode when she could so easily have left out
those letters and no one would ever have known of their existence?
In one respect, the Bianca episode serves as an accurate reflec-

tion of how she never evaded her own unsavory behavior. It also shows how she usually acted when it came to Sartre: his desires, whether valid or not, always came before her own. Coupled with her unflinching honesty, she chose not to hide what she had done.

But that answer seemed only a partial explanation for her anger (or embarrassment) whenever I asked about Bianca. Finally, after several years of tiptoeing around it, I was ready to ask if it had something to do with how she defined her own sexuality and her insistence that she was not a lesbian. Was she afraid that if she admitted to the Bianca affair (which she verified) and to several other same-sex "friendships" (which I was never able to verify as anything more), and now her adoption of her boon companion, Sylvie, that her leading role as feminist icon and luminary would be tarnished? In previous sessions, when we had talked about her feminist activities, she had spoken disparagingly or dismissively of "those" lesbians, so was it possible that she retained some of the prejudices of her conservative Catholic upbringing? She was her usual brusque self in her answers: No, she did not have a preju- diced bone in her body. Yes, she had done things she was careful to say she was "not proud of" rather than admit to anything more, such as (my words here) embarrassment or shame. As for the role history would assign to her, she only hoped her written contribu- tions to her time would be lasting.

Bianca Bienenfeld Lamblin was the only one of Sartre's major relationships with women who was still alive and mentally compe- tent to talk when I was conducting research. Simone Jollivet was dead, and Michelle Vian was suffering from memory loss compli- cated by alcoholism. Dolores Vanetti, whom I did talk to in New York, was an unreliable subject. Olga Bost was angry, and after a brief sentence or two about her and her sister Wanda's sexual relationships with Sartre and Beauvoir, she told me the subject was closed. I searched for Bianca because she was the last pos- sible source. In those pre-Google days I used every reporter's and scholar's trick I could muster, but no one knew anything about her, where she lived or even if she was still alive. Beauvoir claimed she had not seen her for forty years and had no idea what had become of her, or even if she had survived the war. I had access to Beauvoir's address book and her daily appointment calendars. I never saw Bianca Lamblin's name in either one. After several years, I gave up trying to find her.

Imagine, then, my surprise when she published her book, *Mémoires d'une jeune fille dérangée*, in 1993, claiming that she had seen Beauvoir regularly at least once every month since the war ended and that she had been living all that time in Paris, close enough to walk to Beauvoir's apartment had she wanted to do so. She had been married to Bernard Lamblin (who died in 1978), a prominent philosophy professor who had been Sartre's pupil at the Lycée Pasteur and whom Beauvoir had known since his school days. She was also the cousin of the writer Georges Pérec, whom Sartre and Beauvoir knew as well. Much of what she wrote can be described only as her own version of reality or, more accurately, as a fantasy. But it's also perfectly understandable that she would want justification, if not revenge, given her schoolgirl seduction and Sartre and Beauvoir's callous abandonment of her during the war, when as a Jew she had pleaded for their help and received none. Their actions must have paled before the public humiliation when Sartre's letters were published in 1983 and Beauvoir's were published in 1990. My biography was published three years before Bianca Lamblin's memoir, and, not surprisingly, she had issues with it. She was entitled to her own memories, and I did nothing then (and will do little now) to dispute them.

Now, so many years after those conversations with Beauvoir, I realize how difficult, if not painful, they were for her. I think of some contemporary terms used by feminist writers: "self-authorship," "agency," and "control." Self-authorship begins with women who, for whatever the reason, were originally unable to tell their own stories truthfully, or honestly, or objectively. The first story they told may have begun in "bad faith," which was their way of evading their "real truth," defined by the term "agency," or the assumption of taking responsibility for truthful self-definition. "Control" of one's personal narrative can come only through agency. Retroactively applying these ideas to Beauvoir, I wonder, was she claiming her own version of self-authorship when we talked about Bianca so that she could fashion the story of herself to fit the narrative of agency she wanted the world to remember? And if so, had she been doing this throughout our years of interviews and conversations?

It made me think all the way back to our very first meeting and ask myself if, through Bianca, she was simply exhibiting another version of what she had told me about how we would write the book—that she would talk and I would write down what she said, and then (as she gleefully clapped her hands together a single time), we would have her biography?

This is another of the nightmares that brings on the 4 a.m. anxieties among biographers. In the cases of Leibniz and Bianca, I came away without absolute certainty; I had had such high hopes for nailing down the truth about these topics, but in the end I couldn't get through the Lucite curtain. Such circumstances create the galloping insecurities that make biographers worry that they might inadvertently—unconsciously—assign their own truths to the people they write about.

And naturally, when my frazzled brain was reeling with thoughts of Beauvoir and how I was ever going to write about her complexity, this was the moment when back into my life came Samuel Beckett.

36

The afternoon with Beauvoir had been so emotionally overloaded that I was recovering as I usually did, at the Dôme with a ritual glass of white wine in a window seat, scribbling furiously in my notebook. Every question she had answered had only given me another half dozen to worry about, each with the potential to upset her further. As I thought about this, I raised my head to look at the people on the street and saw a man with a familiar craggy face dressed in a sheepskin jacket and turtleneck Irish sweater. But I had to do a double-take, because he walked slowly and carefully, and looked so old and bent that I thought perhaps I was confusing someone else with Beckett. After a few moments, I had no doubt that it was indeed Samuel Beckett.

I had not written to Beckett before I made this trip because I did not want to have any contact with him. My head was so full of things I needed to do in connection with Beauvoir's biography that I did not want anything else to clutter it. I did not want the anxiety that always consumed me before the actual meeting with Beckett, the insomnia the night before, the nervous stomach the day of, and the mental exhaustion once it was over. Nor could I spare the time for him or for most of the many good friends I had made in Paris while I was writing his biography. Unless they had some connection to Beauvoir, I had to politely decline their hospitality and could just chat briefly on the phone. If I could not see the people with whom I could relax and enjoy myself, I could not withstand a meeting with Beckett.

I could have avoided him on this particular evening just as easily as I had done one year earlier. I did not know then that it would be the last time I was in Samuel Beckett's company, so I can't claim that I wanted one last meeting. My session with Beauvoir had left me frustrated but neither confrontational or defensive, so I can't properly describe the particular attitude that made me hail him. Perhaps the unexpected sight of him provoked a sudden and spontaneous reaction that gave me no time to think about what I was doing when I stood up and waved. He saw me, and seemed unsure about who was waving at him.

He stood near the doorway to the Dôme, so I went out to the sidewalk to meet him and offer apologies for not letting him know I was in Paris. I think he said something like, "No doubt you are here to work with *her.*" (I distinctly remember that he did not say Simone de Beauvoir's name: shades of his old animosity.) He told me he was taking a short walk before dining at Aux îsles marquises, a fish restaurant he liked because the staff always ensured his privacy, and he asked if I wanted to join him. The invitation was unexpected, and I had no ready excuse for why I would not because I never made dinner engagements after a session with Beauvoir, so that I could spend the rest of the evening alone, remembering and making notes on what we had talked about.

His invitation caught me off-guard, because in all the years we were working together, I never actually had a meal with Samuel Beckett. We always had drinks, coffee usually, wine sometimes, perhaps some light bar snacks. I always arranged it that way because I knew I would have been too nervous to eat, as I knew I would be on this evening. I lied, blushing as I did so, saying that I was meeting friends later for a casual supper. He suggested that we share an apéritif in the Rosebud (another of his usual haunts), just around the corner.

It was a long, slow walk there, as years of heavy smoking had taken their toll and he was breathing heavily. Once we were seated, I noticed that, for the first time, he had no cigarettes or matches with which to fidget. He asked about the progress of "her book," but once I had given him the answer I gave whenever I did not want to talk about it—everything was fine, moving right along, publication very soon, all well indeed—he shifted the conversation to me personally. Was I still teaching? My children must be fully grown by now; were they finished with university? Did I still live in Philadelphia? He knew from various German scholars that I had been spending a great deal of time in that country speaking about his work at various conferences and symposia, and he knew that I was scheduled to return shortly for another conference. He asked how I found it to work there.

Suddenly I found myself blurting out all the indignities—the hell, actually—that I had gone through since publishing his biography. I gave a highly edited and sanitized version, but at some point my derogatory term "the Becketteers" slipped out. I can still see the expression on his face: I think it stunned him. He did not repeat it and neither did I, but I knew it sank in. I think he said something like how "unfortunate" it was, but I can't remember the exact context, whether he meant their behavior or my various "agonies," as I half-jokingly termed what they had put me through. I do remember, however, that he told me how he had decided early on that he would never respond to his critics. He did not advise me to follow his rule, but I am sure that was his implication. And then he changed the subject entirely to tell me that he was "working with Jim now."

It took me a moment to comprehend that he was talking about James Knowlson, who was writing a biography that would not be published until after Beckett's death. Just as I had a lot to say about the Becketteers, I found that I had a lot to say about other biographies besides mine, and I launched into it. I said I welcomed any future books that would be written about him because there were obviously so many incidents, events, and relationships that I had only managed to touch upon and that needed fuller exploration. Slyly, and with gleeful purpose, I also said I thought it would be good for readers to have his and Knowlson's "authorized" biography as opposed to my "designated" one. I could not resist telling him that authorized biographies sometimes bore the taint of "the gospel according to the subject, written by the earnest supplicant." As mine had been written independently and was already out there, no doubt Knowlson would have to acknowledge it, if only to rebut or reject my findings. It was almost too bad that he would be metaphorically looking over his shoulder at me and my book all the while that he wrote his. How smug I was as I said this, and how much I relished saying it! Samuel Beckett, true to form, said nothing.

I talked so much that my wineglass was left mostly untouched, but it was getting late, so I started to gather my things. Until then he had not said anything specific about the Becketteers' behavior, but I think he was alluding to it when he volunteered one of the last things he ever said to me: "You must never explain. You must never complain." Indeed, there have been many times since then when I have been ready to lash out in retaliation for a bad review or an unkind comment, but every time I have remembered these words and I have never explained and never complained.

I did not know then that it was the last time I would be in Samuel Beckett's company. The unexpected encounter was so highly charged and emotional that I had to replay it in my mind and make notes about it in the *DD* for many days afterward. At the time I thought about how all my pent-up emotions had burst out, and I marveled at how quietly, graciously, and thoughtfully Beckett had received them. Later, when I became a seasoned biographer, I wished I had taken the time to send him a letter explaining how much it meant to be able to tell him all that had happened to me since the moment when he asked if I would be the one to reveal him as a charlatan. I wished that I had told him how grateful I was for allowing me to reveal him as the extraordinary man I believed him to be, and what an honor and a privilege it had been to know him.

I left Simone de Beauvoir in a very good mood when my Paris sojourn ended. The rest of 1985 had the usual interruptions, albeit welcome ones, of giving lectures and writing articles about Beckett. Mostly, however, I went to my desk every morning and stayed there until early evening, putting what I thought were finishing touches on an almost finished book. By the end of the year, I knew I was ready to publish, because no one was telling me anything new. That was, and still is, the moment when I know the research is finished. It is also the moment when the nonfiction writer's worst fear arose—that some new and unexpected and possibly upending information will come to light that might destroy the entire thesis or premise of the book. I felt secure, however, that I had covered all my bases, and I thought I was ready to go to Paris for my final fact-checking trip before publication.

I scheduled the trip for one month, the last two weeks of February and the first two of March 1986, timed to coincide with another of Hélène's *vernissages*, the opening of a large show of her paintings hosted by Yvette Roudy at the Ministry for the Rights of Women. It was a bittersweet evening for me, as my enjoyment of the paintings was diminished by the need to spend time apologizing to so many wonderful women about why the Penn conference had failed.

Hélène was thrilled and delighted with her evening, particularly because she was sharing it with the sister she idolized. If Simone reciprocated these warm feelings, she did not show it. I kept comparing it to my own attitude toward my younger sister when we were children, the little fly who buzzed around me in adoration while I swatted her away, the little pest. I would revise my thinking about Simone's behavior several days later, when I learned that she had been ill and was exhausted by the activity connected with Hélène's eight-day stay as her houseguest, the constant comings and goings of their many feminist friends, and having every journalist in Paris imploring to photograph and write about the famous sisters.

Hélène was especially delighted to see me because she knew that, like her, I had been invited to participate in a conference at Stanford University in April arranged by the Center for Research on Women and the American Simone de Beauvoir Society, where her paintings would be exhibited as soon as the Paris show ended.

Simone walked over to us as we were having this discussion and gave me quite a scare: she appeared to have trouble recognizing me, and I had to say my name twice. I wondered if something might be seriously wrong.

After all our years of intimate conversation, to have to tell her who I was and remind her that we had an appointment for the very next afternoon was disconcerting, to say the least. It was even more perplexing when she said no, no, she could not see me for at least the next eight days, since she would be fully occupied with her sister. We had corresponded before my departure and laid out a schedule for many more meetings than usual, agreeing that our first order of business was to get the manuscript in final shape. The room was overheated and overcrowded, hot and noisy, and I had landed the day before with a terrible cold that gave me an excruciating headache. I left fairly early, distressed by Beauvoir's behavior but too sick to do more than crawl into bed and try to sleep.

The next morning I was awakened early by the ringing telephone. It was Beauvoir, apologizing for her behavior the night before. She said the room had been too hot and there had been too many flashbulbs going off and people pressing her with things they wanted her to do. She had not been herself last night, and of course we must keep to our schedule. She would see me at the usual time that afternoon, four o'clock, and I could have as much time as I needed throughout my stay. I was greatly relieved.

There were no arguments or disagreements that month. I saw her several times each week, we spoke on the phone on other days, and when I thought I needed more information about some of her recent feminist activity, she phoned some of the women she worked with and arranged for me to meet them. She was in good spirits and fine fettle throughout, even doing something she almost never did: making jokes. She had always been serious and professional with me, on guard to make sure all my questions written on the little cards were asked and answered. My two-word phrase for my rapport with her was "strictly business." It was unusual to see her relaxed, smiling, and offering a refill of the ritual scotch. And when

I left her on the last day that I saw her, she made the most unusual gesture ever. Tall woman that I am, short woman that she was, she clutched at my arms just above the elbows and gave me a slight shake. I liked to think that it was her way of giving me a hug, and I was thrilled to have it.

I flew home, ready to put the finishing touches on the book before the Stanford conference, and I told Jim Silberman and Ileene Smith, the young woman who had been assigned to edit it, that they would have the manuscript as soon as I returned from Stanford, probably by the first of May.

Instead I went to Simone de Beauvoir's funeral in Paris in April.

37

I knew something was wrong the moment I set foot on the Stanford campus, when I could not find Hélène on the day the conference began. Two days earlier she had been happy and radiant at her *vernissage*, after which I left her for a hasty trip to Los Angeles to interview the screenwriter Ivan Moffat.* After looking everywhere, I phoned and finally reached her at the home of her host, Yolanda Patterson, who was then the president of the International Simone de Beauvoir Society. Hélène said she had been hoping I would call because she had something important to tell me: "Simone is in the hospital with pneumonia, and we think it is very serious."

I had difficulty taking this in, considering how positive and joyful she had been at our last meeting. I had to ask Hélène to repeat what she said several times, and I remember stammering over and over, "But she was so well when I left her!" Hélène said she was too upset to continue the conversation on the phone and asked me please to come at once to the Patterson house. She requested that I not tell anyone at Stanford, as she did not want to upset the conference-goers with this news.

I was further shocked when I arrived. Hélène had been so spritely and happy two weeks earlier in Paris and she had been exuberant two nights before, at her exhibition's opening. Now she was holding tightly to her hostess's arm as she came to greet me, her face ashen and her walk a shuffle. We embraced, and she held

---

* He told me he had been "conned" by Beauvoir and Sartre into marrying Natalie Sorokin, the "Natasha" with whom they had both had relationships.

me longer than usual as she whispered in my ear that this was very serious and she was deeply upset that Sylvie was deliberately keeping her from her sister.

She told me that just a day or two after I had left Beauvoir, she had complained of severe stomach pains and been rushed to the nearby Hôpital Cochin, where doctors ran tests that found nothing amiss. They sent her home when she appeared to be recovering well, but within another day or so she developed "pulmonary complications" and was taken back to the hospital.

Even though Simone had been readmitted just hours after Hélène boarded her flight, Sylvie had waited almost four full days to tell her, and not with a phone call but with a brief telegram. Since Hélène's first impulse was to fly home immediately, she telephoned Sylvie, who insisted that the only reason she had waited to pass on the news was to ensure that things were under control. Hélène was not to come, because Simone was responding to treatment and there was every indication that she would recover. Hélène was still so worried that she decided she could not attend that day's program, even though she was to be the guest of honor and most of the sessions were dedicated to the relationship and rapport between the two sisters.

I stayed by her side for the rest of the day, sitting in the kitchen drinking coffee and listening enraptured as Hélène tried to divert her worry by entertaining us with more memories of her and her sister's childhood. I was scheduled to speak that evening before the final celebratory banquet, and Hélène decided to attend because she wanted to hear me and say goodbye to the many new friends she had made during her brief stay. As it was already the middle of the night in Paris, she knew there would be no further news from Sylvie. When we left the house, gracious lady that she was, Hélène took it upon herself to cheer me up, for her hostess and I both sported long, anxious faces. I was driving a rental car, a Renault, and Hélène complimented me for having chosen "a good French vehicle." On the campus, the three of us were soon surrounded by well-wishers, and even though we thought we were being cheer-

ful, people who knew us well asked if something wrong had kept
Hélène from that day's sessions. To them all, we made the excuse
that her long flights and layovers and then the excitement of her
exhibition had exhausted her.

That was the night of April 12, and we were to fly on the
thirteenth to our respective homes. When we said goodbye, we
embraced tightly, and both of us were crying. I wrote what she told
me in the *DD*, that we must *"have courage. I tell her yes, we must
be strong. We say this but I think we both know that the end will not
be far off."*

I spent my last morning in San Francisco with my son, then
in graduate study at San Francisco State University. Hélène went
directly to the airport for the early-morning flight to Paris, which
required almost a day-long stopover in Dallas. I also had a long
layover, in Cincinnati, and as the head cold I had had in Paris had
never really gotten better, by the time I reached Philadelphia, I
was in terrible sinus pain.

At noon the next day, April 14, my phone rang. It was Hélène,
still in California. She had delayed her flight after Sylvie phoned
her on the night of the twelfth to let her know that Simone had
taken a bad turn and to suggest that Hélène should stay there and
await further news. When Sylvie did not call again, Hélène tried
repeatedly and unsuccessfully to reach her. She was unable to do
so until after Simone died. Hélène was devastated that Sylvie had
not called to tell her. Conference organizers worked frantically to
get her onto a direct flight with an upgrade to business class, but
nothing was available, and the frail little lady gamely shouldered
her bag and began the long, sad flight to her beloved sister's funeral
in a middle seat at the rear of the plane.

And now Simone de Beauvoir was dead. After I spoke to
Hélène, I made a black-bordered box in the *DD* around this brief
statement: *Simone de Beauvoir died today, 4 p.m., in the Hôpital
Cochin in Paris. Official cause of death is pulmonary oedema."* And
then I just sat there, unable to move.

Almost immediately my friends heard the news and came to

volunteer their help. I sent one to the dry cleaner's with the black suit I would need for the funeral, and I put another to working the phone to get me on the first plane to Paris. The American friend with the Paris apartment came by to give me the keys and tell me to stay as long as I needed. Then the phone began to ring. First journalists in Paris from *Libération, Figaro, Le Monde,* asking for a comment, then from various American papers and periodicals. My children called from New York and San Francisco to offer comfort, and my husband canceled meetings and left work early. I went into my office and shut the door tightly, something I never do, as I always want to be alert for whatever is happening in the rest of the house. I wrote another entry that night: *"Von comes home early absolutely bereft, feeling as if he has lost someone dear. He was unable to work all day long. Both kids are sad. Katney worries that I'm still too sick to fly to Paris; Vonn Scott keeps saying 'But you didn't tell me she was sick when you were here. What can I do to help?' Amazing how we all feel such loss. Loss. Loss. Loss. I don't think I realized how much I liked her until now that she's gone. No—I didn't realize until now that I more than liked her: I respected her, sure; but I think I loved her, too."*

There was little time to mourn privately. On April 15, I took the only flight I could find: last-minute, via Frankfurt on Lufthansa with a connection to Paris. I had given Hélène the phone number in my friend's apartment, and she phoned shortly after I arrived. She asked if she could come to tea the next afternoon, and of course I said yes. She told me Sylvie was waiting for my call so that she could give me information about the viewing and the funeral and invitations to several private gatherings before and after. Hélène warned me, "You must be sure to address her now as Madame de Beauvoir when you first speak to her, for she is now Simone's legally adopted daughter and the inheritor of her estate. You may call her Sylvie after that, but first you must pay her the honor." I followed protocol when I reached Sylvie on the phone, and I did the same the first time I saw her; afterward, we returned to our usual greetings of Sylvie and Deirdre.

The viewing was scheduled for Friday, April 19. Beauvoir's casket lay in a grim little room just off a lounge at the Hôpital Cochin. I remember a concrete floor and no decoration—no flowers next to the casket, only a few chairs brought in for the old and infirm. Hélène's husband, Lionel de Roulet, sat in one of them. He was recovering from surgery for inner ear problems that created vertigo, and he was still very weak and fearful of falling. His wife, very tired and frail, did not sit but stood beside him to be ready to greet the friends who had been invited to share this private moment. I greeted Sylvie, then went to Bost, *"who looks like a sleepwalker. Everyone is there: four ministers (former) that I know: Jack Lang, Laurent Fabius, Yvette Roudy, Lionel Jospin. I see Élisabeth de Fontenay, Claudine Serre, lots of others I know in the room.*

"Simone de Beauvoir looked bloated and yellow. The red rag [as I called her turban] *was on her head and she was in the (by now) ratty looking red robe. They had her head propped up in the coffin which gave her fat double chins she did not have in life. She had some sort of what looked like incipient ring-worm or open sores on her face. Hélène said she looked like she was sleeping but I thought she looked terrible. The hardest moment came for me as we filed past because at the same time as we were saying our last goodbyes, there were very businesslike little French men noisily and officiously screwing down huge screws into the coffin so they could close it."*

A cortege formed after the viewing. Lionel went to a friend's house because he was too weak to make the final journey to the Cimetière du Montparnasse, where Simone was to be interred with Sartre and share his tombstone. Hélène went in a car with her two cousins Jeanne and Magdeleine, the irrepressible childhood friend Geraldine (GéGé) Pardo, and the young feminist who had been such a help to her, Claudine Monteil. The rest of us walked. Marie-Claire Pasquier came to stand beside me, as did Geneviève Fraisse and Marcelle Marini, still dealing with her husband's recent death from cancer. Judy Friedlander, an American friend to us all, and the publisher Françoise Pasquier completed our little group.

I knew a real feeling of community as we marched with so many different people. There were young mothers with babies in strollers. A father with a toddler on his shoulders told us that she was too young to understand the occasion, but when she was older he would tell her that she had attended the funeral of a great lady. There were African men and women in colorful native dress, among them a group of women who said they had come from several African countries and who bore banners proclaiming themselves the daughters of Simone de Beauvoir. There were middle-aged women dressed in what I call "academic shabby," with long hair and little round glasses, all proudly proclaiming that they had been on the barricades with Sartre and Beauvoir during the 1968 student uprisings. The famous were there—the actress Delphine Seyrig, who had joined Beauvoir in feminist protests, and another actor who my French friends told me was "one of those famous ones you see all the time but whose name you never remember." Claude Lanzmann and Claudine Serre exchanged words with the lawyer-photographer Gisèle Halimi when they thought she was snapping photos too aggressively.

A small fracas interrupted our reveries and turned our sad faces into smiles and laughter when a taxi driver who had been honking his horn was told to shut up and show respect because this was the funeral of a very important woman. When told it was Simone de Beauvoir, he parked his cab and joined my small group, linking arms with us and saying we should probably sing patriotic songs at some point.

The cortege passed slowly down the rue Saint-Jacques because the crowd, estimated at between three and five thousand, pressed close to the hearse. People wanted to touch it, and it was swamped with flowers. It took quite a while for police to make enough room for it to pass. The car traveled slowly through Montparnasse, the arrondissement where Beauvoir had lived her entire life. Eventually it reached the boulevard du Montparnasse, where waiters stood respectfully outside the Dôme, the Select, and La Coupole, in honor of the woman to whom they had served countless meals and drinks. It wound its way to the boulevard Edgar-Quinet, past the building with Sartre's last apartment, and finally to the cemetery entrance. The crowd had become so dense that the police escorts took to bullhorns to yell *"Circulez!"* ("Keep walking!") in an attempt to get the crowd to let the several vehicles in and to close the gates behind them. The young and the enterprising climbed the high walls to look down on the gravesite, but everyone else just stood outside, even though they could not see or hear what was happening.

"The crush was frenetic. Lanzmann read the end of 'Force des Choses' and 'Adieux.' We all stayed—inside the cemetery and outside the gates—it seemed forever. Even though it started to rain, no one wanted to leave."

Eventually a small group left to gather in an apartment on the rue Gay-Lussac, where friends of Hélène had sheltered Sartre and Beauvoir during the '68 uprisings. We heard stories of how they watched when students on the street below tore up the cobblestones to make barricades and weapons to hurl at the authorities, and how the scent of tear gas was so strong they had to keep the windows closed. Hélène asked me to sit with her, Jeanne, Magdeleine, and GéGé, and between bouts of sobs and tears they told me stories of the elder sister she so loved who was now gone and how worried they were about how the younger one would cope. Hélène clutched my arm and whispered, "Simone always took care of me. Now it is all up to me to take care of myself." I had no words of comfort to offer, but I did put my arm around her shoulder. The gesture sufficed; she leaned in and we stayed that way for a long time.

It was getting late and I was exhausted. Reliving the moment later that day: *"I am suddenly deeply affected emotionally and I get very shaky and weepy. I know that I need to leave. I say goodbye to Hélène and Lionel with tearful embraces, and I promise Jeanne and*

Magdeleine that I will make one more visit to Meyrignac later [this]
*year. We agree that we will laugh and tell more stories about 'the
antics of Simone and Sartre.'"*

I walked over to the Jardin du Luxembourg and sat in a café,
drinking a large *café crème* and trying to unwind: *"Now that I am
alone, I can think about what has happened on this day. I try to read
a newspaper; the rain stops and a few rays of the last of the sun peek
through the clouds; I drink the warm milky coffee and feel better.
Emotions under control now. I take the bus back to Bac/St. Germain
and the apartment."*

In the apartment I managed a light dinner of fruit and cheese
between telephone calls with friends, most of whom had been with
me on that last sad walk from hospital to cemetery. *"We all seem to
need to touch base in our common emotional distress. Marie-Claire
Pasquier tells me that on her way home, she 'bought flowers for the
living—myself!' I go to bed and fall into deep sleep. At last this day
is done."*

The next few days were devoted to all sorts of follow-ups before
my departure. I added to my impressions of the funeral those of
Sylvie, Bost, and Lanzmann, and I conferred with several journalists who had followed the crowd. I met with Claude Courchay, who
had been so distraught by Beauvoir's sudden death that he became
ill with *"zonas"* (shingles) and was unable to attend the funeral. He
could not accept that his dear friend was gone, so I found myself
in the curious position of having to offer comfort when I so badly
needed it myself. After all this activity, I telephoned Sylvie for a
brief conversation, just long enough to settle that I would probably
need to make another visit to Paris in the near future to confer
with her and do my last fact-checking. She asked me to wait several
months, and I told her I would probably wait until the fall. I did
not tell her then that I would make one last push for new materials,
anything that recent events might have brought to light, but I was
certainly going to ask her when I returned.

At home, the book was waiting for me. For months I had been telling anyone who asked that it was almost finished, even though I kept realizing the need to cover "just one more topic," or perhaps "just one more chapter." But on my last day in Paris, when I walked the streets in gloom and steady rain, I stopped short with a stunning realization: the biography was nowhere near done. What had been a living, breathing, feisty document about a writer who was actively engaged in the writing life had to become a final, finished, and definitive account. With Simone de Beauvoir's death, her canon was forged in perpetuity. Her life required a different focus and a suitable ending.

And then I had another thought that literally left me breathless: "*I have to write this bloody book all over again, starting at the beginning and ending with something very different from the one with which I started.*"

38

Life, as always, had a way of intruding on almost every plan or schedule I have ever made. As soon as I returned from Beauvoir's funeral in Paris, I found requests for more articles about her than I could possibly have written. Elaine Markson told me to try to write as many as I could, for all the publications were prestigious and would be excellent publicity for the forthcoming biography. There were also multiple requests from scholarly journals that wanted articles on Beauvoir and, to my irritation, on Beckett. I did not want to think about him or his biography until I had sorted out all my thoughts and ideas about Beauvoir, and—to my surprise and concern—my far too emotional responses to her death. From the end of April until the beginning of September 1986, I worked on the book in fits and starts between other writing tasks. My calendar was filling up for the year to come with invitations, such as the one to preside over a day-long Beckett symposium at a Maryland university and to speak about Beauvoir at Harvard's Center for European Studies with Sartre's most recent biographer, Annie Cohen-Solal. I accepted all this, not only to stoke prepublication interest in the book but also for the eventual review of my credentials for promotion to full professor.

I wrote the Beauvoir biography on my first computer, a huge, heavy, and expensive IBM with only 64 kilobytes. I used the program called Wordstar when I started, and by the time I finished nine years later, I was using Wordperfect. These days, with Windows messing up my writing life by updating itself with new complications every other day, I still mourn Wordperfect, which was exactly what its name said. I also had a 10-megabyte external hard drive because the book, with its seven or eight full drafts, used up all the computer's memory. Not trusting it, each day I saved everything onto a floppy disk and then printed what I wrote. My children called me their friendly local paranoid because of my anxiety that I would inadvertently delete or otherwise find a way to destroy what I had written. I did not go as far as some of my writer friends, who stored their printed manuscripts in the refrigerator or freezer just in case their houses caught fire, but by the time I finished the book, I had a seven-shelf bookcase filled with variously colored file folders that indicated the status of each revision. I went through a color spectrum, from beige to yellow, orange, red, blue, and green, which as my favorite color I thought would be the last. Now that I had to rewrite yet again, the only color left to buy for the final text was purple, a sad color that seemed fitting.

To this day I cannot cope with all the sophisticated possibilities computers offer, but I loved writing on one from the very first. When I used typewriters, as fast as I was composing a sentence, I was already thinking of three other ways I might phrase it better. Many reams of paper were sacrificed before the computer freed me to create every sentence I could imagine, one after the other, then to cut, paste, and rearrange the words until I had exactly the sentence that I wanted. A few of my notes from the period reveal how I agonized over the writing:

> 6/25: *Today I re-wrote the first six pages of Chapter 7 three different times in three different ways. Maybe I'm trying for too much historical erudition and documentation. Maybe I should just get on with the life.*

> 6/26: *I am mired in detail, but I had better write it all, passionate purple prose or not. I can decide at the end what to cut.*

> 7/22: *Including revisions, I have 15 pages I think I can keep. I seem to be making a lot of statements about SdB and her relationships with women. They need to be integrated where appropriate.*

7/30: Euphoria short-lived. Too much I can't figure out where to put in. Must find the way to weave—intersperse—make it all agree. So hard.

And so it went, throughout a hot and sticky Philadelphia summer. Getting nowhere fast, with the ancient and noisy room air conditioner in my office that I called the "B-29" blasting away, I decided I needed to change direction by putting the book aside and trying something different. I began by typing all Beauvoir's letters to me to see if there were any nuggets there that I might explore independently. Perhaps if I wrote a single self-contained episode based on something in the letters it would start the writing juices flowing. On "8/13" I wrote: *"Finished typing SdB's letters to me. They were deeply moving. Knowing her as I do now, I can place the evolution of her deepening affection for me and her trust in my work. Seeing this makes it very hard to work on the book because the shape of it has changed so much since her death. I think I am going to leave it that way, much of it as I originally wrote it, and then try to explain why I did so in a preface. Then it would stand as a sort of critical 'explication de la méthodologie.' But that, too, remains to be decided."* By September I was able to clarify the main problem with reshaping the text: *"What makes it all so difficult is that now I have to fit in so many different concepts & ideas in the early part of the book to show the basic development of her personality, so that her later behavior will be understandable, especially when it comes to fitting her work into her life."*

This was a fairly obvious conclusion, but I was a long time coming to it. I felt very good when I had the breakthrough, because immediately after, *"I wrote about ten pages that got her through meeting Sartre, and I had it happen in the middle of a chapter, uneventfully, in the ordinary course of things, because that was how it actually did happen—two students aware of each other who finally met."*

Things progressed smoothly after that, and I thought I had the manuscript well enough under control to make my last trip to France before publication in early October. For the first time in a long time, Von was able to come with me, and we looked forward to fitting some personal time in among all the work I had to do. Each of us had been so busy professionally during the past year that we felt the need to slow down and pay attention to our relationship. I was especially cognizant of my absence from family life, not only with husband and children—even though the children were now grown and living independently—but also with my brother and sister, with whom I have always been close. My mother was retiring from her work as a cardiac intensive-care nurse and planning a move to California to live near my brother. There were many decisions that involved us all during this move, and I felt I had not participated in all that I should.

And yet when I turned off the computer and shut the door to my office on the eve of departure, the guilt I felt over abandonment had nothing to do with my personal life but everything to do with my work. I was still struggling with the dilemmas of a woman of my generation, torn between home and profession, always feeling that attention given to one meant serious neglect of the other. As I had pushed deeper into revisions, I had begun more consciously to view my subject through my own lens. How did Beauvoir manage to avoid such doubts and conflicts throughout her life? How did she keep so single-mindedly focused on the professional? Or did she? I was still sorting this out.

For the first (and the last) time, I dreaded having to go to Paris, the city I have always loved, which now evoked *"so many feelings of desolation and loss. Just awful."*

My anxiety was compounded by a round of terrorist attacks in Paris that led the government to require visas for all travelers. In an unseasonal and unrelenting heat wave that enveloped the entire East Coast at the end of September, Von and I had to go to New York and stand on line outside the Consulate General for three hours. When the officer asked the reason for my journey as he affixed the visa to the passport, he offered "condolences for your loss."

Security was tight when we flew, a commonplace now but most unusual then. When we landed at Orly Airport, *"French kids in police uniforms looking scared, carrying Uzis. A loud boom all over the airport while waiting for luggage. Everyone jumps, thinking it's a bomb, then we all laugh sheepishly. Everything so different now."*

The apartment we rented for the month of October was on avenue Reille in our beloved Montparnasse, bright and sunny and overlooking the reservoir, which made it seem as if we were in the country looking out onto a green field. We walked through Parc Montsouris remembering how the old men had nodded their approval when *le papa* had come jogging along well after *les enfants*. We went back to the little market on the rue d'Alésia where the clerks had welcomed our family as part of the neighborhood. We walked past the bakery where Madame had kept us up-to-date on increases in the price of butter. We found everything changed: the old men were not in the park, the small market had become a *supermarché*, and a large apartment building was under construction where the bakery had been. It seemed that every physical thing connected to happy times was gone and now all we had were memories.

I had a bit more archival research to do on this trip. Several films and television documentaries had been rushed to completion after Beauvoir's death, and I needed to see them at the Centre Simone de Beauvoir, since they were unavailable elsewhere. Here I ran into bureaucratic roadblocks until I managed to convince the curators of my limited time in Paris and they let me see them all in one long day. I was not so fortunate with archives at the Bibliothèque de l'Arsenal, where a French friend who was a historian of drama had found several interviews Beauvoir had given years before about her dramatic writings and her limited interest in theater. My friend thought I should see them, but I didn't quite know where this information would fit in the biography and wanted to take copies home to digest later. Photocopying was not permitted, however, so I had to spend several long days sweating metaphorical bullets as I copied them in longhand with a pencil. Each night I had to ice my swollen wrist before I could think about holding a fork to eat my dinner.

But the most important appointment was with Sylvie, who said we should meet at Beauvoir's apartment. I knew I needed to gird myself to enter 11 bis, rue Schoelcher. The golden sofas and the jewel-like chairs were still there, as were the Giacometti lamp and the tiny sticklike figures on the shelf above where Beauvoir always sat. The plaster cast of Sartre's hands was still on the table in the center of the room. The little tray of fountain pens and the small writing pad were still on the coffee table, but the woman who had given everything such vibrant life was gone. How was I going to cope?

Sylvie had asked me to come in the late afternoon, when she was finished with her teaching day. Dusk was falling and she had not yet turned on the lights. At first I found her *"snippy, even snotty."* This demeanor intensified after she let me turn on the tape recorder, and for almost an hour she proceeded to run down every single person in Beauvoir's life, especially Hélène. At the end of the rant, she suggested we meet at her apartment next time, for she was removing everything from Beauvoir's so she could sell it. She also told me she was preparing Beauvoir's letters to Sartre for publication, "and many people will not like them." She did not answer when I asked directly who these unhappy people would be, but having read the letters myself, I had my suspicions. Surely Sylvie would withhold the ones that were the most wounding; surely she would not publish such ugliness and cruelty against people whose only sin was to love Simone de Beauvoir. Unfortunately, I would be proven wrong when the book appeared. Sylvie printed Beauvoir's harsh and brutal comments about her sister's life choices as a married woman and her professional ability as a painter. Hélène was devastated when she read them, and the emotional pain she suffered lasted the rest of her life.

Despite Sylvie's negativity at the start of that initial meeting, it ended on very good terms. I knew we were on good footing when she took an unopened bottle of scotch from the refrigerator and said we must have a drink, *"comme d'habitude,"* this time unwatered, *"pur, sans eau."* I think I had put her at ease by sticking to questions that were mostly about clarification of certain dates or events, all basic fact-checking, and because I had not pressed her on her plans for the damning letters. There was nothing to raise hackles or inspire controversy. She seemed surprised by the depth of my knowledge and the sophistication of some of the opinions I voiced, for more than once she made a snide remark about how unusual it was for an American to have such insights into things French. I just smiled and pretended to be grateful for the compliment.

She told me I should give her two days to collect some documents she knew I had not seen because they had only recently been unearthed in the rue Schoelcher cellar: letters from fans, admirers, and persons who had had insignificant roles in Beauvoir's life. Some were interesting, but most contained information I already knew. There were several notebooks I had not seen, compiled during Beauvoir's years of teaching, which dealt with material for her classroom lectures rather than her writing or thinking. None of these documents was what I hoped to find: the Leibniz dissertation, for example, or the manuscripts of her novels. However, it was good to see all these things because they confirmed everything Beauvoir had told me during our interviews: that she was holding nothing back, and that if my book had been published before her death, there would have been no surprises or contradictions and nothing to prove wrong what I had written. I thought it ironic that her death could, in many ways, allow me to relax. And reading these documents confirmed again that no one was telling me anything new, which meant that my primary research was indeed complete.

I saw Sylvie several more times, recording what she told me and taking copious notes. By the time we parted, I had unlimited permission to quote any document for which she held the copyright and to use whatever photos I wanted. She had agreed to honor the conditions under which I worked with Beauvoir and would put no obstacles in my path. Everything was working out so perfectly that even though there was going to be time for fun with my husband in the days ahead, all I wanted to do was go home and get back to my office, my computer, and my manuscript. And then Sylvie threw an unexpected curveball.

When I told her that I hoped to be finished with revisions and the last of the writing by the following spring, she insisted that I had to come back in February, because she was sure that she would have found "other things" in the rue Schoelcher cellar by then. Even though Beauvoir had told me repeatedly that there were no manuscripts of any of her writings (her mother had had to use the paper to cover jam and jelly jars during the war), there was always the hope that she had missed something. Hope sprang eternal in me: what a coup it would be to find the manuscript of *The Mandarins* or *She Came to Stay* . . . Yes, I told Sylvie, I would return in February, even though I was not sure I would have either the time or the money.

I had just spent a fortune paying the Centre Simone de Beauvoir for permission to use their copyrighted photos, and I had just written a huge check to a French graduate student who claimed to have spent hours chasing down obscure publications but had found nothing at all. And of course there was the current trip, with the extra expense of the car rental to take us south to Beauvoir's cousins. I had visions of what was left of my fellowship money evaporating in dollar signs, as if in a cartoon bubble that floated over my head. Nevertheless, I was in Paris, and I meant to make the most of it.

———

Von and I began our tourist adventures in Paris, where we had a little time for window shopping on the Right Bank. I will never forget the sight of the entire Japanese sumo wrestling team coming out of Hermès, huge men all decked out in blue-and-white kimonos, their outfits punctuated by brilliant orange shopping bags filled with luxury goodies. We still bemoan leaving the heavy Nikon at home that day and having only our memories of the sight. We spent a day rambling through the château country, another exploring Normandy, and another at Mont-Saint-Michel. Our itinerary was supposed to take us next to Goxwiller to see Hélène, but Lionel de Roulet was back in the hospital for another operation and she was exhausted by worry and long days of sitting at his bedside, so we changed it to go directly to Uzerche in southwest France to visit the two cousins, Magdeleine and Jeanne, at La Grillère and Meyrignac respectively.

It was our second trip to Beauvoir's two elderly cousins but the first when we were to be their houseguests. Our first stop was the village of Saint-Germain-les-Belles and the family estate of Magdeleine Mantis de Bisschop. The large manor house at La Grillère had been sold years before and was now "the property of a rich man from Nice," but the Mantis family had kept some of the estate's land, and when Magdeleine married she moved into a house on that property. When she was widowed, she had had a new, smaller house built for herself so that her daughter could live with her family in the larger house where she had been raised. We stayed with Magdeleine in the smaller house and visited her daughter, Agnès, her husband, Jean, and Isabelle, the only one of their three children still at home. The entire visit was pure and simple fun. At the age of eighty, Magdeleine had so much energy and enthusiasm for life that her devoted teenage granddaughter told me she was usually exhausted after a day in her company and had to go to bed early, while her grandmother stayed up to read until the local television station went off the air.

We seemed to be eating all the time during those few days:

large breakfasts and midmorning coffee with Magdeleine, bounteous lunches prepared by Agnès and Isabelle, afternoon tea with Agnès and Jean, and (thankfully) simple suppers once again with Magdeleine. In between, we walked the grounds and she described in detail all that we saw. That tower was the dovecote where Magdeleine had hidden Sartre when he showed up unannounced and uninvited. That back doorway at the château was the entrance to the house's kitchen, from which she had spirited bread and cheese in her apron to feed Sartre. That path over there—that was how Simone had walked to the dovecote when she sneaked out of Meyrignac to spend her nights with him. I had seen it all before, on my first visit, but that had been a hasty one, and even though I had taken copious notes, much of it had not settled into my mind. Now, to take our time and see it all again, listening to the stories Magdeleine told us of Beauvoir and Sartre's early years, I found myself transported back to those moments. I told Magdeleine that I could envision clearly the years when theirs had been pure intellectual passion, and she chortled: "Yes, and also pure lust."

On Sunday morning we prepared to leave for Meyrignac, the home of the other cousin who had been Beauvoir's girlhood playmate, Jeanne de Beauvoir Dauriac. We had been told repeatedly by Hélène and Magdeleine that Madame Dauriac was like them but also very different. Each cousin had known exactly how she wanted to live her life and so, too, had Jeanne. She had wanted to marry early and have children (she had nine) and become the mistress of her family estate. She had succeeded in her desires and lived her life contentedly, in her own way and on her own terms. Jeanne was far more formal than her cousins and would always present herself as Madame Dauriac, and that, they said, was how we should address her. Jeanne's cousins loved her dearly, but both made gentle fun of her haute bourgeois propriety as they advised us on how to behave properly at Jeanne's Sunday lunch. As we left Magdeleine, she told us to make sure we stopped by the florist in town to buy our hostess a tasteful bouquet of flowers, and to arrive precisely at 12:30. When we phoned Hélène to update her on our travels and relay these instructions, she laughed and said we had given her the only cheer during a long worrisome day at Lionel's bedside.

We arrived promptly at Meyrignac, and in trepidation, but despite the formality of the occasion and the perfection of the luncheon table's setting, it was a rollicking occasion. Madame Dauriac was charming and gracious, and some of her nine adult children (and their children) joined us for spirited conversation in two languages, as some wanted to practice their very good English. We listened enthralled to stories about Simone's antics, so much so that we probably did not pay proper attention to Madame Dauriac's descriptions of the excellent food, almost all of it raised or grown on the estate.

Later she showed us the many changes to the property since Simone's childhood. Her bedroom, for example, had been converted to a bathroom. But despite the interior changes, the exterior and some of the formal rooms remained exactly as Beauvoir described them in her memoirs. In preparation for the visit, Von had reread *Memoirs of a Dutiful Daughter,* and he turned to me with a huge smile to say that from the moment we entered the house, he could envision her there. Later we saw the kitchen (only slightly updated since young Simone's days), where all the women gathered to gossip and cook. We were escorted to a position at the window to see the tree under which Simone would sprawl, refusing to engage in such demeaning activities as canning and preserving: "Simone preferred to keep her nose always in a book, and her father was usually there scolding while her mother glared from the kitchen window." Everything came alive for me that weekend, and I like to think that I was able to channel that energy into the biography's chapters that covered those years.

On the drive back to Paris, my head was filled with ideas and the rewrites they would require. I filled several small notebooks while Von drove, and several more on the flight home. Back in my office once again, I looked at the colorful manila folders on my bookcase, smiling particularly at the green ones, which were originally intended to hold the final draft. As I read through the notes I had compiled since Beauvoir's death, my euphoria gave way to panic. With every page I turned, it was horrifying to realize that these notes were as much about me as they were about her. They were *my* thoughts, *my* reactions, responses, emotions. How was I going to turn this mess into *her* biography? After all, it was her life, and how was I going to write the end of it?

39

Obviously I would need to start a different set of folders, and I went right out to buy them. The only color I had not yet used was purple, so green gave way to purple and that's what the final version became. When I brought them back to the office, I was so paralyzed by the overwhelming thought of starting all over again that I simply sat and stared at them.

And then my thoughts shifted to Beckett. I had managed to keep him out of mind during the Paris sojourn, knowing that I probably would not run into him on the street because he had become quite infirm. Sitting paralyzed in my office, I spent more hours than I'd like to admit reflecting on how I had written his biography and how different it had been to work with him. All our meetings had been so formal. He may have thought we were "just two friends having a conversation," but each time we met, Mr. Beckett and Mrs. Bair were always exceedingly courteous and polite to each other. Such formality created distance, and distance allowed objectivity, so I didn't even have to think about it as I wrote.

I was wondering how I might impose similar objectivity on my work with Beauvoir when the phone rang late one afternoon in October 1987 and a colleague asked if I had heard the news of Beckett's death. I did not react emotionally, as I had done to the news of Beauvoir's. Instead, in those pre-Internet days, I thanked her, hung up, and calmly phoned a journalist friend in Paris, who told me that no, the famous writer who had just died was not Beckett; it was Jean Anouilh, in Lausanne, Switzerland. I was genuinely happy that my colleague had been mistaken, but my thoughts had zoomed originally to professional matters: a new paperback edition of the Beckett biography was in the works, and I was relieved that I would not have to rewrite the ending. I remember shaking my shoulders as if to clear my head, wondering what made me think of him so coldly.

With hindsight, I think it was because of the formal distance between us, which I was more responsible for creating than Beckett was. I created that distance deliberately, because as a woman, I felt I had to. I was determined to act as a professional scholar completely free from any hint of inappropriate behavior, with Beckett or anyone else. This approach evolved naturally from my entire professional life to that point, starting with my first job as a journalist at *Newsweek*.

At a later reporting job I learned from a caring editor not to make "smart-ass" rebuttals to insinuations that I had traded sexual favors for scoops. To this day, I keep on my desk two lines of doggerel cast in hard type by a compositor: "I don't think it is fair/to see a mini [skirt] on Dee Bair." I keep it there to remind me of how far women have come since I began to work with Samuel Beckett. However, the 1970s were still the bad old days, and in the end, how I presented myself really didn't matter; the old boys' club members still wrote whatever they wanted about professional women.

Those attitudes were beginning to change when I began to write about Beauvoir in the early 1980s. The larger women's movement mirrored my own struggles as women began to reclaim their place in history and demand to take their places in all walks of professional life. Simone de Beauvoir was a role model, as she had been subjected to every outrageous sling and arrow throughout her life even as she remained dedicated to her writing career. By her last decade, feminist women all over the world used her tenacity as their example. When she espoused causes and joined protests, they lined up behind her. In effect, she was a sister in arms, and I always thought her advocacy of feminist issues was one of the reasons she welcomed me so warmly. She simply wanted someone to consider all her work, and for her, the personal hardly mattered; all she cared about was ensuring that her many contributions to contemporary culture would be recognized by generations to come.

I admit, it was probably easier for two feminist women to reach a rapport as they worked together than for an Old World gentleman to confide in a woman he hardly knew. This was a question I had had ample opportunity to explore in the programs and panel discussions I attended once I began to write about Beauvoir. The subject was usually framed as "Can a Woman Write About a Man (or Vice Versa)?" and I was usually paired with a man who had written about a woman. In almost every instance, the audience had no problem agreeing that men could certainly convey the essence of a woman's being, but a woman writing about a man—well, that was another thing entirely. My contributions to these discussions were usually met with skepticism at best, dismissal at worst.

And the more profound and troubling question of whether a woman subject was even worthy of biography usually simmered just below the surface. During a colloquium of distinguished scholars at Harvard's Center for European Studies, I was invited to talk with Annie Cohen-Solal about the political activity of our biographical subjects. Annie did little more than read passages or summarize what she had written in her book about Sartre, but I slaved over my lecture. My book was due to be published in several months, and so I presented much hitherto unknown information about some of Beauvoir's political writings and opinions. It was tailored expressly for the interests of the politicians and political scientists (almost all male) in the audience. I could see many of them taking copious notes as I spoke, so I looked forward to what I thought would be a spirited Q & A. When it came, every question directed to Annie was indeed about Sartre's politics, but every single question directed to me was about Simone de Beauvoir's sex life. Literally, I almost cried.

Clearly the Beckett biography could not serve as a template or model for the Beauvoir biography. He was still living and working when I finished writing his, which freed me from feeling an intense need to make it a final, finished document; he was still writing, and something new was happening to him every day. I have long held the view that no biography is ever definitive and none can serve as the be-all and end-all. It can only be the book that a generation or two finds necessary, informative, and satisfying. I believe it was Margaret Atwood who rightly said that each generation needs its own biography, for how can we have the arrogance to think that we have provided all the answers when we don't even know the questions future generations will ask?

So my ultimate obligation with Beckett's biography had been to gather every bit of information I could find and tell the truth as I discerned it. I joked that I could not write a sentence saying "It was a nice day" until I checked weather reports for three weeks before and after that day in every newspaper published in Beckett's immediate area. As I've said, for every person who volunteered a version of an encounter with Beckett, I wanted at least three others, if not five, to tell the same version independently. It was the first biography of Beckett, and therefore accuracy had to be primary. Most important, it was his life, and as I had played no role in it, there was no reason for me to appear in any part of it.

Asking that question led directly to Beauvoir: why then, had I departed so far from this point of view when I wrote about her? I found a partial answer when I was contacted by an editor who asked me for a blurb for one of his biographies, written by a woman about a woman. The author was prominent then, and as she and the editor are still working together today, I won't name them here. The editor volunteered that I might not like his writer's book because her writing was so different from mine. He said that I was *"very careful not to place myself as an obstruction before my readers, whereas [his writer] always puts herself in the way, so that in order to understand her subject you must first let her tell you all about herself, until finally you are weighed down by her sensibility and are so inundated by her persona that you've almost lost sight of who she is writing about."*

The thought of my being placed in such a category scared the writing life out of me. I immediately started to purge anything that might be construed as a personal, emotional opinion and to replace it with prose so clinically detached that all the liveliness was gone. The computer screen filled with revision after revision before I found a positive rhythm, and just as I was settling into putting *her* life back into *my* book, my "other lives" intruded and I had to put it aside for the better part of the year.

I was well into my second year of fellowship in 1987, which allowed me to be away from the university and happily ensconced in my home office, when I received a call from the English Department chairman. He told me that the full professors "*were embarrassed*" that despite all the honors and accolades I had been receiving, I had not yet been considered for promotion to full professor. My first response was delight that my colleagues thought so well of my contributions, but, to mix metaphors, warning flags flared quickly. I had been away from the campus for almost two full years, and such absences never made academic hearts grow fonder; it only made them jealous. Even though I had a solid contract for the second book, I knew that my promotion could be fully denied or at the very least postponed until it was published, and perhaps even then until after it was reviewed. Also, preparation of a promotion dossier—compiling my writings, lectures, reviews of other books, and professional appearances; securing letters of recommendation from students; assembling a list of the many times I represented Penn at public events; and collecting testimony from people in public or nonprofit agencies throughout Philadelphia with whom I had cooperated in many different ways—all this was a very serious and time-consuming process and could take several months, at the very least.

I did not voice these concerns to the chairman during that initial phone conversation. Instead I said I realized that I could spend the time preparing this massive dossier only to have none of it taken into consideration because the all-important second book had not yet been published. He said that would never happen in my case, and in fact I would not even need to submit the entire manuscript, as no one would have the time to read it anyway, so why didn't I just select "several hundred good pages that would give the flair and flavor of the book"? Reluctantly, I agreed to go forward, but only after he gave his word that the promotion would not be denied because I had not submitted a published second book. He assured me repeatedly that this would never happen, "given that everything else is so outstanding."

It took almost five months to compile the dossier, and all the while I was preparing it, I drove my friends and family (according to my husband) "round the bend" with my "rampant paranoia." I submitted it at the start of the fall term in 1987, full of apprehension about the outcome and desperate to return to my writing. The first four hundred pages of the book were fairly final, and I thought they gave its "flair and flavor." The full professors had two months to read through the dossier, and the meeting to vote on it was scheduled for Friday, November 13, at 4:30 p.m. Less than an hour later, the chairman phoned to tell me that by a vote of seven to two (barely a quorum), they had decided it would be in my "best interests" to deny promotion until the book was published. There had not been much to discuss, they said, because I had submitted only a partial manuscript.

I had to ask him to repeat this before I found voice to protest that he had given his word that this would not happen. He equivocated and obfuscated, and while he did, visions of Alice's white rabbit disappearing down the rabbit hole floated through my mind. He spouted one contradiction after another, and nothing he said made sense. I kept repeating that he had given me his word that the reason for denial would not be the submission of a partial manuscript, and now he had to deliver; if he did not reconvene the meeting and ask for another vote, he would have my resignation on his desk by the following Monday. He snickered and said he knew that that would never happen. In a rage, I wrote his exact words in the *DD*: "*Nobody resigns tenure, especially not you.*" It was all I could do to tell him goodbye—politely—before I put the phone back in its cradle—softly.

My husband came home shortly after and found me in my office working on the first draft of a letter of resignation. When I showed it to him, he said he owed me a profound apology: *"Von said he thought I was being paranoid but he was very wrong: 'They are truly insane.'"*

What depressed me the most about this so-called review was that of the seven negative votes, four had been cast by women full professors. Sisterhood was sadly absent.

It did not take long for news of the rejection to find its way onto the university grapevine, and my phone rang steadily all weekend. Two words were used by everyone: first they were "stunned," and then they were "outraged." From university trustees to members of other departments, from the distinguished external scholars who had written on my behalf to my bewildered students, no one could understand what had happened. The only person who called from the English Department was the chairman, and his increasingly contradictory messages were one of the finest examples of "cover your ass" tactics I had ever seen. All I had to do, he said, was to resubmit the following year—a brand-new dossier. In a subsequent conversation he said I should withdraw my resignation letter and resubmit the original dossier the following spring. At one point he said that if the book had still not been published, perhaps the department would want to wait until the entire text was in galleys; or perhaps not, perhaps it would be best to wait until the book was in print. Or perhaps I should wait until the reviews were in. I stood firm each time: he had given me his word and he had to keep it. He went so far as to make statements to the student newspaper: *"They let him shake his jowls in righteous indignation and make me look like a hysterical crazy person. I remain silent but resolute."*

Because each department had complete autonomy, there was little the dean or the provost could do to resolve the stalemate. When the chairman was asked to explain, he told them that "the decision was to decide not to decide because it would be in [her] best interests." People who had been in that meeting told me that "nothing he said made any sense." My conclusion was a tired "Yea, verily." A dear friend in another department phoned to caution me of the seriousness of my decision to resign. I listened carefully to his thoughtful arguments before telling him how I had wasted the better part of a year on this review, and how my book had been delayed for yet another time by departmental politics. I said I was aware of the financial pitfalls ahead, but I simply did not want to endure any more of these humiliations. This latest snub was one outrage too many. His conclusion also went into the *DD: "In other words, you are not willing to stick your nose in one more bucket of shit so they will have no other choice but to let you into the club."*

Yes, I said, that was exactly right. I had always been a major contributor to my family's finances and I would need to find a way to replace my salary, but I was truly lighthearted when I said this. Despite being a professor for thirteen years, I had always maintained my "freelance mentality," and I had no qualms about resuming the improvisational writing life. In fact I looked forward to the freedom it would bring. It was going to take another year to finish writing Beauvoir's biography and a second one for the yearlong publication process, so that would make it ten years from start to finish for my second book, 1980 to 1990. Without the academic interruptions I could have published it in six or seven at the most. I knew I was lighting out for strange new territories when I resigned, but I never looked back.

Whenever I am asked if I miss academic life, I always say that there is one thing I do regret: the pension I don't have. But I have taught since then as a visiting professor or writer in universities in the United States and everywhere else, from Europe to Australia, and those experiences have brought nothing but pleasure and the sheer joy of experiencing so many different ways of looking at the subjects that interest me. I have taught biography courses in which clever students have delighted me with their insights into the genre, and I have helped several to publish well-regarded biographies of their own. After long periods of solitude in my office, when all I did was put my own words into print, these encounters have been wonderfully refreshing. It has been so nice to be able to leave the classroom energized and mentally enriched, and to know that the experience will not be soured by a department meeting to follow. I never did know how to play academic politics, and I realize how fortunate I have been to be free from them, and to have spent so many years doing work that I love.

And so it was back to the biography, the writing punctuated this time by assignments I accepted happily for the needed income but also for the sheer pleasure of writing them. I established a good rhythm with the book, was pleased with the structure, and looked forward each day to resuming where I had left off the night before. My *DD* became filled with notes of a kind that I sheepishly referred to when talking to other biographers as "the Deirdre Bair Theory of National Biography."

I formulated my "theory" or "thesis" after I was asked countless times what it was like to write about persons whose cultures and societies were different from my own. The Americans, I said, will footnote you to death as they overwhelm you with sources to convince you of the validity of their interpretation. They produce doorstoppers, the huge bricks that show off every bit of research they have done. The British are quite different, as they tell enthralling stories in the most elegant prose styles, but when readers look for citations and references, they are most likely to be told to trust the writer, dear reader. Oftentimes sources and citations are few and far between. The French are entirely different from both: they will create a theoretical box, and if they have to break the biographical arms and legs of the subject to fit him or her into that box, they will cheerfully do so. I was reminded of a French writer who told me he was going to write a biography, too, just as soon as he found a subject who fit his thesis.

I was factoring all these thoughts smoothly into the final Beauvoir manuscript until I came to another of those moments of insight that required a major rewrite of much of the text. I read through all the biographies of Sartre that had been published to date and came to a startling revelation about my own book. To contrast just two of them, Ronald Hayman's with Annie Cohen-Solal's, I noted: *"His seems more thoughtful than hers. She restates much information already known while he does pretty much the same but strives to interpret it. Basically, both are acceptances of known truths and restatements of Sartre's writings."* And then came the insight: *"Interesting that neither gives that much space to SdB."*

What terrified me was the fact that in my biography of Beauvoir, Sartre appeared on almost every page, from before their first meeting to her death several years after his. How had he insinuated his way so deeply into what was supposed to be Beauvoir's life, and why was there such a lopsided discrepancy? The British critic Peter Conrad gave me a partial answer when he reviewed a biography of Thomas de Quincy. Borrowing Joseph Conrad's term, Peter Conrad said that de Quincy had made himself "a silent secret sharer" in any book written about him.

I asked myself, *"Is this what I did with Sartre when I wove him so deeply into the fabric of her life?"* And then: *"If my intention is to validate her life and work, what do I do about him!?!"*

40

Nelson Algren came back to the forefront of my work while I was thinking about Sartre's role in Beauvoir's life, and writing about her relationship with him helped me to integrate Sartre where I thought he belonged. Her letters to Algren had been bought by Ohio State University, and at the end of 1987, I was trying to free time to go to Columbus to read them, while cognizant that I had promised Sylvie to return to Paris in February 1988 to read any further letters or manuscripts she might have found. It was quite a shock to receive a *"harsh and hysterical"* letter from her just after the new year, denying permission to quote from the Algren letters or from any of Beauvoir's correspondence with Sartre that I had already seen. *"Her letter was a vicious and nasty put-down, but at the same time a great relief because I don't have to go to Paris in February. Even better, I can now interpret the Algren break accurately as the devastating romantic split it really was."* The problem of how to write about Algren was settled, but that of my "secret [and meddlesome] sharer," Sartre, would be solved more gradually.

Sylvie could do whatever she wanted now that she was Beauvoir's legal heir. She could obstruct my book if she chose, because I did not have a formal contract or written agreement with Beauvoir that covered rights and permissions. I was writing her biography the same way I wrote Beckett's, on a metaphorical handshake, which in my naiveté was how I had originally thought all biographies got written. I knew better by the time I began Beauvoir's, but I still asked for and received this informal trust. I was very lucky, because I continued to create myself as a biographer as I went along, and it was the only way I knew how to work in the genre.

Sylvie knew everything about our informal arrangement, and she also knew that Beauvoir had expected her to honor it, which made it all the more upsetting not just for me but for everyone who had known or loved Simone de Beauvoir after Sylvie began to dismantle or destroy everything from Beauvoir's beloved apartment to the agreement with me and the several others I knew that she had had with writers and filmmakers. In the end Sylvie backed down from her position and I was able to write the book exactly as I felt it needed to be written. But to this day, despite the fact that Beauvoir's letters to Nelson Algren at Ohio State have been read, used, and even quoted in other books, Sylvie has never allowed any legitimate scholar or writer to read Algren's letters to Beauvoir, all of which she holds in her possession.

I cannot understand why she still maintains this ridiculous position, but my primary emotion in 1988 was relief that I did not have to see her in person, for fear that my very presence might provoke her to take hostile action. When I thought about it, I concluded that her volatility was actually an indirect benefit, as it led me to think carefully about how I portrayed Sartre and Algren. The content of the Algren letters in conjunction with Sartre's gave me immense freedom to write about Beauvoir's relationships with these two men and to write about the letters themselves. Those she exchanged with them were useful for corroboration, validation, and interpretation. They provided background for everything from where she and they were at any given time to what they told each other they were thinking and doing, reading and writing. The letters became one more valued source to ensure the accuracy of my written text.

It was much the same with Beauvoir's memoirs, which I had read for the first time long before I ever thought I would write about her. Like so many other women, after that initial reading, I was (to use one of her favorite expressions) *"totalement bouleversée,"* totally blown away. There was so much in them that I could imagine was relevant to women at every stage of life, from bookish awkward teenagers who yearned to break free from stultifying families and expand their horizons, to young adult women trying to sort out human relationships, to mature women who had experienced both successes and failures in life and work and who cast cold hard eyes upon Beauvoir's decisions in light of their own. There was an unflinching honesty within the four volumes, but when I began to write about her, especially after I conducted so many interviews with the people who knew her best, I thought there was another facet of the memoirs that required exploration and explanation.

In my earlier versions of various chapters, I had praised her for her directness and the way she faced everything head-on, no matter how unpleasant or embarrassing. Now as I wrote, I was questioning her evasion, the degree to which she never told anything truly personal. A prime example was when she told Nelson Algren how difficult it had been to keep him out of the story when she wrote about Chicago in *America Day by Day:* "I have to find a way of saying the truth without saying it." I thought this personal element was regrettably missing from the memoirs, because it was what truly defined and explained her. In her written version of her life, she told readers where she went and what she did, what she wrote and what she thought. But she did it all dispassionately, as if she were the observer of her own self. It seemed as if she, the woman Simone de Béauvoir, was the silent secret sharer hidden behind the shadow of Beauvoir the writer. I knew that I needed to probe her evasion. I saw it as the biographer's task to tell what she left out, and how best to do it was the question constantly before me.

I thought back to my many conversations with Beauvoir, when I would inquire about an event or encounter in her memoirs, and how my questions would inevitably boil down to "Yes, but how did you *feel* about that?" Her response was almost always the same: first there would be silence while she thought about it, then perhaps a toss of the head, a flick of the wrist, and finally her dismissive answer, always something along the lines of "It happened, it's life; there is nothing you can do; best to get on with it." I would not give up and would try to find another way to ask my essential question. "I've just told you," she would say. And down would slam the Lucite curtain.

Thus it was up to me to interpret so many aspects of her life, and that is where the testimony of those who were closest to her became important for what I wrote. In the memoirs she wrote of her "perfect" compact with Sartre: "Our way of life was so exactly what we wanted that it was as though it had chosen us." Why then, I wondered, when she and Sartre were enjoying an evening in one of their favorite bars with friends and members of their "family," did she sometimes leave the table and go to sit alone at another table to consume vast quantities of wine and sob uncontrollably? Lanzmann, Bost, Pontalis, Pouillon, and many others observed this behavior and told me about it, how as suddenly as she started to cry she would stop, dry her tears, stand up, shake her shoulders, and return to the group as if nothing had happened. This unhappiness was hardly the image of perfection. Beauvoir also believed that everything about her childhood was dark and black. I could accept those thoughts about the clothing worn by her mother and her aunts but not her family's apartment, which was filled with light—I had seen it myself, thanks to the current owners. I remembered what Hélène told me: "That is what my sister believed, and you must allow her to have *her* memory of *her* life." And so I thought long and hard about how to explain such discrepancies without inserting myself into the text as the ultimate authority. I called this phenomenon the difference between personal truth and historical reality, and decided that places had to be found for both.

I knew I was not going to write hagiography, but to what degree, if any, should I act as her advocate, or if not that, as her debunker? Finding the proper voice consumed me. I remember trying to puzzle this out over a dinner at the home of Aileen Ward with several distinguished biographers from her famed biography seminar: Frederick Karl, Kenneth Silverman, Carole Klein, and Maynard Solomon. Perhaps because we were dining, we bandied food metaphors about until we concluded that the biographer's job was to "whet the appetite without providing the full meal." By that, we agreed, those of us who wrote literary biography should ensure that our readers ended our books by wanting to turn immediately to our subjects' writings and to read more about the historical times in which they lived.

I have followed this dictum with every biography I have since written, but I was particularly concerned with doing so when I wrote the chapter about *The Second Sex*. Of the entire book, that is the one I am still not sure works in the way I intended. Instead of giving an *explication de texte*—a summary of the work—I wrote a history of its evolution, from when Beauvoir first got the idea for it and how she wrote it to how it was received by readers, particularly its impact on American readers. I even gave the evolution of its initial flawed translation by the harassed zoologist H. M. Parshley. In effect, I wrote a capsule biography of her book within the larger biography of her life. My intention was to give the full spectrum of responses to it—from the hostile, bitter, sarcastic, and demeaning to the shock of the new, the recognition among women of common anxieties and concerns. Beauvoir gave them hope as she addressed their questions about how to navigate their private and personal spheres and how to find possibilities for engagement with the larger public world. This chapter is still the one that garners the most interest whenever I am asked to speak about Beauvoir's life and work. It mirrors the response to all my biographies, from those who say that the best (or worst) thing about my writing is that I never tell readers what to think but expect them to form their own opinions. And the individual writing that draws this divided response most of all is the chapter on *The Second Sex*.

The writing proceeded smoothly once it became my only occupation, and by mid-1988, I submitted the manuscript to Jim Silberman at Summit Books. I appreciated his insistence that we not rush, that we have the book's appearance and promotion reflect what he called "the excellence" of the content; rather than hurry its publication to late 1989, he decided to hold it until the beginning of 1990. Jim believed that the intelligent general reader suffered cabin fever during the darkest winter nights after the holiday season, and the period between January and March was the perfect time for books such as mine. He was entirely correct, for enough readers were interested in an "old Frenchwoman nobody cares about anymore" that they made it a bestseller that won accolades, was widely translated, and remains in print to this day.

Jim selected Ileene Smith, then at the start of her distinguished career, to work with me, and from the beginning it was a meeting of two minds as we pored over every line of the text. We were on a strict deadline, because she was heavily pregnant with her first child. My book and her son entered the world together, and Ileene and I smile every time we reminisce about how she spent her last hours before becoming a mother editing my last chapter.

As the publication process unfolded, I had the better part of a year to think about what I had written. There is always so much more to do once the manuscript leaves the writer's hands and before it becomes a book. There are photos to select, acknowledgments to write. But I also left for last the very first, and perhaps the most crucial, part of the book: the introduction. I had followed the same practice for the Beckett book, and it became the one true parallel with the Beauvoir biography and with every book I've written since. Writing the introduction at the end allows me to express what I think the reader needs to know before delving into the life, to tell what drew me to the subject and why I think an understanding of his or her life is important for insights into the work. Only at the end of the process could I clearly articulate these seemingly straightforward answers.

When I give talks at conferences or lectures in classrooms, I am often asked to talk about my aims and intentions when I write biography. With the Beauvoir book, I talk about the struggle to write tellingly while also finding the necessary distance to express myself objectively. Obviously I began as a partisan with a bias, attracted to her life because of respect and admiration for her work. The task was to tell this to my readers while convincing them that I presented a version of a life they could trust. It led me to thoughts of what, if anything, the two biographies had in common and what gave each such a separate identity that neither could serve as a model for how to write any other.

In both cases I felt it was an almost unbelievable privilege to know and write about these two giants of contemporary culture. One could argue that because of Beckett, theater changed irrevocably after *Waiting for Godot,* and because of Beauvoir, the contemporary feminist movement ignited with *The Second Sex.* Throughout the seven years I worked with Samuel Beckett, I often thought that if my experiences were ever dramatized, they might fall somewhere between thriller and high drama at one extreme or somewhere between Oscar Wilde's comedy of manners and Feydeau's farce at the other. My years with Simone de Beauvoir had me marveling at the courage this daughter of Catholic minor nobility had shown when she broke away to live a life of freedom from social constraints and to write a book that would change the way more than half the human race lived their lives.

I usually tell people that biographers are not supposed to have feelings about their subjects. And then I admit that of course I have feelings—positive feelings—because how could I (or anyone) spend every day and night for all those years with someone for whom I did not feel something, from admiration and respect to genuine affection and perhaps even a kind of love? I know there are biographers who come to disapprove of or even despise the people they write about, but I could never write a book like that. The reader would sense it and would neither enjoy nor respect it. My job while I am writing is to put feelings aside and become Desmond MacCarthy's "artist under oath." But when I am finished, I have the freedom to say what I really think, and in the case of these two, a single word leaps immediately to my mind: respect. I respected them, and I did so with unqualified admiration.

Samuel Beckett and Simone de Beauvoir had purity of vision, certainty of the rightness of their conduct, the worth and value of their writing. Beckett insisted that "nothing matters but the writing." Time and again he said, "I could not have gone through the awful wretched mess of life without having left a stain upon the silence." Simone de Beauvoir refused to let herself be turned into a monument. She regretted being known as France's "sacred monster," but if this dubious distinction meant she had influence among the generations that followed, she was willing to let it stand. For me, Beckett and Beauvoir were role models. I respect their contributions to contemporary culture and society, and with humility, I am grateful for having known them. But I admit that filtering the variety of my experiences and the fervor of my admiration required multiple revisions before I arrived at what I hoped would be a discreet and understated record of the originality and achievement of both writers.

Most biographies of "the greats" don't appear until after their subjects are dead. It was good that I had no idea this was the custom when, as a brash young woman who thought she was on a mission, I decided to write my first one. Writing each of these books brought so many changes to my own life, and they have influenced all my work between the years when I began to those of the seasoned professional I have become today. No doubt Beckett and Beauvoir were pleased with my enthusiasm, but they also probably thought me amusing and exasperating in equal part.

While I wrote the introductions to each of those biographies, I went through many emotional upheavals as I relived every moment from the long years of researching to the final written words. Approaching each conclusion became an exercise in dread as well as anticipation, so much so that I could barely bring myself to write their concluding passages—a feeling I experienced once again as I struggled with this conclusion, too.

All sorts of emotions resurfaced as I remembered the stunning realization that it was all over. Seven years of spending every single day thinking and writing about Beckett, followed by a decade of doing the same with Beauvoir, had come to an end. It was time to move forward with another life, my own, and it was impossibly hard for a long time. I found myself walking aimlessly from room to room or sitting motionless at my desk, sometimes bursting into tears and sobs that so upset my beloved bulldogs that they put their heads on my knee or pawed at my leg, hoping to comfort me with little whimpers of concern. After a while I knew it was time to stop polishing the copper pots in the kitchen (they always shone when I wasn't writing and were badly tarnished when it was going well) and get myself going again.

I've had similar wanderings about the house lately, for it has not been easy to write about myself. Throughout my writing life, I have always kept myself scrupulously out of everything. I am that curious anomaly, the writer who reveals intimate facts about the lives of others while keeping the facts and events of hers closely guarded and private. Incongruous, perhaps, that I have revealed so much about others while telling nothing of myself, but like Beckett, I believed sincerely that I was "dull and without interest."

In the biographies, the final question for which I needed an answer was, how does one sum up the achievements of a lifetime? Indeed, as I write this, how do I conclude my journey down the lanes of some of my most fascinating memories? As I wrote both books, I would occasionally leaf through books by some of the writers I called "the greats": Rousseau, Voltaire, Virginia Woolf, Saint Augustine, Pascal, James Joyce, Montaigne. I always found something in them that spoke to my general condition, and I had a habit of copying their remarks, aphorisms, or definitions into the margins of the notebooks I dedicated to the author I was writing about. I suppose the most fitting conclusion here would be to share the words that rang truest for me most of the time.

Joyce provided an example (one that he cribbed from Flaubert, but never mind) that I followed for everything I wrote: "The artist, like the God of the creation, remains within or behind or beyond or above his handiwork, invisible, refined out of existence, indifferent, paring his fingernails." (I did keep myself refined out of existence, but I was never indifferent and didn't bite my nails; I just picked at my cuticles.) Pascal had the perfect *pensée* to help me open up and confide my own experiences to the permanence of print. When he thought about how his life was "swallowed up . . . in the eternity that precedes and will follow it," he "[took] fright." When I began to write this bio-memoir, I was, like Pascal, "stunned to find myself here rather than elsewhere . . . Who sent me here? By whose order and under what guiding destiny was this time, this place, assigned to me?" It led me to ask myself what had ever made me think that Samuel Beckett "needed" a biography and I was the one to write it? Saint Augustine provided the answer for what drew me to Beauvoir: I had become "a question to myself. Not even I understand everything that I am." And Rousseau gave me hope that sustained me during each biography, but especially within this bio-memoir: "My purpose is to display a portrait in every way true to nature, and the person I portray will be myself. Simply myself."

If I managed to do that, then I have succeeded, and I am content.

ACKNOWLEDGMENTS

This is the book I thought I would never get around to writing, so I want to begin with a grateful nod to my family and the many friends who spent years urging me to do it. Aileen Ward, the distinguished scholar and writer, mentor and friend, to whom this book is dedicated, was among the first. Twenty years ago, I promised to write it as a gift for her eightieth birthday; today I regret that she is no longer here to receive it.

My children, Vonn Scott and Katherine Tracy (Katney) Bair, whose growing-up years paralleled my biographical adventures, were the best of sports to put up with me throughout their childhoods. Now that they are in their adulthoods, I appreciate how seldom they roll their eyes at my antics. Their support for so many years means more to me than I can say. I am delighted that our family's closeness continues in our next generation when my granddaughter, Isabel Anna Courtelis, tells me how my adventures in forging a feminist identity have value for her generation.

I began to write this book during the academic year 2017–2018, when I held a fellowship at the University of Connecticut Humanities Institute (UCHI). I cannot express my gratitude strongly enough to Director Michael P. Lynch and Associate Director Alexis Boylan for selecting me to participate in the brilliant program and to enjoy the congenial working spaces UCHI offered. Talking to them about their research and writing has enriched mine tremendously. I also thank all my UCHI colleagues for their generous suggestions and support, especially Harry van der Hulst, Tracy Llanera, and Alicia LaGuardia-LoBianco. My administrative needs were smoothed by Jo-Ann Waide-Wunchel, while Nasya al-Saidy patiently guided me through my various computer woes.

As my UConn year was winding down in March 2018, I took a tumble that resulted in a fractured left tibia and fibula. I spent a month in a rehabilitation hospital, another non-weight-bearing six weeks at home, and a long and slow ten-month progression to learn how to walk again. My beloved sister, Linda B. Rankin, gave up six weeks of her life to be my nurse. My dear friend Allison Stokes replaced her to provide another week of constant care. My children were there every step of the way, and my brother and sister-in-law, Vincent J. and Judith Bartolotta, gave me much needed emotional support. My son-in-law, Niko Courtelis, cheered me with a constant stream of stamps and cards. Visits from Tracy Crutchfield and Cynthia Stretch got me through many dreary hospital days. Deborah Henderson saw to my shopping and household errands. Thomas Henderson was always ready to solve any problem—computer or otherwise. My Oronoque Forest neighbors gave good cheer through frequent visits, and I thank Linda deVicino, Janis Eisenberg, Arnold DeMaio, Gary and Susan Toole, Arline Winters, and Jack Zalcman. Dr. Michael Patrick Leslie was the surgeon who made me into a bionic woman with metal plates and screws, and physical therapists Bohdanna (Billie) T. Zazulak and Wendy Novick helped me learn to walk again. Dr. Tara Sanft was an inspiration.

Flowers, phone calls, and visits from friends were lifesavers, and I thank Neil Baldwin, Ted Botha, Patricia de Maio, Jane Kinney Denning, Walter Donahue, Theodor Itten, Evelyne Gottwalz-Itten, Diane Jacobs, Susan Munger, Donald and Diane Pette, Leon and Myrna Bell Rochester, and Maeve Slavin.

I owe special thanks to Sydney Stern for never hesitating to join me enthusiastically on adventures biographical and otherwise. Marion Meade helped me to overcome my trepidation of revealing myself with her sound advice and encouragement. Colleagues at the Women Writing Women's Lives Seminar cheered me on, as did my colleagues on the Authors Guild Council, where I extend special thanks to Mary Rasenberger and Diana Rowan Rockefeller. My friend and fellow traveler down Beauvoir byways, Mary Lawrence Test, was the best first reader and first editor any writer could wish for, and I can't imagine submitting a book for publication without her initial response to it. I also thank Mark Lehberg for explaining how best to write about legal issues. Terrance Gelenter smoothed my way every time I was in Paris while writing this book. I benefited from conversations with Rosemary Sullivan, biographer and poet, who always had a theme or idea worth pursuing. And I will never forget how Nancy MacKnight was a calming presence at the nervous start of my Beckett years.

I thank my visionary publisher, Nan A. Talese, for this, my third book under her imprint. Daniel Meyer has my admiration and respect for his guidance throughout the editorial process. I thank Carolyn Williams for additional editorial care, Emma Joss for publicity, and Sarah Engelmann for marketing. Liz Duvall was my excellent copy editor, and thanks to Bette Alexander, Maria Carella, Lorraine Hyland, and Michael J. Windsor at Nan A. Talese/Doubleday. Kristine Dahl was not only my trusted agent, she also helped me to persevere through shared stories of broken-foot adventures. I also thank her assistant, Tamara Kawar, for her attention to my many needs and questions.

Most of all, I thank Samuel Beckett and Simone de Beauvoir for allowing me to spend the better part of two decades in their company and for the extraordinary opportunity to write about their lives and work. It was a privilege for which I will be eternally grateful.

A NOTE ON THE TYPE

This book was set in Caledonia, a typeface designed by W. A. Dwiggins (1880–1956). It belongs to the family of printing types called "modern face" by printers—a term used to mark the change in style of the type letters that occurred around 1800. Caledonia borders on the general design of Scotch Roman but it is more freely drawn than that letter. This version of Caledonia was adapted by David Berlow in 1979.